SENDING MONEY

FOREX, REMITTANCES, MIGRATION AND THE FINTECH REVOLUTION

The Evolution of the Cross-Border Financial Services Industry

PART II
2001-2030

Hugo Cuevas-Mohr

This book is a memoir. This is a work of nonfiction. It reflects the author's present recollections of experiences over time. No names have been changed, no characters invented, and no events fabricated. Some events have been compressed, and some dialogue has been recreated. The interviews were real, and most of them were recorded.

The author makes no guarantee of any results obtained by using this book. It is not intended to be a source of financial, compliance, entrepreneurial, legal, or consulting advice.

The book is not intended to discredit, denigrate, hurt, or defame anyone. Although the author has made every effort to ensure that the information in this book was correct at press time and while this publication is designed to provide accurate information about the subject matter covered, the author assumes no responsibility for errors, inaccuracies, omissions, or any other inconsistencies herein and hereby disclaim any liability to any party for any loss, damage, or disruption caused by errors or omissions, whether such errors or omissions result from negligence, accident, or any other cause.

Copyright © 2023 by Hugo Cuevas-Mohr

The first version of this book was written and published in Spanish in 2022. This is not a translation; the book has been rewritten extensively.

All rights reserved. No part of this publication may be reproduced, distributed, or transmitted in any form or by any means, including photocopying, recording, or other electronic or mechanical methods, without the prior written permission of the author, except in the case of brief quotations embodied in critical reviews and certain other noncommercial uses permitted by copyright law. For permission requests, write to the author.

Quantity sales. Special discounts are available on quantity purchases by corporations, associations, and others. For details, contact help@crosstechpayments.com

Orders by U.S. trade bookstores and wholesalers. Please contact help@crosstechpayments.com

Printed in the United States of America
First Edition

Book Design by: Maria Alexandra Rodriguez
Cover Design by: Oladimeji Alaka

www.crosstechpayments.com

Contact: help@crosstechpayments.com

TABLE OF CONTENTS

Special Thanks 9

Chapter 1. A New Reality 11
    The 9/11 Attack: Fund Transfers 12
    Terrorism Comes Into Play 15
    Post 9/11: Facts are Revealed 17
    The Real and the Perceived Threats 18
    Funds from Illicit Activities 25
    Remittances Studies Begin 27
    Regulations Evolve 32
    Cross-Border Payment Consulting 39
    The Kroll Report 44
    @Red Internacional 46
    Banco Union - DR 46
    The Sale of TITAN 47

Chapter 2. Consolidation: The Market Shifts 49
    Preconceptions and Bias 51
    MTOs for Sale 54
    Vigo Remittance - US 55
    Dolex Dollar Express - US 56
    Ria Envia - EEFT 58
    Small World - Choice 60
    Travelex - Coinstar - Groupex - Sigue 61
    Uniteller 62
    Moneygram 64
    Western Union 68
    Commercial Banks and Remittances 71
    Serving Remittance Clients 72
        Origination 72
        Destination 75
    Banking Partnerships and Derisking 78
        Australia 87

  The Philippines 89
  Spain 90
  Are there solutions for Derisking and Debanking? 90
 Financial Inclusion vs. Bancarization 91
  The War on Cash 95
 Aggregators Evolve 97
 Postal Services 99

Chapter 3. The Digital Age Takes Hold 103
 Regulating Innovation 105
 New Kids on the Block 108
 How fast is the market changing? 110
 The US 110
 Europe 112
 The Digital Dilemma 114
 Xoom 116
 ZEPZ (WorldRemit - Sendwave) 117
 Wise (Transferwise) 119
 Remitly 121
 Transfergo 122
 Azimo 124
 Papaya Global 125
 PaySend 127
 Flywire 128
 BITSO - B2B 129
 MMOs - Communication & Payments 131
 Public Companies 134
 Going Public: The Collapse of UAE Exchange 140

Chapter 4. Cryptocurrency and Money Transfers 143
 Basic Crypto Advantages 146
 Crypto and Remittances 148
 Use of Crypto by Consumers 150
 Industry Partnerships 154
 Central Bank Digital Currencies - CBDCs 157

Chapter 5. Cross-Border Payments 2030 163
 Market Growth 166
 Remittances (P2P) will continue their upward trend 168

Businesses & Individuals, B2P & P2B 171
Business Payments (B2B) 172
Government Payments 173
Humanitarian and Relief Programs 176
Intra-regional Remittances 179
Coopetition: Banks and Fintechs 182
Neobanks 184
The future of Derisking and Debanking 190
The FedWire, RTP and FedNow Battlefront 191
Integrating Services and Partnering 194
Domestic Payments and Cross-Border Payments 194
Embedded Finance 196
Integrating Complimentary Services 198
Integrating Payment and Communication Services 200
Mobile Money and Wallets 204
eCommerce and Payments 207
Travel & Tourism 212

Closing Remarks 215

Appendix One. Conferences 217
IMTC - CrossTech 217
Remtech Awards 220
Fintech Conferences and Events 221
Remittances and Development 222
Global Forum on Remittances,
Investment and Development 223

Appendix Two. The Associations 227
NFBIs Associations 227
The US 229
The Money Services Roundtable 230
MTRA 230
IOREM 231
Europe 231
Remesas.org 232
AUKPI (UKMTA) 232
South America 233
Fintech Associations 235

List of Graphs 239

List of Tables 240

List of Interviews 241

Abbreviations & Acronyms 243

DEDICATION

I dedicate this book to all the individuals who developed the fertile history of the non-bank international financial services industry, supporting migrants and forging the foreign exchange, remittances, and cross-border payments sector.

In this dedication, I also want to include all the visionaries who proudly develop today's fintechs and are reaping the rewards of the battles fought before their time. Everyone in the cross-border payments industry is a maverick. In the words of Barack Obama: *There are always too many things to look out for, too many barriers to break and too many challenges to overcome. Change is difficult but always possible.*

SPECIAL THANKS

I want to thank all my colleagues, who have taught me everything I know and given me their stories and anecdotes, successes and achievements, and their pains and frustrations that contributed to this book. I want to thank my teammates at Universal de Cambios, Titán Intercontinental, Titan Payment Center, Serviexpreso, NYFX, Rapid-o-Giros and UNO Money Transfers, and the correspondents and agents who were our business partners.

I want to thank all the companies, colleagues, and friends I have consulted for and advised in my career for their trust and reliance.

I thank everyone who contributed their interviews, comments, and advice and my team at CrossTech, who have contributed to bringing out this project ahead.

Every work is built based on a family that supports, emotionally and materially, the life of one another. This work is no exception.

I want to thank Lucía Salazar and Carlos Mauricio Muñoz Bermeo, who helped me get this project off the ground, and their support with the interviews.

I appreciate the hospitality of my friends who gave me a sheltered harbor, where this book saw many of its pages written.

I would like to thank my colleagues and CrossTech Directors, Erick Schneider and Daniela Cuevas, who read many chapters of this book and gave me their comments and feedback.

CHAPTER 1

A NEW REALITY

Major historical events are often memorable because they bring us immediately back to where we were —and who we were— when they happened. On September 11, 2001, I was traveling in South America, and my wife, who was in Miami, called me to get to a TV and watch the news. I saw with disbelief the Twin Towers collapsing on top of the same train station in Manhattan that I used to come and go to the NYFX office as an employee in 1992-3. I will walk to NYFX's office at 61 Broadway from that destroyed subway station under the towers. I immediately tried to find out if Roger Freed and the people at NYFX, recently sold to AFEX. I finally heard a few days later that the disaster affected none of them.

One of the first significant changes we all experienced as travelers was airport security as we flew from one country to another to meet customers and prospects. Boarding times and processing upon arrival became longer and longer. Security measures became increasingly strict in the US and worldwide; that was the new reality.

> As terrorism invaded the scene, the remittance industry entered a new era.

The transition took time, as many internal and external factors played a role. Ethnic MTOs serving Latin America that had been struggling for more than a decade had shut down, and a few who had survived were expanding. Traditional US companies such as WU and MGI were undergoing corporate transformations, growing their agent base and developing new business partnerships with banks, NBFIs, and large retail chains. By then, Federal and state regulators in the US and other countries were gaining a deeper understanding of our sector and the role check cashers, exchange houses, money transmitters, and MO providers played.

The first reports and studies on remittances appeared at the turn of the century, as their importance became more apparent. The presence of Hispanics in the US moved from the farm workers hidden in the fields or the out-of-sight urban dwellers to impacting the broad society. This presence was slowly transforming the panorama.

THE 9/11 ATTACK: FUND TRANSFERS

The Financing of the 9/11 Plot is well documented, and the funds transfers' role was analyzed in detail. *A Terrorist Financing Staff Monograph*[1] that is part of the National Commission on Terrorist Attacks Upon the United States reveals how the funds were moved internationally without raising any red flags. The introduction of the monograph is worth quoting:

> To plan and conduct their attack, the 9/11 plotters spent somewhere between $400,000 and $500,000, the vast majority of which was provided by al Qaeda. Although the origin of the funds remains unknown, extensive investigation has revealed quite a bit about the financial transactions that supported the 9/11 plot. The hijackers and their financial facilitators used the anonymity provided by the huge international and domestic financial system to move and store their money through a series of unremarkable transactions. The existing mechanisms to prevent abuse of the financial system did not fail. They were never designed to detect or disrupt transactions of the type that financed 9/11.
>
> Neither the hijackers nor their financial facilitators were experts in the use of the international financial system. They created a paper trail linking them to each other and their facilitators. Still, they were easily adept enough to blend into the vast international financial system without

---

[1] Terrorist Financing Staff Monograph: Appendix A: The Financing of the 9/11 Plot - https://bit.ly/3sSggdF

doing anything to reveal themselves as criminals, let alone terrorists bent on mass murder. The money-laundering controls in place at the time were largely focused on drug trafficking and large-scale financial fraud and could not have detected the hijackers' transactions. The controls were never intended to, and could not, detect or disrupt the routine transactions in which the hijackers engaged.

From this report, I want to highlight the use of cash, traveler checks, bank transfers, Debit and Credit Cards, and money transfers for the financing of the terrorist attack on 9/11:

1. The financing of terrorists in the US amounted to around US $300,000

2. The hijackers received assistance in financing their activities from two facilitators based in the United Arab Emirates: Ali Abdul Aziz Ali, a.k.a. Ammar al Baluchi (Ali), and Mustafa al Hawsawi and one based in Germany, Binalshibh.

3. Ali wire transferred a total of $114,500 to the plot leaders Shehhi and Atta after they arrived in the US in May and June 2000.

4. On June 29, 2000, Ali sent a $5,000 wire transfer to a Western Union facility in New York, where Shehhi picked it up.

5. Over the next several months, Ali sent four bank-to-bank transfers directly to a checking account jointly held by Shehhi and Atta at SunTrust Bank in Florida: $10,000 on July 18, $9,500 on August 5, $20,000 on August 29, and $70,000 on September 17.

6. On June 13 and June 21, 2000, Binalshibh sent $2,708.33 first and $1,803.19 later, from Hamburg to Shehhi in New York using Moneygram. Binalshibh also sent two Western Union transfers from Hamburg to Shehhi in Florida, wiring $1,760.15 and $4,118.14 on July 25 and September 25, 2000, respectively.

7. On February 23, 2001, the French terrorist Zacarias Moussaoui declared $35,000 to Customs when he arrived from London, and he deposited $32,000 into a Norman, Oklahoma, bank three days later. In early August 2001, Binalshibh sent $14,000 in two wire transfer installments.

8. The 13 muscle hijackers who arrived in the US between April 23 and June 29, 2001, brought cash and traveler's checks. One hijacker opened a new bank account and deposited $9,900 days after arriving. Six hijackers purchased traveler's checks totaling $43,980 in the UAE and used them in the US for expenses and to open bank accounts in Bank of America and SunTrust.

9. One of the muscle hijackers, Banihammad, also set up a bank account at Standard Chartered Bank in the UAE, accessible by an ATM debit card and a VISA card. After he arrived in the US on June 27, 2001, he made cash withdrawals with both cards; he used the VISA card to purchase the 9/11 plane tickets for himself and one other terrorist and to pay his Boston hotel bill on the morning of 9/11.

10. From September 5 through September 10, 2001, the hijackers consolidated their unused funds —roughly $40,000— and sent them by various means to the UAE. US and UAE authorities seized some of the funds after the attack.

11. The extensive investigation into the financing of the 9/11 plot has revealed no evidence that the hijackers used hawala or any other informal value transfer mechanism to send money to the US.

Table 1 summarizes the information above to better visualize the money involved in financing the terrorist attacks.

TABLE 1: The Financing of the 9/11 Terrorist Attacks in the US - 2000-2001

YEAR	DATE	AMOUNT	MEANS
2000	May-June	$114,500	Bank Wire Transfer
	June 29, 2023	$5,000	Western Union
	July 18	$10,000	Bank Wire Transfer
	August 5	$9,500	Bank Wire Transfer
	August 29	$20,000	Bank Wire Transfer
	September 17	$70,000	Bank Wire Transfer
	June 13	$2,708.33	Moneygram
	June 21	$1,803.19	Moneygram

YEAR	DATE	AMOUNT	MEANS
	July 25	$1,760.15	Western Union
	September 25	$4,118.14	Western Union
2001	February 23	$35,000	cash (declared)
	August	$14,000	Two Bank Wire Transfers
	April 23	$9,900	Cash
	June 29	$43,980	Traveller Checks
		$342,270	

It is important to note that in several instances in the monograph, there is an attempt to exempt every financial services institution in the UAE, Germany, and the US from responsibility for not flagging these transactions. The report also states: *Contrary to persistent media reports, no financial institution filed a Suspicious Activity Report (SAR) in connection with any transaction of any of the 19 hijackers before 9/11, although such SARs were filed after 9/11 when their names became public. The failure to file SARs was not unreasonable. Even in hindsight, there is nothing to indicate that any SAR should have been filed or the hijackers otherwise reported to law enforcement.*

TERRORISM COMES INTO PLAY

Somalia's Al-Barakat Bank case is perhaps one of the most high-profile cases of injustice committed by US LEAs to an MTO in search of headlines and exposure[2] to showcase to the public their work against the threat of terrorism.

The al-Barakat Group, Arabic for *blessings*, is a corporate group founded in 1985 in Somalia to handle inward remittances under the leadership of Ahmed Nur Ali Jumale. By 2001, al-Barakat was active in 40 countries, and it was one of the largest private employers in the country. It handled around $140 million a year from the Somali diaspora using formal and informal (Hawala) channels.

On November 7, 2001, The US and UAE officials confiscated a total amount of US $2.1 million in simultaneous raids against 12 company offices around the world, alleging that the organization provided funding for

---
2 Terrorist Financing Staff Monograph: Al-Barakaat Case Study The Somali Community and al-Barakaat; Chapter 5 - https://bit.ly/3Ce7Z6k

Al Qaeda and an associated group, Al-lttihad Al-lslamiya (AIAI). The big headlines came immediately: President Bush traveled to FinCEN's offices and, along with the Secretary of the Treasury and the Attorney General, announced the action at a press event, describing the company's owner, Jumale, as a *friend and supporter of Osama bin Laden*. Treasury Secretary Paul O'Neill described the company's offices as *a major source of funding, intelligence, and money transfers for Bin Laden*. He later announced: *We estimate that $25 million were diverted from al-Barakaat's network of companies each year and redirected to terrorist operations*.

The U.S. government designated al-Barakat as a terrorist entity, placing it on OFAC lists and asking other countries to do the same. Jumale was arrested in the United Arab Emirates while charges were being pressed against him. This time, the issue was terrorist financing, and decisive action had to be demonstrated. Once again, an ethnic MTO would be the target.

After investigations involving the analysis of thousands of documents in the US and the UAE, interviews with Jumale and other company officials, and internal discussions between the US LEAs (differences of opinion that brought the FBI and OFAC into conflict), they concluded that no evidence of terrorist financing or criminal activity existed that would show, with certainty, incriminating links or suspicious transactions. Since other governments were involved, the situation became complicated. The authorities quietly —with no apology or public statement— returned the confiscated funds, began to remove the group from the sanctions lists, and continued to do so for several years. The company resumed operations in 2014, but only in February 2020 was it finally removed from the official records; I do not doubt that it will continue to appear in risk databases for decades. The harm was done.

I have helped companies that have been unable to clear their names from compliance systems that highlighted news or charges that never came to fruition, and it is an uphill battle that takes a lot of patience.

Somalia's difficult existence as a single nation and the activity of al-Shabaab, the Muslim paramilitary group active in the country, renders the provision of remittances for the more than one million Somalis in the diaspora an enormous challenge for service providers. Traditional remittance companies in this country, such as Dahasbill and Amal, have had serious problems working with commercial banks in the countries where they operate and have continually had to seek alternatives for their treasury management and payment compensation despite the support of multilateral agencies.

POST 9/11: FACTS ARE REVEALED

One of the most disturbing books about the reaction of the US to 9/11 is found in Ron Suskind's 2007 book, *The One Percent Doctrine*[3]. The book was written with wide access to the former director of the CIA, George Tenet, as well as to other CIA officials and a host of sources at the FBI and in the State, Defense, and Treasury Departments. It portrays US President George W. Bush as an incurious and curiously uninformed executive and Vice President Dick Cheney as the puppeteer, who in tandem with CIA's director George Tenet, repeatedly pushed CIA staff members to come up with evidence to support the White House public statements. The term *intelligence on demand* was coined.

A NY Times report[4] by Michiko Kakutani on Mr. Suskind's book mentions the role First Data and its affiliate at the time, WU played after 9/11:

> In *The One Percent Doctrine,* Mr. Suskind discloses that First Data Corporation —one of the world's largest processors of credit card transactions and the parent company of Western Union— began cooperating with the FBI in the wake of 9/11, providing information on financial transactions and wire transfers from around the world. The huge data-gathering operation, in some respects, complemented the National Security Agency's domestic surveillance program (secretly authorized by Mr. Bush months after the Sept. 11 attacks), which monitored specific conversations as well as combed through large volumes of phone and Internet traffic in search of patterns that might lead to terrorism suspects.
>
> Despite initial misgivings on the part of Western Union executives, Mr. Suskind reports, the company also worked with the CIA and provided real-time information on financial transactions as they occurred.

---

3 Ron Suskind: The One Percent Doctrine, Deep Inside America's Pursuit of Its Enemies Since 9/11; Simon & Schuster, May 2007 ISBN:9780743271103, 0743271106 - https://bit.ly/3sSxDek
4 Michiko Kakutani: Personality, Ideology and Bush's Terror Wars; The NY Times, June 20, 2006 - https://nyti.ms/3ZmiGNS

The National Commission on Terrorist Attacks Upon the United States[5] states in its introduction that it is essential to distinguish between the media coverage and the facts that the public was led to believe. In discussing the funding of al Qaeda, the commission stated:

> Contrary to common belief, Bin Ladin did not have access to any significant amounts of personal wealth (particularly after his move from Sudan to Afghanistan) and did not personally fund al Qaeda, either through an inheritance or businesses he was said to have owned in Sudan. Rather, al Qaeda was funded, to the tune of approximately $30 million per year, by diversions of money from Islamic charities and the use of well-placed financial facilitators who gathered money from both witting and unwitting donors, primarily in the Gulf region. No persuasive evidence exists that al Qaeda relied on the drug trade as an important source of revenue, had any substantial involvement with conflict diamonds, or was financially sponsored by any foreign government. The United States is not, and has not been, a substantial source of al Qaeda funding, although some funds raised in the United States may have made their way to al Qaeda and its affiliated groups. Prior to 9/11 the largest single al Qaeda expense was support for the Taliban, estimated at about $20 million per year.

THE REAL AND THE PERCEIVED THREATS

Let's examine a graph on the terrorist incidents, fatalities, and non-fatal injuries from terrorist attacks worldwide from 1970 to 2020.

---

5 The National Commission on Terrorist Attacks Upon the United States; Chapter 1 Introduction and Executive Summary - https://bit.ly/463IbWa

GRAPH 1 - Incidence, fatality, and injury from terrorist attacks, World, 1970 to 2020

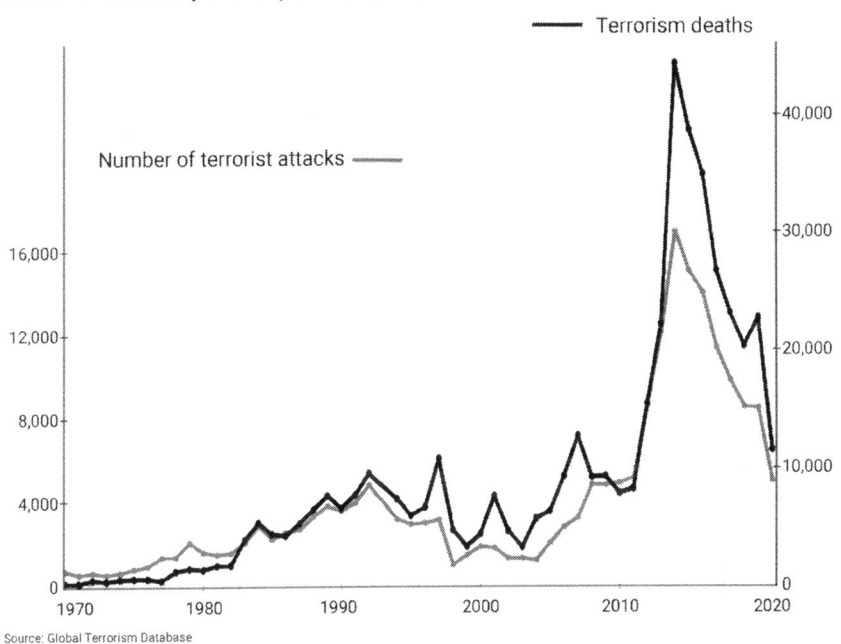

Source: Global Terrorism Database

Although the number of incidents was pretty low from 1998 to 2004, 900 to 1000 incidents per year, fatalities (7,129), and non-fatalities (28,187) peaked in 2001 with the 9-11 attack on the NY World Trade Center and other US targets. Of the 7,129 world fatalities in 2001, 42% were from US incidents, 47 for the year, and 77% of the non-fatalities, which shows us how massive the US incidents that year were, compared to world data. In the US, in 1970, 468 incidents were reported, and in 2020, 103[6].

Dale L. Watson, Executive Assistant Director of the Counterterrorism/Counterintelligence Division of the FBI, in his 2002 report[7] explained:

> The terrorist attack of September 11, 2001, marked a dramatic escalation in a trend toward more destructive terrorist attacks which began in the 1980s. Before the September 11 attack, the October 23, 1983 truck bombings of US and French military barracks in Beirut, Lebanon, which

---
[6] Hannah Ritchie, Joe Hasell, Edouard Mathieu, Cameron Appel and Max Roser; Interactive charts on Terrorism, Global Change Data Lab, UK - https://bit.ly/449xv7Z
[7] Dale L. Watson: Hearing before the Senate Select Committee on Intelligence, Washington, DC, February 06, 2002, Federal Bureau of Investigation - https://bit.ly/3XBVRVo

claimed a total of 295 lives, stood as the most deadly act of terrorism. The attacks of September 11 produced casualty figures more than ten times higher than those of the 1983 barracks attacks.

The September 11 attack also reflected a trend toward more indiscriminate targeting among international terrorists. The vast majority of the more than 3,000 victims of the attack were civilians. In addition, the attack represented the first known case of suicide attacks carried out by international terrorists in the United States. The September 11 attack also marked the first successful act of international terrorism in the United States since the vehicle bombing of the World Trade Center in February 1993.

Watson continues in his report explaining Jihad:

However, the threat from Al-Qaeda is only a part of the overall threat from the radical international jihad movement, which is composed of individuals of varying nationalities, ethnicities, tribes, races, and terrorist group memberships who work together in support of extremist Sunni goals. One of the primary goals of Sunni extremists is the removal of U.S. military forces from the Persian Gulf area, most notably Saudi Arabia. The single common element among these diverse individuals is their commitment to the radical international jihad movement, which includes a radicalized ideology and agenda promoting the use of violence against the "enemies of Islam" in order to overthrow all governments which are not ruled by Sharia (conservative Islamic) law.

The terrorist attacks have sparked a new paranoia about migrants. The incidents in the US and Europe, the threat of Al-Qaeda, and the radical international jihad movement brought increasing pressure on migrants. The fears were now directed at Middle Easterners and everyone from a foreign country that could be connected to any religious network, including Indians, Sikhs, and other dark-skinned migrants.

US and European governments needed to ensure the public believed they were doing their jobs through big press headlines. The immediate concern was to find out how the terrorists were financed and, soon after, to uncover how cells were supporting these terrorists by sending monetary help. Islamic groups and organizations were now on the list, and their suspicious activities were the target.

In a hearing[8] examining the role of charities and NGOs in the financing of terrorist activities held before the US Congress Subcommittee on International Trade and Finance, Senator Evan Bayh wrote:

> Since September 11, the United States has designated seven foreign charitable organizations as having ties to al Qaeda and has shut down two prominent U.S.-based charities with alleged ties to Osama bin Laden and the Taliban. The assets of the largest U.S.-based Islamic charity, Holy Land Foundation, have been frozen based upon information linking it as a funding vehicle to Hamas. At least $2.4 million in U.S. charitable funds have been seized, and an undisclosed amount has been frozen in Bosnia and Somalia.

The Holy Land Foundation for Relief and Development (HLF) and five of its leaders were convicted by a federal jury in November 2008 and sentenced in May 2009 on charges of providing material support to Hamas, a US-designated foreign terrorist organization.

All Islamist religious groups and NGOs were investigated. I want to highlight the case of the US v. Sami Omar Al-Hussayen[9], where a Michigan-based charity known as the Islamic Assembly of North America (IANA) was accused of having as its mission to raise funds and recruit individuals for terrorist acts. On February 12, 2003, Al-Hussayen was charged, and funds were seized. He was an Islamic graduate student at the University of Idaho. He was prosecuted under the material support to terrorism statutes for designing, creating, and maintaining websites that federal prosecutors viewed as supportive of terrorism. The case drew a lot of controversy. He was acquitted in 2004 but had to plead guilty to immigration charges and deported. His wife and three children left with him.

When the target shifted from money laundering to terrorist financing, the bad actors, the undesirables, shifted from Latin Americans and Blacks to other ethnic groups in a new set of frightening stories. The predisposition of Muslims to be terrorists raised the suspicions of all remittance companies sending money to the Middle East and, as we saw, NGOs doing

---

8 The Role Of Charities And Ngo's In The Financing Of Terrorist Activities; Hearing before the Subcommittee on International Trade and Finance of The Committee on Banking, Housing, and Urban Affairs of The United States Senate - https://bit.ly/3PIhtgM

9 Alan F. Williams: Prosecuting Website Development Under The Material Support To Terrorism Statutes: Time To Fix What's Broken, Legislation and Public Policy, Vol. 11, No. 2:365, New York University - https://bit.ly/3rgPydV

humanitarian work in this region, especially in the most needy countries, arguably the riskiest ones.

As I mentioned in Chapter 4 describing Hawala, after 9-11, there was a large number of investigations done regarding Hawala Networks and how modern laws could regulate this ancient method of transferring value so they could continue to operate in a more transparent manner that would please regulators.

Under US and European pressure to fight terrorism, the wars in Iraq, Syria, and Afghanistan, and the dismantling of ISIS support networks, countries in the Middle East started seeking ways to formalize payments and remittances.

The UAE, Saudi Arabia, and other EMEA states were concerned that if IVTs, Hawalas, and Hundis were not thoroughly regulated, they might go completely underground due to the pressure of the US and the EU. In an attempt to study ways to regulate them and demand records, the UEA Central Bank organized the First World Hawala Conference in Abu Dhabi in May 2002, followed by a second one two years later, in 2004. By the third conference in 2005, the IMF had laid the groundwork for hawala regulation in its document *Regulatory Frameworks for Hawala and Other Remittance Systems*[10]. The fourth and final conference on the subject was held in Abu Dhabi in 2007[11].

From a historical perspective, 9-11 caused several changes in the global financial system, an impact that continues to be studied by academics and researchers.

On an industry level, the USA Patriot Act[12] (Uniting and Strengthening America by Providing Appropriate Tools Required to Intercept and Obstruct Terrorism Act) established new regulations and reports. It also enhanced the role of the Compliance Officer, which became a key executive role in most institutions. Many ethnic companies that provided services to the Middle

---

10 Regulatory Frameworks for Hawala and other Remittance Systems; International Monetary Fund, Monetary and Financial Systems Dept., Washington, D.C, 2005, ISBN 1-58906-423-2 - https://bit.ly/3UCH5Me
11 The Central Bank of the UAE: Communiqué; The Fourth International Conference on Hawala, Abu Dahbi, 18-20 March 2017 - https://bit.ly/3r5DgBM
12 USA PATRIOT Act; FinCEN - https://bit.ly/3bspV1Z

East and extensively to India, Nepal, and other Asian countries unrelated to 9/11 ceased operations by that time, unable to continue existing despite calls to moderate the prevailing policy for fear that these services would go entirely underground.

Losing access to banking was undoubtedly the primary cause of these closures. During that time, as a consultant, I helped many MTOs serving corridors in the Middle East and North Africa to get bank accounts and find ways to channel their transactions to aggregators and third countries to survive while maintaining the necessary regulatory transparency in case they were audited or targeted. Long hours were spent with compliance professionals with moderate success. Some MTOs using Hawala or Hundi informal payment services restricted their use to well-known clients within extremely closed communities, hoping to remain in business.

An IMF blog post by Dilip Ratha, one of the most respected authorities in remittances in the World Bank, sums it up[13]:

The intense scrutiny of money service businesses for money laundering or terrorism financing since the 9/11 attacks on the World Trade Center has made it difficult for them to maintain accounts with their correspondent banks, forcing many in the United States to close.

While regulations are necessary to curb money laundering and terrorism financing, they should not make it difficult for legitimate money service businesses to maintain accounts with correspondent banks.

Using a risk-based approach to regulation—in which only suspicious transactions are checked and small transactions below, say, $1,000 are exempt from requiring proof of identity and address—can reduce remittance costs and facilitate flows.

After the attacks on the Pentagon and the World Trade Center, Eddy Cuesta recalls the abrupt changes for MTOs in the US:

In the 90s we did a number of compliance reviews to ensure that there were no money laundering issues. We spent a lot of money analyzing

---

13 Dilip Ratha: Economics in Action: What Are Remittances?; IMF - https://bit.ly/3fiUWap

whether structuring existed. But each new regulation required us to invest more money in systems, in a compliance officer, name given later to that role. But, basically, after the Twin Towers event, we were all taken out; the banks would not let us deposit money. Banks started closing the accounts, and a few increased their fees tremendously; they were taking advantage of companies like ours. Increasingly so, they began to add more conditions. We looked for help, talked to members of Congress, and reached out to many people in government for support. We needed time, help, and resources. Ultimately, the big companies took the market, and the small ones were pushed out[14].

> **Given the challenges ethnic businesses faced and the difficulties obtaining bank accounts, very few of them survived. Antiterrorism measures that had little or nothing to do with remittances reinforced this challenge.**

The increase in hate crimes against Muslims and anyone regarded as a Muslim was immediate following the 9/11 attacks[15]: the first recorded hate crime in the US occurred in Mesa, Arizona, four days after 9/11, when a Sikh American citizen, Balbir Singh Sodhi, was murdered[16]. He wore a *pagri* on his head, had a large mustache and long beard, and worked in his own gas station. In the first month after the 9/11 attacks, the Sikh Coalition[17] documented over 300 cases of violence and discrimination against Sikh Americans throughout the US.

Because of their distinctive turbans that make them very conspicuous, the Sikhs remain one of the most persecuted ethnic groups in the US and Europe. According to the FBI's data, Sikhs were among the top two most targeted faith groups for hate crimes across the US in 2021, behind the Jewish American community. Between 2020 and 2021, anti-Sikh hate crimes

---

14 Virtual interview with Eddy Cuesta, July 21, 2022, recorded and transcribed by Lucía Salazar
15 Kiara Alfonseca: 20 years after 9/11, Islamophobia continues to haunt Muslims, Anti-Muslim hate crimes spiked after 9/11 and during the Trump administration. ABC News, September 11, 2021 - https://abcn.ws/3bpg1yg
16 My dad was killed in first hate-crime after 9/11; BBC News, September 13, 2021 - https://bbc.in/3QdrLmh
17 The Sikh Coalition is a national organization founded in 2001 and based in New York with additional staff in California, Illinois, and Washington, DC. - https://bit.ly/45MQhCN

increased by 140 percent, from 89 incidents to 214. The FBI is still working with local police in the US to ensure that the large number of unrecorded hate crimes are documented.

FUNDS FROM ILLICIT ACTIVITIES

To understand the scope of the flow of funds from illicit activities, it is important to understand that criminal activities arise from a variety of sources. The perception of risks faced by financial services providers has to be expanded considerably. Banks and their regulatory agencies must broaden their risk perception so the bias against the *low-hanging fruit*, ethnic businesses, and companies serving ethnic clients are not risk-assessed unfairly.

Table 2, published in 2005[18], estimates the flow of funds from illicit activities.

TABLE 2: Global flow of funds from illicit activities in billions (US $bn)

Global Flows	Low (US$ bn)	%	High (US$ bn)	%
Drugs	120	11%	200	12.50%
Counterfeit products	80	7.50%	120	7.50%
Fake currency	3	0.20%	3	0.20%
Human Trafficking	12	1.10%	15	0.90%
Illegal arms trade	6	2.00%	10	0.60%
Smuggling	60	5.60%	100	6.30%
Organized crime	50	4.70%	100	6.30%
Crime subtotal	**331**	**31.20%**	**549**	**34.30%**
Price manipulation	200	18.90%	250	15.60%
predatory pricing	300	28.30%	500	31.20%
Fake transactions	200	18.90%	250	15.60%
Business subtotal	**700**	**66.00%**	**1000**	**62.50%**
Corruption	30	2.80%	50	5.10%
Gran Total	**1,061**	**100%**	**1,599**	**100%**

18 Raymond W. Baker: Capitalism's Achilles Heel – Dirty Money and How to Renew the Free-Market System, John Wiley and Sons (2005) - https://bit.ly/44Usm34

Matthew Green, a journalist and social science teacher who specializes in using news in education, summarizes in an article[19] the four main areas of the impact of 9-11 in our societies:

1. The rise of continuous wars in the Middle East (such as Iraq, Afghanistan, Palestine and Syria)
2. Changes in the view of immigration and the continuous increase of deportations (resulting, for example, in the construction of border walls and fences)
3. International Movement Control (resulting in increased airport security)
4. Big Surveillance (which explains the massive investment in surveillance of the US and European governments inside and outside its borders).

It is widely argued that governments have used the terrorism threat to increase their surveillance and control mechanisms. As university researchers Kevin D. Haggerty and Amber Gazso stated: *the terrorism threat provided a convenient opportunity for the security establishment to lobby for increased surveillance capacity, despite lingering questions about whether such devices can achieve their professed goals*[20].

The International Federation for Human Rights is actively looking for ways to balance controls and the rule of law: *Ostensibly to fight terrorism, extraordinary and particularly repressive legislation was adopted in a large number of countries, even in democratic countries [...]. Many authoritarian states adopted similar laws, which they also used to legitimize the repression of opponents and human rights defenders and to criminalize any other type of social protest*[21].

Many opponents of the U.S. Patriot Act criticize it because it creates large government surveillance and tracking apparatuses, which, in turn, have caused resentment among supporters of privacy and civil rights, as opposed to the people who defend the need for surveillance and control mechanisms. A

---

19 Matthew Green: How 9/11 Changed America: Four Major Lasting Impacts (with Lesson Plan); The Lowdown, KQED, September 8, 2017 - https://bit.ly/3Q6hVmk
20 Kevin D. Haggerty and Amber Gazso: Seeing beyond the Ruins: Surveillance as a Response to Terrorist Threats; The Canadian Journal of Sociology / Cahiers canadiens de sociologie Vol. 30, No. 2 (Spring, 2005), pp. 169-187 - https://bit.ly/3EC6XRB
21 International Federation For Human Rights: Terrorism, surveillance and human rights - https://bit.ly/3r59MYq

widely quoted article by New Zealand philosophy professor Jeremy Waldron titled *Security and Liberty: The Image of Balance* made the following point: *We should be even more careful in giving up our commitment to the civil liberties of a minority, so that we can enjoy our liberties more securely*[22].

REMITTANCES STUDIES BEGIN

Besides the considerable changes to compliance and risk-based perception and the new realities facing the industry after the 9/11 attacks, the new century saw the beginning of the publishing of reports on remittances and a major development: remittance data began to be gathered.

Based on bibliographic references from documents published by CEPAL and some of the symposia held in the late eighties and early 1990s, the first analyses of remittances were probably published by Oded Stark, an economist at the Center for Development Research of the University of Bonn in Germany, Harvard University and Bar-ilan University in Israel[23,24,25].

In his presentations and publications, Manuel Orozco, a Nicaraguan native, was one of the first academics to work on remittances. He studied at the National University of Costa Rica and earned his doctorate and master's degrees from the University of Texas in 1999. As a result of his studies in foreign policy and international conflicts, he gained a deeper understanding of migration. In Latin America, the Cold War manifested itself through the Cuban revolution (1958), Colombia's guerrilla movement (1964) and the Nicaraguan Salvadoran revolutions (1980), causing great internal and external displacements. Through the analysis of these socio-political crises, Manuel becomes aware of the importance of remittances within the countries affected by violence. In 1992, he wrote a remittance article with Father Segundo Montes, a martyr of the UCA, followed by a publication by FLACSO, and

---

22 Jeremy Waldron: Security and Liberty: The Image of Balance; Journal of Political Philosophy 11 (2):191-210 (2003) - Este artículo luego apareció en el libro "Civil Rights and Security" publicado en 2009.
23 Robert E.B. Lucas, Oded Stark: Motivations to Remit: Evidence from Botswana, Journal of Political Economy, vol. 93, N° 5, pp. 901-918, October 1985 - https://bit.ly/43xeZFD
24 Oded Stark, J. Edward Taylor, Shlomo Yitzhaki, "Migration, remittances, and inequality: a sensitivity analysis Using the extended Gini index", Journal of Development Economics, vol. 28, 1988 - https://bit.ly/3O5WLq4
25 Oded Stark: Migration in LDCs: risk, remittances, and the family, Finance and Development, vol. 28, N° 4, December p. 39, IMF eLibrary, Index 1991 Volume 28 - https://bit.ly/3PKzlI7

he organized the first remittance event in Washington with Carlo Dade, a member of the Canadian Foundation for the Americas, in 1999[26].

In 2002, Rodolfo O. de la Garza, B. Lindsay Lowel, and Rafael Alarcón, with contributions from Manuel Orozco, Louis DeSipio, Deborah Waller Meyers, and J. Edward Taylor, published *Sending Money Home*[27], a seminal book on remittances, migration and development. This was followed in 2012 by *América Latina y el Caribe: Desarrollo, migración y remesas*[28] [Latin America and the Caribbean: Development, Migration, and Remittances], a book by Manuel Orozco that became a study guide in many institutions across the continent. The scope of his work is extensive. In addition to his leadership in the Inter-American Dialogue on migration and remittances for many years, he has taught seminars and courses at Georgetown University in Washington, D.C., and other universities.

In 2012, Manuel founded RIO (Remittance Industry Observatory), an industry Think Tank that collects statistical information from companies in the sector, analyzes trends, and conducts consumer surveys and mystery shopping to obtain a scorecard for rating MTOs. However, he believes his greatest accomplishment is showcasing the importance of remittances to increase families' savings through financial education.

At the symposium *La migración internacional y el desarrollo en las Américas* [International Migration and Development in the Americas][29] held in San José, Costa Rica in September 2000 by ECLAC, CELADE, IOM, IDB and UNFPA[30], ECLAC's Executive Secretary, José Antonio Ocampo, stated:

> Remittances are clearly one of the most positive expressions of migration. Remittances are widely perceived as crucial because of their sheer magnitude: remittances to Central America in 1998 were estimated to be

---

26 Private Communications with Manuel Orozco in May 2022
27 Rodolfo O. de la Garza et al.: Sending Money Home: Hispanic Remittances and Community Development, Rowman & Littlefield Publishers, January, 2002, ISBN-13: 978-0742518865
28 Manuel Orozco: América Latina y el Caribe: Desarrollo, migración y remesas, Editorial Teseo, August, 2012, ISBN-13: 978-9871867233
29 Simposio sobre la migración internacional y el desarrollo en las Américas, San José, Costa Rica: CEPAL, CELADE, OIM, BID y FNUAP; September 2000 - https://bit.ly/3ztKDXd
30 Comisión Económica para América Latina y el Caribe (CEPAL) Centro Latinoamericano y Caribeño de Demografía (CELADE), División de Población Organización Internacional para las Migraciones (OIM) Banco Interamericano de Desarrollo (BID) Fondo de Población de las Naciones Unidas (FNUAP)

US$3.5 billion. These resources accounted for 16% of El Salvador's GDP, 5% of Nicaragua's, and similar levels in several Caribbean island nations. Even though Colombian remittances are smaller, they account for half of the coffee exports".

In this event, Adella Pellegrino quoted Russell and Teitelbaum, who estimated in 1992 that remittances were US $43.3 billion in 1980 and had climbed to US $65.6 billion in 1990. The authors believe remittances would rank second behind crude oil in international trade. The discussion and the race to effectively estimate remittances began. In the same report, Wendell Samuel comments on the absence of reliable data: *the accuracy of estimates of migrant remittances is rather dubious, and very little empirical research has been done.*

To document its growing importance for the region, the MIF, an autonomous fund managed by the IDB, began analyzing remittances in 2000[31] due to their increasing importance for the region. In subsequent years, the MIF held 14 conferences in nine countries and conducted 12 studies and 6 surveys among remittance senders from the industrialized North to their families in five countries in Latin America. Funds were also invested in several entities to develop their remittance programs.

Through the IDB's work, remittances were given their rightful place, began to be seriously accounted for, and made the media and politicians understand the remittance markets and, slowly, the industry as a whole.

Latin American central banks, as well as regulatory bodies, developed and participated in symposiums and events where the industry began to make a presence. It was the efforts of the IDB, then the CEMLA, and the World Bank that brought remittance and payment service providers into the spotlight.

The research surrounding remittances that came to light after the year 2000, was a significant contribution to the development of the industry changing the perception of the business world and bringing major changes to the sector.

---

31 BID-FOMIN - Remesas - https://bit.ly/3zNqUDs

In Washington, D.C., from June 28-30, 2005, IDB's Multilateral Investment Fund (MIF) held the first international forum on remittances and their nexus to technology, financial services and housing for immigrants and their families in their native countries[32]. The second forum was held in 2007, also in Washington, D.C. at the IDB headquarters[33]. At the third forum in 2009, the United Nations International Fund for Agricultural Development (IFAD) took the initiative and started the Global Forums, with Tunisia hosting the first one[34].

In 2005, Dilip Ratha and Samuel Munzele Maimbo edited the book[35] titled, *Remittances: Development Impact and Future Prospects* which compiled and condensed into nearly 400 pages the facts then known about the sector and recommended ways for governments, public servants, and development agencies to expand the market and improve the lives of migrants and their families. The contributors of this book presented papers at the *International Conference on Migrant Remittances: Development Impact, Opportunities for the Financial Sector and Future Prospects*, organized by the Department for International Development and the World Bank in collaboration with the International Migration Policy Programme, in October 2003, in London. It was the *who is who* of remittances studies at the beginning of the century: Abdusalam Omer, Abul Kalam Azad, Admos O. Chimhowu, Antonique Koning, Barnabé Ndarishikanye, Caroline Pinder, Cerstin Sander, David C. Grace, Devesh Kapur, Gina El Koury, Ildefonso F. Bagasao, James P. Korovilas, Jenifer Piesse, John Page, Manuel Orozco, Nikos Passas, Norbert Bielefeld, Raul Hernandez-Coss, Richard H. Adams Jr. and Roger Ballard.

Dilip Ratha started working at the World Bank in 1992, and in the more than 30 years at the bank, he was crucial in the studies of remittances and their importance. Dilip was born in Sindhekela, Balangir, Odisha, in India where he completed his school education and later graduated in Economics and Mathematics. After completing his Master's degree at Jawaharlal Nehru

---

32 Interamerican Development Bank (IDB) Multilateral Investment Fund (MIF); IDB fund to hold international forum on remittances, June 28-30; June 21, 2005 - https://bit.ly/3Bq90I9
33 International Fund for Agricultural Development (IFAD), Multilateral Investment Fund (MIF); International Forum on Remittances 2007, Washington; 18 - 19 October 2007 - https://bit.ly/3cIlL6q
34 International Fund for Agricultural Development (IFAD); Global Forum on Remittances 2009, Tunis 22 - 23 October 2009 - https://bit.ly/3Q6JbAR
35 Dilip Ratha y Samuel Munzele Maimbo: Remittances: Development Impact and Future Prospects; Washington, DC: World Bank (2005) - https://bit.ly/3SmnH4C

University, he received his PhD from the Institute of Statistics (ISI) in New Delhi in 1988. In 1992 he joined the World Bank and moved to the U.S. The industry worldwide owes Dilip a great deal for making remittances part of most governments' plans, which, along with migration, are essential components of any development effort. Throughout his writings, studies, presentations, programs, and broad understanding of migration, Dilip has demonstrated the importance of remittances on both sides of a corridor, origin and destination, and we are grateful for his perseverance and dedication.

The Migration and Remittances Team of the Development Prospects Group at the World Bank, Dilip Ratha, Irena Omelaniuk, and Sanket Mohapatra, published the first Migration and Remittances Brief[36] in June, 2006. The briefs, like the issue 38 that was published in June 16, 2023, contains an analysis of remittances and migration trends, the major sociopolitical events and their impact, with a worldwide view and region by region.

> **The briefs are an invaluable tool for governments, regulators, industry, that have contributed to understanding the market since they were first published.**

The role of multilateral organizations, the analysis and research of countless experts on the subject, and the role of trade union representatives, all contributed to bringing the reality of remittances to the public eye and pulling them from anonymity –and informality and stigmatization– in which they had lived for almost two to three decades. Multilateral organizations believed, in the beginning of the century, that only banks should be in charge of paying remittances and contributing to financial inclusion and did everything that they could to facilitate their entry into the remittance business. This view has evolved with the role of fintechs and MMOs in the financial inclusion of large populations of underserved customers, shifting the view that only banks could be the vehicle for the financial benefit of people without economic means.

---

[36] Dilip Ratha, Irena Omelaniuk, and Sanket Mohapatra:Migration and Remittances Brief 1, The Migration and Remittances Team, Development Prospects Group, World Bank, June 28, 2006 - https://bit.ly/3XLGqdv

REGULATIONS EVOLVE

In October 2001, at an extraordinary plenary session, FATF issued eight recommendations - which in 2004 would become nine - requiring all states to adopt and implement them immediately, in addition to the 40 recommendations on money laundering originally signed in 1990. The UN General Assembly had approved the UN Convention for the Suppression of the Financing of Terrorism in December 1999, and the UN Security Council passed Resolution 1373 for member states to step up their fight against financial networks supporting terrorists.

> International organizations and governments began to improve the regulation of NBFIs by providing a legal and juridical framework more in line with the relevance they were acquiring in all markets, gained from a new understanding of the industry.

As remittance data was acknowledged and the efforts to change the concept of financial inclusion to incorporate NFBIs, regulatory entities began to issue laws and licensing processes that changed the sector fundamentally, modernizing it. Many countries went through similar processes in the new millennium's first decade as information sharing became more widespread. Some countries took longer to address the need for clarity and formalization of NBFIs but most eventually did it. By the second decade of the millennium, regulatory agencies would face the challenge of regulating a new breed of NBFIs, the fintechs.

The changes that occurred in Europe were the most decisive steps towards transforming laws to allow NBFIs to grow and expand, laying the foundations for the brewing payment revolution.

The concern over terrorism financing, the need to combat drug trafficking, the control of corruption in governments and tax evasion and tax havens, made the policy makers aware of the need to increase control and report requirements over the financial services market.

Both NBFIs and banks had to pay more attention to incoming and outgoing transactions, gain a better understanding of their clients and the origin of the funds transferred, and develop better risk matrices.

Financial investigation units (FIUs) became more sophisticated and pursued investigations through international agreements, which led to more information exchange and common strategies.

Multilateral agencies were promoting functional rather than institutional regulation. It implied the need to review previous regulations to increase market transparency and, most importantly, to encourage domestic and international competition of all financial services providers, NBFIs and banks.

The vision of improving cross-border payments among EU members also transformed payments among non-EU European countries, former African and Asian colonies and by extension, the entire globe. This happened in 2007[37] with the approval of the Payment Services Directive (PSD), which aligns the legal frameworks for money transfer services in the EU by creating the Payment Institutions (PIs), a single license for all payment service providers, excluding banking institutions or electronic money issuers, EMIs. For example, EMIs can have virtual wallets, where they *hold* the public's money - funds are held in a custodial bank account - while PIs handle transactions as money in transit only. This is a simplified explanation of a more complex topic at the regulatory level and has specific aspects according to each jurisdiction.

The PSD has succeeded in aligning payment services regulations in all member states, including remittances; many updates have been released since it was first published[38], and it will continue to be updated as the market evolves. The PSD also introduced the Single Euro Payments Area (SEPA), the initiative that allows payments to be made from an account located anywhere in the area with the same conditions, efficiency and security as domestic payments in each country. Other non-member countries have joined SEPA, such as Iceland, Liechtenstein, Monaco, Norway, San Marino, Switzerland, and Andorra.

As for EMIs, the EU had already published the Electronic Money Directive (EMD) in 2000, which provided the opportunity for quasi-bank companies, with lower capital requirements than banks, to offer prepaid services, such as virtual wallets or cards that store value, such as gift cards. The

---

37 IFAD: The use of remittances and financial inclusion; A report by the International Fund for Agricultural Development and the World Bank Group to the G20 Global Partnership for Financial Inclusion September 2015 - https://bit.ly/3KTxGLJ

38 From Remittances to M-Payments: Understanding "Alternative" Means of Payment within the Common Framework of Retail Payments System Regulation; The International Bank for Reconstruction and Development / The World Bank, October 2012 - https://bit.ly/3x1AW1T

UK, a leading market for payment developments, prompted the Financial Services Authority (FSA) to issue a series of recommendations that made this country a very attractive place to establish operations before Brexit changed all that. The Electronic Money Association (EMA)[39] was formed in 2001 to represent the growing industry.

Moneybookers, created by German entrepreneurs Daniel Klein and Benjamin Kullmann in 2001, was the first e-money institution to be authorized in the UK. It was renamed Skrill in 2011. At that time, the company had more than 25 million users and over 120,000 corporate customers[40]. PayPal Europe was also licensed in 2001.

During the first years after PSD was introduced, the UK attracted the majority of MTOs obtaining PI licenses, passporting these licenses to other EU member states, and deploying services in an organized and transparent manner, resulting in a significant growth of NFBIs on the continent.

The UK, however, would leave the EU after the public referendum on June 23, 2016 led to 51.9% of voters supporting the exit, much to the dismay of all the sector. The British government invoked Article 50 of the Treaty in March 2017, initiating a two-year process that was to conclude with its exit on March 29, 2019. This deadline was extended several times due to the complexity and disagreements in the negotiations and internal parliamentary disputes, until January 31, 2020.

In 2020, 401 Payment Institutions (PIs) were operating in the UK, of which 52 PIs and 38 EMIs became licensed that year. In 2021, the UK granted 152 licenses: 107 PIs and 45 EMIs. Buu, in 2022, there was a significant slowdown in issuing EMI licenses in the EEA and the UK. In 2022, more authorizations were revoked than EMIs authorized in the UK. UK EMIs have had to adapt to post-Brexit requirements on serving EU customers: ten did so in 2020, nine in 2021, and four in 2022[41].

With Brexit, UK companies with locally granted licenses no longer had the option of *passporting*[42]. Ireland and the Netherlands were the first choic-

---

39 EMA: History timeline - https://bit.ly/3QmnJrc
40 Remus Zoica: Everything You Need To Know About Moneybookers – Past, Present and Future, Comprehensive Guides, Updated April 11, 2022 - https://bit.ly/3TKdyje
41 E-Money Trends 2022, TheBanks.eu, 19 December 2022 - https://bit.ly/3rysfw0
42 FCA: Payment Services and Electronic Money – Our Approach: The FCA's role under the Payment Services Regulations 2017 and the Electronic Money Regulations 2011, November 2021 (version 5) - https://bit.ly/3eumWHq

es; language and a welcoming attitude were key. Other EU member states such as Lithuania, Estonia, Cyprus, and Malta decided to compete as host countries for fintechs that were emerging, promoting simplified licensing processes and reducing investment barriers. Unfortunately, some of these countries let their guard down regarding control requirements and audits, staining their reputation. They have been eagerly changing their controls to prevent their PIs from being banned in other jurisdictions.

In 1998, Spanish regulations required licensing from the Banco de España (Bank of Spain, BDE)[43] for MTOs to operate. Previously, only registration was required. New control measures were implemented as a result of this regulation.

During the turn of the millennium, Spanish banks concluded that they had a great opportunity to attract migrants and their intention was to offer remittances to them at a very low price or even for free to clients of the bank. In 2002, BBVA announced[44] the opening of dedicated stores in different Spanish cities to offer remittance services. The bank opened 130 *Dinero Express* branches, while other banks followed suit with similar strategies: Banco Santander acquired Latino Envíos, Banco Popular launched Mundo Credit opening 59 branches and La Caixa unveiled Caixa Giros. Just six years later, BBVA announced[45] the closure of the operation, keeping 15 points as restructured bank branches and relocating 230 employees. Failure to understand migrants and remittances made the bank lose more than 7 million euros in this venture; it only acquired 138,000 users. In 2008, BBVA had a 7.2% market share and was ranked sixth in the national ranking - the top-ranked Spanish institution. Similar measures were taken by the other Spanish commercial banks. Santander, Caja Madrid and La Caixa didn't establish specific ethnic channels. Banesto, which had purchased Cambios Sol in 2004, sold the company to MGI.

Movistar Remesas later joined the banks' unsuccessful attempt to provide money transfers to migrants. This new division of Telefónica started

---

43 BOE: Real Decreto 2660/1998, de 14 de diciembre, sobre el cambio de moneda extranjera en establecimientos abiertos al público distintos de las entidades de crédito.- https://bit.ly/3L2pCIC
44 BBVA crea Dinero Express para captar clientes entre los inmigrantes; EL PAIS Empresas, Cinco Días; October 24, 2002 - https://bit.ly/3A1GRF7
45 BBVA cierra el 90% de las oficinas de su filial Dinero Express; EL PAIS Empresas, Cinco Días; November 7, 2008 - https://bit.ly/3JW9CY3

operations in 2010. Apart from providing money transfers, Movistar Remesas intended to grant consumer credit, offering customers advance payments on their pending bills (e.g. electricity, water, gas or telephone). After three years, Telefónica decided to abandon the sector permanently. Their announcement[46] stated that *"a sufficient volume could not be reached to justify continued activity"*.

One issue in Spain that I want to comment on is the regulation of agents. At the time agents were mostly *locutorios*, calling shops, offering communication services; these services changed with the rapid evolution of telecommunications: first there were calling cabins, then calling cards, toll free numbers with codes and then VOIP (Voice over IP - internet calls). In theory, *locutorios* were required to be agents of only one licensed company in order to prevent agents from structuring by using several providers. In practice, this requirement was never met. Most of the *locutorios* were forced by client needs to offer different services based on preference, ethnic group served and pricing. The Banco de España (BDE) registered the agents based on the company or the individual's name, with their Tax Identification Code, but the address of the commercial establishment was not required. Agents established several companies at the same location and worked with different money transfer companies.

In 2007, Spain adopted the EU PSD regulation, and restrictions on exclusive agents were removed. It has been reported that by 2015, more than half of the 15,000 *locutorios* that existed in Spain before 2007 had disappeared. More than 50 MTOs entered a *validation process* to adjust to these new EU measures and become Payment Institutions (PIs). The Spanish Association of Money Transfer Agencies (ANAED - *Asociación Nacional de Agencias de Envio de Dinero*) became the Spanish Association of Payment Institutions (AENPA).

One of the major changes brought about by the PSD in most of the countries was the *reduction* of the minimum capital requirement for licensed entities, now called Payment Institutions (PIs). In Spain, prior to the PSD, the minimum capital was €300,000 for those MTOs authorized to manage remittances of workers domiciled in Spain, and €1.8 million for those authorized to manage any type of international transfers. The new requirement ranged from €20,000 to €125,000 depending on the services provided by

---

46 Santiago Millán Alonso: Telefónica decide liquidar su filial de envío de remesas; EL PAIS Cinco Días, May 14, 2013 - https://bit.ly/3CaFhD3

the entity. In addition, in Spain domestic payments were allowed for PIs, a service limited to banks and the Postal Service. Furthermore, a series of measures were put in place to promote greater transparency in the market, which allowed BDE to increase its control and enforcement of the sector. PSD2, the second instalment of revised regulation was done in 2018[47].

> **The cultural ties between Spain and Latin America is the reason behind the majority of remittances from Spain to that region, which is over 60%.**

By 2021, Colombia was the main destination country for remittances (€1,089 million), followed by Morocco (€1,022 million), Ecuador (€784 million) and the Dominican Republic (€545 million). With 78% and 63% growth respectively, Honduras and Pakistan are the countries experiencing the highest growth since 2017[48]. In the EU, about 53% of total personal remittance flows in 2020 occurred within the Member States, i.e., EU residents predominantly sending money to each other. However, there are considerable discrepancies: in countries such as Poland (98%), Spain (93%), Greece (91%), Lithuania (84%) and Italy (82%) outbound personal remittances went mostly to markets outside the EU. For Portugal, where the main remittance destination is Brazil, 66% of outbound remittances are sent outside the EU.

Unlike Spain, the banking sector in Portugal handled foreign exchange and remittances until the adoption of the European regulation. Portugal has even taken more time to adopt some of the EU measures. Pedro Santos, a Real Transfer executive, describes the scene: *"There were no MTOs here. In Portugal, it was banned. In Portugal, remittances have always been regulated by the central bank, and only banks and post offices were allowed before 2002. In 1997-98, there was a Brazilian company called Cambitur - which in 1994-95 was one of the largest companies in Brazil - developed a special program working with banks, but the Central Bank suspended it because they were making payments directly to an English company; that was forbidden and it was suspended"*[49].

---

47 European Central Bank (ECB): The revised Payment Services Directive (PSD2) and the transition to stronger payments security, May 2018 - https://bit.ly/3eyytFP
48 España dispara un 33% el envío de remesas a Marruecos en la pandemia; Cinco Días, September 21, 2021 - https://bit.ly/3RBuRS0
49 Entrevista virtual, grabada y transcrita, realizada a Pedro Santos, el 25 de mayo de 2022, por Ana Karina González.

Regulations evolved in that time in most of the countries originating remittances in North-South corridors. In Japan, for example, foreign exchange transactions, and remittances, were restricted to banks licensed under the Banking Law before the Payment Services Act (PSA) was adopted in April 2010. However, there were certain companies called banking agents that deposited remittance funds in banks. One of these companies was called Japonesito Express, a Peruvian-Chinese business that sold music and nostalgic products to Peruvians and other Latin Americans on the island, while also providing shipping services. I personally met the owner who described Colombian and Dominican remittances coming mostly from *nightlife girls* that made him close late to protect them from returning to their apartments with cash. Suspicions regarding the origin of the funds the company handled led to its closure by the Japanese authorities and the leverage of fines. It took the owner many years to prove the legality and transparency of the orders the company handled. Anyway, the reputational damage led to the closure of the business.

As in Vietnam, the Philippines and Korea, there is an extensive Chinese colony in Japan. Remittances from Japan to China reached US$5 billion in 2018, followed by Korea (US$1.6 billion), the Philippines (US$1.3 billion), Vietnam (US$500 million), Brazil (US$375 million) and Peru (US$150 million)[50].

Japan has a large Peruvian and Brazilian population due to the migration of Japanese to these countries in the XIX century. A treaty in 1899 led to the first arrival of 790 Japanese to the port of El Callao; more than 20,000 would follow, mostly men. Japanese-Peruvians will soon reach 100,000 by the middle of the XX century and now the country has more than 200,000 inhabitants who consider themselves Japanese. The only Asian president of a Latin American country was Alberto Fujimori, of Japanese descent. In Brazil, more than 2 million people consider themselves Japanese. In the later part of the century Brazilian and Peruvian Japanese descendants have migrated to Japan; there are more than 250,000 Brazilian migrants in Japan and 60,000 Peruvian. There are even Japanese denomination of these descendants: issei for the migrants born in Japan, *nissei* their children, *sansei* the grandchildren and *yonsei* the great-grand children.

---

50 Statista: Value of remittances sent from Japan in 2018, by country of destination - https://bit.ly/3x0111c

Kyodai Remittance is the brand of Unidos Co, Ltd. Unidos was established in 2000 to support the money transfer for the Peruvian community in Japan. Under the 2010 Act, Unidos was registered as a money transfer company. City Express, InstaRem and Japan Money Express, which also work with WU and MGI, have been very active industry players in this market.

Regulation evolved in the US too, mostly concerning compliance related requirements, controls and reports. More than ten years have passed since FinCEN issued the BSA regulations defining the categories of MSBs in 1999. Besides the work done by the US States[51], the Federal government decided to hold public meetings which began in 1997, lead by FinCEN, giving members of the financial services industry an opportunity to discuss the proposed MSB regulations and any impact they might have on their operations. Meetings were held in Vienna, Virginia, and New York on July 1997, San Jose, California and Chicago on August, and Vienna, Virginia, on September. *The Definitions and Other Regulations Relating to Money Services Businesses* rule was published in the Federal Register on May 12, 2009, the comment period ended in September 9, 2009 and the final rule was released on July 21, 2011. Besides a detailed clarification on what constitutes a MSB, the rule included the federal registration of NBFIs, whether they had a licenses in one of the states or not, including foreign MSBs doing business in the US[52].

CROSS-BORDER PAYMENT CONSULTING

Consulting for the industry also began in the first two decades of the new century. A few legal counsel firms have helped money transfer companies since the 80s and 90s. One of them is Merle, Brown & Nakamura[53] in New York. Pierre Merle —now retired— entered private practice in 1983 after ten years as General Counsel for a money transmitter and foreign payments business. Hervás Abogados[54] began operating in 1988 in Madrid, Spain, and has managed ANAED, the Asociación Española de Entidades de Pago, since 1998. Certainly, there were others that I should recognize.

---

51 Thomas Brown: 50-State Survey, Money Transmitter Licensing Requirements, UC Berkeley Law School, Paul Hastings LLP - https://bit.ly/3F4ujjO
52 Federal Register/Vol. 76, No. 140, Thursday, July 21, 2011, Rules and Regulations: Definitions and Other Regulations Relating to Money Services Businesses - https://bit.ly/3XRv5bM
53 Merle, Brown & Nakamura, P.C. - https://bit.ly/3ZhOLGv
54 Hervás Abogados - https://bit.ly/3EC6FtX

Many specialized Legal, Regulatory, and Compliance consultants began their work after the Patriot Act in the US and the developments of the PSD in Europe, as MTOs needed outside help to face the regulations and the challenging work of evolving their risk practices; companies needed to adapt quickly to the new environment. Connie Fenchel, a friend and mentor who came in 2011 to help IMTC with the development of compliance courses, helped develop a compliance culture, as well as Mike McDonald and David Landsman, and the compliance professionals they inspired.

In 2001, Charles Intriago created the Association of Certified Anti-Money Laundering Specialists (ACAMS), the world's first certification board for individuals with compliance functions within institutions.

In his early days, he was assisted by John Byrne, Al Gillum, Mike McDonald, Saskia Rietbroek, and Dan Soto, who, ten years later, in an interview with Karla Monterrosa-Yancey[55], proudly recalled his contribution to making the compliance function important as well as promoting, from the beginning, its crucial monitoring and control role. The development of the CAMS certificate was a major undertaking. Al Gillum reflected in the interview: *The exam writing process has been one of the most challenging tasks that I have been a part of. We took great effort to make sure that there was a viable process in place so that the exam would stand up to any committee that would like to audit the process.* The CAMS designation for Anti-Money Laundering (AML) professionals was a major step in the evolution of the role of compliance professionals worldwide. ACAMS got all Compliance Officers certified, to the point that, without this diploma, their reputations would be questioned.

Compliance officers from the industry took the ACAMS exams but always complained that they aimed more at banks than the more transactional companies from the NBFI world. This is why the NMTA in 2006, and later on the IMTC in 2010, developed compliance seminars more specific to the compliance function in the remittance and foreign exchange sector, with the support of the experts that ACAMS developed and trained. Compliance

---

[55] Karla Monterrosa-Yancey: A Look-Back: 10 Years of ACAMS; ACAMS Today, September 2, 2011 - https://bit.ly/3dS6FMs

certificates designed to answer regional or country-specific issues emerged in many countries, and the compliance activity became standardized globally. With IMTC –now CrossTech– we have developed certification seminars taught in different countries[56]: Brazil, Mexico, Guatemala, Cuba, Nigeria, Kenya, Turkey, Spain, Belgium, UK, India, and The Philippines. In May 2023, at the CrossTech Payments event in Miami, we developed the first compliance seminar devoted to B2B money transfers. Cross-border Business payments are set to grow exponentially in the next few years and Compliance Professionals must understand KYB –Know your Business– and the different risks associated with B2B.

There were no money transfer consultants in the business space at the time. I seriously questioned my future in the industry during this time of transition. I felt that my time as an executive in the sector had ended. I did not see my role in the future of the industry. Returning to academia was appealing to me. I sought positions in university departments in the US and Europe that might hire someone with my expertise in migration and remittances. A PhD was in order. In those days, I had a couple of opportunities to work in the multilateral sector. However, I was skeptical of the funding of some bank remittance projects under financial inclusion umbrellas. I also knew that it would be challenging for me to adapt to the internal culture of these organizations unless I would make a career in them.

Leon Isaacs, a renowned industry consultant, told me in an interview for this book[57] that in 2007, he faced the same dilemma. After working in several companies in the sector, he realized how little regulators and multilateral agencies knew about it, despite all the reports beginning to analyze and quantify remittances. Public sector experts did not understand the high cost of remittances and frowned upon the sector, claiming they were exploiting poor migrants with excessive costs. He decided to create DMA Global, his consulting firm. He began working on a wide range of projects that showed that the private and public sectors are capable of working together since their ultimate goal is to boost the sector's competitiveness.

---

56 These evolving Compliance Courses have been created with the help of many experts in the field: David Landsman, Connie Fenchel, Zory Muñoz, Joe Ciccolo, Lourdes Soto, Laura Goldzung, Amy Greenwood, Kathy Tomasofsky and members of CrossTech's Compliance Council.
57 Personal Interview with Leon Isaacs on April 8, 2022.

Leon realized that his work in Africa, the region with the greatest challenges and needs, would be his focus. With his practical experience in remittances, he helped governments and the international donor community understand the needs and challenges of the private sector and, at the same time, helped explain development agencies' perspectives to the private sector, making him the world's leading expert on this topic. He considers that one of the greatest achievements in his career was to raise awareness among public and private entities on the African continent about the changes needed to further improve the delivery of financial services at all levels.

Some of my industry colleagues began to ask me for consulting, particularly in expanding their distribution chains and determining which existing correspondents would be best suited for contracts and agreements to expand. Developing partnerships, as I had done for TITAN for many years, slowly became a source of income. During that time, the technological capacity of service providers was already becoming a determining factor in establishing the needed integration, besides reputation and compliance know-how.

In 1997, TITAN began a new phase when the partners and the Board of Directors decided to dismiss the manager who had led the company through its most difficult years, Ricardo Londoño, and to establish a new management team. The company hired Juan José Botero as CFO, and the Board asked my sister Michele to help them temporarily as the COO to support this new phase. She had to bring a new partner to Rapid-Envios in Miami so she could dedicate time to her work at TITAN.

Soon after, TITAN offered me to become a strategic and marketing consultant to lead the new international development vision and recover some lost relations with correspondents. The idea was to reestablish the company's image in the industry, develop direct marketing plans inside and outside the country, and represent the company in international industry events and meetings. Teamwork with the company's commercial director, Olga Patricia Medina, led us to carry out campaigns with the senders and their families in Colombia through promotions for Mother's Day, Father's Day, the first day of school, Christmas, and other regional festivities. Thousands of *novenas* —booklets with prayers for family gatherings in the nine days leading up to Christmas Eve— were distributed to hundreds of MTO agents in the US and Europe. These marketing campaigns were very successful and led to the best ten years the company experienced in its history.

> I founded Mohr World Consulting in Miami in 2001 —now CrossTech Consultants— to take care of the consultant projects brought by colleagues from the industry as they began new companies or needed my help with a large variety of projects.

Beatriz Navia, who became TITAN's Compliance Officer, recalls these structural changes in the company and her work:

> The Compliance Officer as a requirement from the Superintendency in Colombia happened in 2000. I was appointed Compliance Officer since my legal background helped me understand the laws and regulations. That was it. The purpose was to monitor the company's operations to ensure no money laundering transactions were coming through; the idea was to prevent money launderers from using the company's services. The team I had consisted of six dedicated people. We had software that listed the number of transactions per individual, their value, and the frequency. As they were family remittances, we knew that they should arrive once or twice a month, and the amount was a fixed amount that a sender would send to their family after paying their living expenses; that was 95% of the business: family remittances. At the start, we had to issue a form for every transaction and send it along with a copy to the Banco de la República; it was called the "exchange declaration", even if it was for US $50. It was a lot of work, but the new management team was very supportive. I participated with Hugo in many compliance events in the US, Argentina, etc[58].

The technology race in the industry, not only for the system to help in transaction monitoring but also to make operations more efficient and process money transfers faster, needed major investment in resources, people, and equipment. The need to provide payment information back to the sending company, both to help with the cash flow and provide information to the MTO, the agent, and the sender, was one of the great challenges of the time.

---

58 Virtual Interview with Beatriz Navia, on April 28, 2022, conducted, recorded and transcribed by Lucía Salazar.

THE KROLL REPORT

As a consultant for TITAN, I led the investigation that the company undertook by contracting the services of Kroll in Miami to investigate any legal or regulatory events, reports, or briefings from any government or regulatory agency in any place in the world, related to TITAN and any of its partners and employees in senior management positions, as well as its major correspondents and their owners.

Kroll is a global risk management consulting firm headquartered in New York City and founded in 1972 by Jules B. Kroll as a research firm for the financial sector. Kroll describes itself as a company specializing in risk management. With such a report in place, it could help the company establish and manage bank accounts in the US and Europe.

Kroll's final report was comprehensive and detailed, resulting from a lengthy and resource-intensive investigation. Four main points were covered in the final document:

1. An analysis of Operation Chimborazo: The report detailed the operations and legal events that occurred in each country, as well as press articles, legal concepts, regulatory reports, etc. According to the study, no charges were filed in any country, and no further legal action was recommended, such as lawsuits, corrections, etc. Kroll's advice was to be proactive in company relations with authorities, participate in industry events, etc., to manage its public relations more effectively.

2. Although already settled, the report also examined the 1985 charges against Cuevas Asociados and its partners. Concerning those charges, neither the U.S. nor any other country had any legal proceedings or reports from governmental authorities or control agencies that should be followed up or analyzed relating to this case..

3. Kroll's report extensively analyzed the potential existence of links between the company, its partners or its directors, whether commercially, legally, or through judicial proceedings, with Oscar Fernando Cuevas Cepeda's illicit activities. His connections with Colombian politicians, such as former Colombian president Andrés Pastrana and his arrests, years after his sentence in the US was commuted and he was deported, allegedly under a certain kind of deal with US

authorities, had been extensively discussed in the news[59]. Press articles and publications alluding to the family relationship between him and the owners of TITAN had created some reputational damage that needed to be addressed. Kroll found no evidence of police investigations, charges, connections, or significant threats. Kroll's only suggestion was to monitor media coverage and the issue of clarifications by specialized firms, if needed.

4. From 1995 to 2003, an Argentinian Special Investigation Commission, led by the Chaco Province Deputy Elisa María Carrió (widely known as Lilita Carrió), a lawyer, professor, and politician, tried to bring charges against former President Carlos Menen. Lilita Carrió was convinced of the corruption allegation and eagerly tried to untangle a large web of cover-ups. In her investigations, she discovered links between President Menem and Oscar Fernando Cuevas Cepeda and tried to connect this relationship to Operation Chimborazo, through family ties. Additionally, links of Oscar Fernando Cuevas Cepeda to former Peruvian president Alan García were also reported by her, resulting in headlines in the Peruvian press. Kroll found that this Special Commission did mention in its 2001 final report Hugo Cuevas Gamboa and Operation Chimborazo without building any case or making any wrongdoing allegations. Consequently, after an analysis by Kroll's team in Argentina, they recommended there was no need for clarifications or doing anything else.

The final report of the Argentinian Special Investigation Commission, led by Ms. Carrió, mentions many foreign exchange companies such as Bedford House International, Beacon Hill Service Corporation, Transafex, South Pacific Trade, Mundial Cambios, and others. Money changers in Argentina and the Southern Cone used many of these companies to clear funds from exchange and remittance activities. MTOs in the US and Europe used these companies to be able to provide money transfer services to customers due to the changing government restrictions. Some of these firms closed or were closed down in the following years.

---

[59] Investigan Grupo de 100 Firmas de Papel: El Tiempo, 24 de agosto 1996 - https://bit.ly/3Yd62A0 - Capturado Óscar Cuevas, el rey de lavado de activos en Colombia: El Espectador, 6 Nov 2010 - https://bit.ly/3OcRzja - Policía capturó a Óscar Cuevas, uno de los delincuentes más buscados: El Tiempo, 6 de noviembre 2010 - https://bit.ly/3rUxXsk

Kroll's report was frustrating for TITAN, as there was nothing to be done on a practical level. Still, I think it gave TITAN the confidence to move forward.

@RED INTERNACIONAL

As part of my consulting work, I decided to create a network of Latin American companies that could, working together, develop a common computer system and a single integration with US and European MTOs. Developing a more consistent management of inbound and outbound funds, a forex desk, and better relationships with banks was also part of the wishlist of the Red.

Several companies in Latin America, some of which were part of TITAN's network developed as part of TPC, the aggregator I mentioned in Chapter 9, decided to believe in the proposed integration. Sadly, TITAN's IT system, which was deployed in Venezuela and Perú and was the basis for the development of @Red Internacional was never up to par. Without a common IT system, the network could not realize its full potential.

MORE Money Transfers, which made its appearance in Uruguay in 2003, developed such a system and was able to deploy it in Argentina, Paraguay, Brazil, and Chile. I am proud of having consulted for MORE in its early entrance into the US market, helping in the incremental growth of operations into the markets they were developing.

BANCO UNION - DR

While consulting for Banco de Credito Union in the Dominican Republic, I learned firsthand how the bank's subsidiary —called Remesas Quisqueyana before the bank was founded— developed home delivery of remittances into a sophisticated payment system.

At an early hour, nearly a hundred motorists gather in a courtyard in the center of Santo Domingo, waiting for the sealed envelopes prepared by the cashiers according to the neighborhood they served. With the help of an IT application, the amount of cash is calculated for each envelope to be distributed to the beneficiary of the remittance. Bills and small change are added as part of the funds in the envelope so the recipient, once the amount received has been counted and the receipt signed, can give a tip to the motorist.

Motorists are very familiar with their assigned neighborhoods: they know who the recipients are, when they are home or away, if they worked close by, etc. Since street names are nonexistent, they are the only ones capable of serving those neighborhoods.

Because the tips supplement the motorcyclists' basic salary, the service is relatively inexpensive compared to office payments and even account deposits. I will never forget the day I rode with a motorcyclist to deliver remittances to a neighborhood in Santo Domingo, a perfect example of what NBFIs can do for their clients through market adaptation. The country has implemented many financial inclusion strategies to change this habit and speed up the payment service with moderate success.

In very few countries, home delivery of remittances flourished, mainly due to security and cost concerns. Something similar happened in Nicaragua, and the company Rapid-o-Giros —affiliated to TITAN— founded by Alcides Ruiz, was forced to suspend operations after the bank providing cash for the delivery services decided to suspend the account, leaving the company unable to find an alternative bank.

Another home-delivery operator in Managua was Servicentro, which was acquired by Costa Rican company TeleDolar in 2017. Home delivery of remittances is still available in Armenia, Hungary, Morocco, Vietnam, the Philippines, and Indonesia.

Even if home delivery of different services —groceries, medication— offered by neighborhood stores and small pharmacies in third-world countries had been disappearing, COVID, however, has boosted home deliveries in every country around the world. Obviously, technology platforms have played a crucial role in the post-COVID sustainability of these services, including remittances.

THE SALE OF TITAN

Despite the company's positive results from 1997 to 2005, by 2006, Casas de Cambio Plenas (CCP) began to lose money, as I noted in Chapter 7 describing the Colombian Remittance Market. Competition with banks was impossible to manage, and discriminatory regulations forced them to sell their remittance dollars in a so-called free market where the only buyers were the banks themselves. With no foreign accounts and no ability to offer foreign currency to companies or individuals, CCP were doomed to fail.

The Colombian newspaper El Tiempo published an article[60] by Fernando Gonzalez in July 2009: *Though exchange houses handle not only cash exchange but also money orders and remittances, the truth is that they have little room to operate, and their total disappearance is imminent.*

The only solution, to acquire a *Compañía de Financiamiento Comercial* (CFC) and merge the remittance operations, was pursued but never materialized. Other consultants were hired, and we all reached the same conclusion: TITAN was forced to close down, sell, or merge. Some partners were not ready to move in this direction.

A 2007 requirement by the Financial Superintendency of a capitalization of US $1 million by the company, and in a race against time to meet this deadline, Mrs. Angela Cuevas de Dolmetsch and her family agreed to purchase the remaining 50% of the shares owned by my sisters and me.

Titan tried to stay afloat, reducing staff and operations until it finally declared bankruptcy in 2017.

---

60 Fernando González: Dólar en efectivo: un mercado sin control; El Tiempo, julio 2, 2009 - https://bit.ly/3Qb5iGk

CHAPTER 2

CONSOLIDATION: THE MARKET SHIFTS

When I stood outside the main auditorium of the IDB Conference Center in Washington, DC, waiting for the first international forum about remittances to start, I sensed that the industry was emerging from anonymity. A different future lay ahead, I thought. Besides WU and MGI, a few of the ethnic companies I knew were there, and I greeted their CEOs and Directors before entering the room. I met several bank representatives interested in the industry, which was a welcoming sign. The date was June 28, 2005, my wife's birthday. She was not thrilled about my trip to Washington, so she flew to Colombia to celebrate with her extended family there.

One of the attendees, a Chilean architect, told me all about the IDB building, designed by Skidmore, Owings & Merrill, an architectural firm in the city, that he admired, particularly the design of the interior space, which was impressive. This industry has always brought such a wide variety of professionals from so many different fields, as well as a wide range of nationalities, not to mention the stories of how they became passionate, like me, about remittances and migration.

Once inside the conference room, the first speakers were Bank of Mexico Governor Guillermo Güemes García and IDB President Enrique V. Iglesias. To document its growing importance for Latin America, the MIF, an autonomous fund managed by this organization, had begun analyzing remittances in 2000[61] For an industry that was barely aware of the volumes of its closest competitors in the corridors where they specialized, MIF reported that Latin America and the Caribbean attracted $45 billion in 2004. U.S. Senator Paul S. Sarbanes spoke during lunch in addition to some industry representatives. Representatives from commercial banks, credit unions, microfinance institutions, regulators, and academia were in attendance, which gave me a glimpse of what was to come. The organization encouraged all US and Latin American financial institutions to join the sector. There was a display of technologies used by service providers on the ninth floor, emphasizing small innovative companies.

One month later, on July 25-26, in Miami, I attended the *First Continental Congress of Money Remittance Agents*, organized by three industry colleagues: Dominican entrepreneur Ernesto Armenteros, US Attorney Jorge Guerrero, and Chilean businessman Carlos Grossman.

These three pioneers wanted to create the *American Confederation of Money Remitters* (ACMR). Ernesto Armenteros is a Dominican businessman whose father had acquired Remesas Quisqueyana in New York in the 1980s and was CEO since 1993, responsible for developing the branches and agent network. Jorge Guerrero, an American lawyer, was one of the founding members of the NMTA and one of the first experts in the compliance area -he was Chief Compliance Officer of VIGO- and had started his consulting firm, External Compliance Officer, Inc. in 1999, before founding Optima Compass in 2005. Carlos Grossman, a Chilean businessman, worked extensively with foreign exchange and remittances in his country.

A keynote address by Manuel Orozco of the Interamerican Dialogue and the presence of Don Semisky of the DEA and David Tilzer of the IRS were notable. For the first time, derisking was discussed, and national organizations voiced severe complaints. Freddy Ortiz from ADEREDI (the Dominican Association of Remittance Companies) gave a chilling account of the situation in the Dominican Republic. He later published his book *Errores Gubernamentales En Las Crisis Cambiarias - El Caso De Las Empresas Remesadoras*[62]. Alfonso Garzón Méndez from ASOCAMBIARIA (the

---

61 BID-FOMIN - Remesas - https://bit.ly/3zNqUDs
62 Freddy Ortiz: Errores Gubernamentales En Las Crisis Cambiarias - El Caso De Las Empresas Remesadoras; Santo Domingo : Mediabyte, 2010; ISBN:9789945003079 - https://bit.ly/3dgCNZM

Colombian Association of Exchange Houses) denounced the discriminatory policies adopted by the Colombian regulator towards the industry.

ACMR was not established, primarily due to the diversity of issues the industry was facing at the time. The following year, 2006, the NMTA, now headed by David Landsman, decided to continue holding an event in South Florida, a seminar on compliance on October 30 and 31 of that year. These seminars led to the first IMTC event in Miami in 2010, which I organized with David Landsman and became the flagship event of the remittance industry.

> **The cross-border payments industry began to radically change in the first decade of the new millennium.**

The ethnic companies that survived the 90s in the US and Europe needed more robust capital structures to compete and corporate governance that met the authorities' demands and expectations. Investments in IT —both back-office and remote agent access— and an accelerated need for liquidity had increased the need for working capital. Additionally, commercial banks were unwilling to work with ethnic companies, concerned about reputation and compliance risks based on widespread preconceptions.

Research and information made it clear to investors that the market would continue its exponential growth, and the larger ethnic MTOs that had survived the tumultuous past were ripe for being acquired and transformed. The entry of banks in paying markets and the discriminative regulation saw many NBFIs in the destination countries facing unfavorable competition rules and conditions that gradually caused these companies to close. The market was bound to significant changes.

PRECONCEPTIONS AND BIAS

Even if the industry's image was damaged by the headlines and persecution of the 90s and the apprehension and fears of terrorist financing, many investors were interested in the future of remittances.

The legacy of misinformation and the reconceptions and bias that remittance companies have faced —and still have to face to a lesser extent

—is similar to what the cryptocurrency sector has been managing based on erroneous perceptions and *the few bad apples*. I leave it to the colleagues we interviewed for this book to contribute their opinions on the image that the industry has had to face for decades.

Francisco Sánchez Apellániz, the founder of MONEYTRANS in Belgium, stated:

> I don't really know how some kind of *black legend* arose, managed by the media and journalists, promoted by the banking system, that has targeted us directly, designed to muddy our path. We constantly feel that our industry carries a poor reputation. Why does this industry, with all the effort and all the work we do on a social level, not have better and stronger referents? We know we are very important and impactful, but this message doesn't get easily across. At least this image is not the same for our clients and those who use us daily who appreciate our services.
>
> Colombia has been the most famous case, where regulators and banks obstructed remittances and posed great difficulty for money transfer companies. Money laundering has been used as an excuse, which is totally ridiculous because when you see the amount of money that remittance companies move, fraud and money laundering are very rare cases. Compared to what is published about the financial system with the Panama Papers and all those banks being involved, we should be *the poster child*. The remittance sector is very professional, competitive, and compliant, providing a much-needed service to underprivileged individuals. We are their main competitors for the banking system, so if they can make our lives hard, they will do it. On and on.
>
> The image is better in Europe than it has been in the US. I know all my competitors very well because I get along with almost all of them - and we all want to do our best possible work. We have a major social responsibility with the person sending 50 or 60 euros. That person has worked hard to earn that money, and we have to send that money cheaply and quickly; our clients are always facing emergencies, and there is always someone with a family solving emergencies. Sometimes, they can't leave a hospital because they have to pay, and money must be sent quickly. When floods or earthquakes occur abroad, our offices become very busy, and we must ensure the money reaches families. We have an immense responsibility.

We are trying to do our best[63].

Ernesto Armenteros, who formerly served as executive vice president of Remesas Quisqueyana in the US and Dominican Republic, agrees with the point of view of Mr. Sanchez-Apellániz:

Businesses that serve migrants get shut down by the banks all the time. They threaten us. They tell us that we are vehicles for criminals, which has never been true, when 99% of the laundering goes through the big banks. It is very difficult to launder money using a remittance company, especially with today's filters and AI; But there is a prejudice based on who we are, who we serve, and where we are from. It is unfair, but it is a reality, and we have to deal with it. Working in this industry has a financial and reputational cost, but those of us who are entrepreneurs face it proudly, and eventually, we prove that we are right. It's the same with everything in life, not only with ethnic businesses but anything new and innovative. It is a steep and rough road that, even if you are not prepared for, you must face and try to get as far down the road as you can[64].

Roger Sanchez, the founder of Remesas del Caribe and director of Serviexpreso in Costa Rica, feels the same way about banks and their prejudices about exchange houses and remittance companies:

Exchange houses and remittance companies have carried a very bad stigma because, in the US, remittances, since the beginning, were not liked by the government and its officials. Here, in Costa Rica, many banks closed our accounts. I will ask the bank: *What is going on?* Large US banks threatened local banks, telling them that if they provided accounts to exchange houses or remittance companies, they would automatically close their correspondent accounts. It was tough to work without banks. The comment I always made at the IMTC conferences in Miami, where everyone complained, was that if we are regulated by the same regulator with the same compliance conditions, why do they keep closing our accounts? What made them think that they had better compliance than us? Why do regulators never do anything to help us? It's a question that never got an answer.

---

63 Virtual interview, recorded and transcribed, with Francisco Sánchez Apellániz, on April 12, 2022, by Lucía Salazar.
64 Virtual interview with Ernesto Armenteros, on June 28, 2022, conducted, recorded and transcribed by Lucía Salazar.

Here, in Costa Rica, on several occasions, I had all the paperwork ready to open an account, I have met with bank officials, etc., and they would tell me, *We have a problem. What is it?* They would say to me, confidentially, that banks in the US do not allow them to hold accounts with exchange houses or remittance companies. The US bank was dictating what the local bank could do or not do. Local bank officials were very frustrated because they knew us and they knew the services we provided. Some of them were even our clients. It made me furious[65].

Erick Schneider, an expert in digital cross-border payments, believes that governments manage two different parameters towards some financial sectors, flexible with traditional banks and tough with NBFIs and Fintechs:

When I first joined fintech WorldRemit in 2017, I was stunned to learn that, having worked in financial institutions, how governments and correspondent banks analyze remittances differs greatly from how governments and regulators analyze traditional banks. I worked at Citibank and American Express, which are regulated companies all over the world, so it's interesting to see the regulators revere those companies and how they were very well respected; they're always well perceived by regulators. With NBFIs, there is a noticeable difference. Banks and these companies handle privileged customers, who are considered secure. Businesses that serve people with less access to financial institutions, such as remittance companies serving migrants, get penalized for being outside of the banking industry, not only in terms of cost but also in ways that are entirely incomprehensible from a regulatory standpoint[66].

MTOS FOR SALE

I want to highlight some of the most notorious NBFIs acquired between 2000 and 2010. I distinctly remember when Helio Gusmao, CEO and founder of VIGO, confided with me about his necessity to sell. It was a Monday at noon, and we were having lunch at the Via Brasil restaurant across from his main office on 45th Street in Manhattan. He told me that he had been successfully sending remittances to Mexico through Uniteller,

---

65 Virtual interview with Roger Sánchez, on June 20, 2022, conducted, recorded and transcribed by Lucía Salazar.
66 Virtual interview with Erick Schneider, on June 14, 2022, conducted, recorded and transcribed by Isabel Cortés.

a newly founded company in New Jersey; still, he needed more cash flow to send over $1 million to Mexico over the past weekend. He had to prefund the weekend payments, and the Increasing volumes required more working capital to make timely wire transfers. Despite his efforts to raise funds, he had to explore new avenues.

VIGO REMITTANCE - US

VIGO, one of the most representative MTOs in the US since 1987, was sold in 2003. GMT Group, Inc., formed by Great Hill Partners in partnership with Mario Trujillo, purchased the company from its owners, Helio Gusmao, Flavio Newlands Moniz Freire, and Ivan Newlands Moniz Freire, for US $76.5 million. Great Hill, a Boston-based private equity firm managing more than $1 billion in capital, announced[67] the purchase of Vigo as a leading provider of wire transfers to more than 33 countries worldwide. It was claimed that, as of 2002, VIGO had transferred approximately US$2.5 billion and had experienced annual growth of more than 30% for the past five years.

The sale of VIGO became entangled by a lawsuit from the sellers, an interesting case[68] involving what the acquiring company claimed to be payments to recipients in Brazil using the parallel market, which was essentially true. Stopping payments through the parallel market had caused a major loss. VIGO's sellers sued their buyers, forcing them to deliver the remaining $1.1 million cash in escrow. Buyers were ordered to hand over the missing funds after a judge determined they had carried out the required audits and had made no objections at the time when they should have.

Two years later, Great Hill announced the sale of VIGO[69] to First Data Corp, the company that owned WU at the time, for US $371 million. The press release reported that Vigo operated in 45 states, with more than 3,700 agents and a payment network of 47,000 outlets worldwide. By 2004, Vigo had processed more than 8 million transactions.

---

[67] Great Hill Partners Forms GMT Group, Inc. and Acquires Vigo Remittance Corporation – Press Release, march 31, 2003 - https://bit.ly/3PW7mln
[68] Casetext: Gusmao v. GMT Group, Inc.; 06 Civ. 5113 (GEL), April 30, 2009 - https://bit.ly/3dflWXG
[69] First Data Corp. Announces Acquisition of Vigo Remittance Corp.; Press Release, May 12, 2005 - https://bit.ly/3RYz9DP

VIGO then became WU's third brand after purchasing Orlandi Valuta in 1997.

DOLEX DOLLAR EXPRESS - US

In 1984, Raul Limón founded Consultora Internacional, a well-known FEFC acquired by OBSA and, later, part of Banco Serfin, until Limón re-purchased it in 1999 and sold it to IXE. DOLEX Limón and other partners founded DOLEX in Arlington, Texas, in 1996.

In an interview for this book, Salvador Velázquez, one of its founders, stated: *Early on, we decided not to have agents in the US, but to open our own branches. A total of 550 were opened, including 60 in Spain. We had payment operations in about 40 countries, with about 300 payment correspondents in the destination markets we were serving. When I left the company, we had a vast Latin American payment network, one of the largest. Except for Haiti, we had a way to pay remittances at great exchange rates in every other country*[70].

In 2003, Global Payments Inc., a U.S. public company based in Atlanta, acquired Latin America Money Services and its subsidiary DolEx Dollar Express, Inc. (DOLEX)[71] for US $190 million, keeping most of its top executives[72].

Six years later, DOLEX was sold again. After selling VIGO to First Data (WU), Mario Trujillo began searching, planning, fundraising, and executing a new acquisition strategy. He founded Money Transfer Acquisition Inc. (MTAI), in partnership with Institutional Private Equity Investors, led by Palladium Equity Partners, Prudential, Adams Street Capital, and Parish Capital, and acquired DOLEX in 2010[73]. In parallel transactions, MTAI acquired Spanish company United Europhil, founded in 1989, and Remesas Quisqueyana (RQI), a successful MTO operating in the US focusing mainly on the Dominican Republic.

---

70 Virtual interview with Salvador Velázquez on June 6, 2022, conducted, recorded and transcribed by Lucía Salazar.
71 Rangel y socios retoman control de Consultoría: Vlex.com, dic 1, 2004 - https://bit.ly/47oYHS5
72 Global Payments completes DolEx buy; Dallas Business Journal, November 12, 2003 - https://bit.ly/47uk4la
73 Global Payments Sells Two Companies; Global Atlanta, November 18, 2009 - https://bit.ly/3OQsPOZ

Acquired by the Armenteros Family in 1986, RQI was responsible for paying orders in the Dominican Republic using a unique home delivery service that has become iconic. Using the proceeds from RQI's sale in the U.S., the Armenteros family founded Banco de Crédito Union in the Dominican Republic.

Ernesto Armenteros' comments on selling RQI in 2010:

Several investment funds approached us about buying the company in 2008. Following a failed negotiation with an influential Mexican group, we sold the business to Trujillo's Group; we were handling half a million remittances per month with 1.5 million customers, dozens of branches, and thousands of agencies in 34 states in the US, Spain, and Italy. When we sold the company, we transformed what we had developed in the Dominican Republic into a microfinance bank, Banco de Ahorro y Crédito Unión. We started to focus on bankarization, bringing financial services to the people, offering reasonably cheap long-term financing, adapting financial services to the unbanked, and providing financial inclusion. As a bank, we added over 30 remittance correspondents. We signed agreements with the IDB to develop tools and promote financial inclusion. We grew as a bank and as a remittance delivery platform to third parties[74].

The DOLEX story does not end here. In 2021, ten years after the sale of Remesas Quisqueyana and the development of Banco Union, Ernesto Armenteros had the opportunity to buy back - along with other shareholders[75]- his former company and consolidate one of the largest remittance companies in the US:

Mariano Trujillo called me in 2018 and told me that Palladium wanted to sell the company, so I asked him: *How much are they selling it for?* He gave me a reasonable price, and I said: *Let me see if I can organize a group of investors, and we'll buy it.*" So we organized a group, and together with Goldman Sachs, we purchased the company I had sold ten years ago and the two more companies they had bought. The company served 5 million customers monthly with 600 branches and nearly 3,000 agencies in the

---

[74] Virtual interview with Ernesto Armenteros on June 28, 2022, conducted, recorded and transcribed by Lucía Salazar.
[75] Press Release: Palladium Equity Partners Completes Sale of DolEx; January 27, 2020 - https://prn.to/3rWk5L9

U.S. and Spain. I returned to the company no longer as an operator or director but as a shareholder[76].

In August 2022, the DOLEX-Barri merger was announced[77]. Barri was a Houston, Texas-based MTO managed by Alberto Laureano, an experienced colleague and former director of WU's subsidiary Orlandi Valuta. Alberto is now the CEO of the merged companies. Ernesto commented:

> We now have over 700 branches and over 4,000 agencies throughout the US and Spain. We serve almost 5 million monthly customers with over $12 billion in remittances. Having focused on the banking side of the business for many years, I got again involved in remittances. It's exciting because I have partners who have never been involved with remittances. Today, I am co-owner of one of the largest MTOs in the US; we're smaller than RIA and MGI, but we're pretty close[78].

RIA ENVIA - EEFT

In November 2006, Euronet Worldwide, Inc. (NASDAQ: EEFT), a Kansas-based electronic payments provider, announced the acquisition of Los Angeles-based RIA Envia Inc[79], for $380 million and $110 million in Euronet stock (about 8% stake in the company). The agreement included RIA's branches in France and the Dominican Republic. Irving Barr and Fred Victor Kunik sold the company, originally founded by Jesus Perez Santalla in 1987. The development of RIA had been led by Juan Bianchi, formerly of AFEX, a company these two entrepreneurs had acquired a few years back. Barr and Kunik come from the Check Cashers and Money Orders sector with their firm Continental Express Money Order Co., which has been in business for almost 70 years.

At the time of the acquisition announcement, RIA had 1,100 employees, processed $4.5 billion in money transfers per year, and was considered the third largest remittance company in the world, behind WU and MGI.

---

76 Virtual interview with Ernesto Armenteros on June 28, 2022, conducted, recorded and transcribed by Lucía Salazar.
77 Press Release: DolEx and Barri Announce Merger; August 1, 2022 - https://bit.ly/3eDoBew
78 Virtual interview with Ernesto Armenteros on June 28, 2022, conducted, recorded and transcribed by Lucía Salazar.
79 Euronet agrees to acquire RIA Envia, Inc., the third-largest global money transfer company; Euronet Worldwide, Inc. Press Release, November 21, 2006 - https://bit.ly/3cLoU5C

Consolidation: The Market Shifts

In those days, RIA had more than 10,000 sending agents and 98 company-owned stores in 13 countries, and 32,000 payment outlets in 82 countries.

Juan Cristóbal Bianchi, CEO and Chairman of RIA, a native Chilean, in a 2006 press release, shared a wish that would come true: *Aside from the obvious market opportunities, we believe the Ria and Euronet operating philosophies and cultures will fit together nicely.* Michael Brown, Euronet Worldwide Chairman, and CEO, commented: *This portion of Ria's network dovetails nicely with Euronet's portfolio of banking clients to whom we provide transaction processing services across approximately 9,000 ATMs and our prepaid mobile top-up network comprising 265,000 points-of-sale across 157,000 retail locations.*

AFEX, under the control of RIA, acquired NYFX in 2001 -the company I had worked for in 1992- and in 2021, AFEX was sold to FLEETCOR Technologies, Inc. (NYSE: FLT)[80], owner of Cambridge Global Payments, creating Corpay in partnership with COMDATA and InvoicePay to provide cross-border payment services in 145 currencies to more than 30,000 customers, processing more than US $80 billion annually.

In March 2017, RIA announced[81] its intention to acquire all of MGI's outstanding shares. It was a counter-proposal to magnate Jack Ma's Chinese company, Ant Financial Services Group, affiliated with eCommerce giant Alibaba Group. Trump's administration did not approve Ant's purchase, one of the first signs that the US-China's rivalry was heating up[82]. Euronet's efforts to derail MGI's acquisition by Ant Financial had succeeded, but in the end, RIA failed to purchase MGI.

RIA continues to grow with targeted acquisitions, such as HIFX -cross-border payments for customers and small businesses- acquired in 2014 for US $242 million[83]; XE in 2015 for US $60 million; Innova, a VAT refunding company in 2018; and in 2022, the merchant acquiring services from Greek bank Piraeus, a company's long-time business partner.

---

80 FLEETCOR Completes AFEX Cross-Border Acquisition; FLEETCOR Technologies, Inc., Jun. 1, 2021 - https://bit.ly/3vlJlwt
81 Press Release: Euronet Worldwide Proposes to Acquire MoneyGram for $15.20 Per Share; march 14, 2017 - https://bit.ly/3S9nAcS
82 Greg Roumeliotis: US blocks MoneyGram sale to China's Ant Financial on national security concerns; Reuters, January 8, 2018 - https://reut.rs/3zn1YkL
83 Press Release: Euronet Worldwide Completes the Acquisition of HiFX; May 20, 2014 - https://bit.ly/3BjkiMD

Today, Ria's network comprises approximately 500,000 cash payment points and digital payment distribution in over 170 countries. In 2022, Euronet launched Dandelion, providing fintechs with an API and a real-time connection[84] to its entire payment network.

SMALL WORLD - CHOICE

A merger between Small World (SW) and Choice was announced in 2011[85], with a combined transaction volume of 600,000 per year reported. Thus, Kevin Neuschatz, CEO of Choice, a New York MTO that had grown through several acquisitions, joined Small World (SW), a company founded by its CEO Nick Day in 2005 in London.

From Choice's early days in New York, I remember Kevin's mother, Rita Neuschatz, the extremely meticulous CFO, working in her downtown Manhattan office at the Empire State Building. Sadly, we lost her in 2019. Choice's operations were managed at the time by Iris Aimee Pinedo, a Dominican executive with a background in technology. She worked in the company for 15 years. Iris joined Omnex in 2022.

Equistone Partners Europe, a private equity firm with extensive experience in financial services, acquired FPE Capital's stake in SW[86]. In 2020, SW announced the acquisition of Money Globe[87] a money transmitter in France offering transfers to North Africa. CEO Adelhak Hidani and Money Globe founder and chairman Lahcen Sadeq remained in the company to sustain the company's growth. SW reported 15 million transactions that year.

Nick Day retired in 2022 as CEO of SW[88], and Khalid Fellahi, previously with WU's digital division, was appointed as the new CEO, leading a company with more than US $6 billion in transactions, employing more than 1,000 people worldwide.

---

84 A one-stop shop solution for accessing the most strategic global network available for cross-border real-time payments: https://bit.ly/3Dr9hvg
85 Press Release: Small World Financial Services Group Ltd: Small World and Choice Money Transfer Combine to Create Leading Global Financial Services Group; July 13, 2011 - https://prn.to/3vJ1ftj
86 FPE Capital announces the successful sale of Small World Financial Services - March 26, 2018 - https://bit.ly/3bw8s9d
87 Equistone-backed Small World acquires MoneyGlobe; February 25, 2020 - https://bit.ly/3zZWTjH
88 Small World announces leadership transition; March 10, 2022 - https://bit.ly/3QsAW2p

TRAVELEX - COINSTAR - GROUPEX - SIGUE

In May 2006, Washington State-based Coinstar announced[89] the purchase of Travelex Money Transfer Ltd. for US $27 million. Coinstar is known for being a leader in the so-called *4th Wall*, the wall in supermarkets and stores that offer products and services to customers behind the checkout cashiers. With the addition of money transfers, Coinstar hoped to enhance its offering and strengthen its existing electronic payment products, such as prepaid long-distance cards, phone recharges, gift cards, and prepaid debit cards. Since migrants used these services, they believed remittances were the only missing service in their product portfolio. Coinstar is also known for its self-service coin-counting machines and *Redbox* DVD rental kiosks, a business line acquired in 2009.

Travelex, founded in 2003 in London, UK, was the third-largest company at the time, with 17,000 points in 138 countries besides its own branches. TMT's 2005 earnings were approximately US $5.8 million, with a negative EBITDA of about $10.4 million.

Mohit Davar, CEO of TMT, commented on the purchase: *We look forward to joining forces with Coinstar to build out our network in North America and around the world.* A successful industry executive with over 20 years of experience, Mohit founded TMT after working with Thomas Cook in London. He led the 1997 start-up of MoneyGram International Limited, the company MGI founded with Thomas Cook. Mohit ran the company until 2003, when MGI acquired Thomas Cook's shares and took full ownership of the subsidiary.

In 2009 Coinstar E-Payment Services announced the purchase of GroupEx Financial Corp.(GFC) for US $48 million[90]. GFC, based in La Mirada, California, was an independent provider of remittances and money orders between Latin America and the United States.

As I mentioned earlier, Groupex was the Money Order Company of King Express, the famous courier company that delivered MOs in Central

---

89 COINSTAR TO ACQUIRE TRAVELEX MONEY TRANSFER: Transaction will add to company's 4th Wall product portfolio and strengthen its E-payment line of business, Press Release, Bellevue, Wash; May 4, 2006 - https://bit.ly/3zQqeNF
90 Caroline Davis: New acquisition connects Coinstar to Latin America; The Seattle Times, July 26, 2006 - https://bit.ly/3vB8T8H

America. At that time, GFC had 375 employees in 23 states. A total of $62 million in revenues was reported for 2006.

The plan was to merge TMT and GFC's European and Latin American markets, now relabeled as Coinstar Money Transfer. Failing to achieve the expected results in the US —adding remittances to its *4th Wall*— and under-performing in Europe, Coinstar Inc. announced the sale of Coinstar Money Transfer to Sigue Financial Corporation for US $41.5 Million in 2010[91]. However, Coinstar Money Transfers had many unresolved issues surrounding its operations in Europe, and Sigue failed to change its course the way it had desired, closing its operations soon after.

Sigue, headquartered in Sylmar, California, is a company founded by Guillermo de la Viña in San Fernando, California, in 1996. He told this story at IMTC MIAMI in 2011, one of our first conferences, and was recorded on video[92]. With its own service centers in Mexico, in the early 2000s Sigue was already recognized as a remittance leader serving the US-Mexico corridor. It purchased Remesas El Cid and Bronco's, and acquired the US branches of BanAgricola of El Salvador and Banrural of Guatemala.

Circling back to Mohit Davar, after Coinstar, he served on the Boards of Directors of leading companies in the sector, such as Eastnets in Dubai and Earthport Plc[93] in London, and was instrumental in the consolidation of The International Association of Money Transfer Networks (IAMTN) founded in 2005, helping IAMTN's founder Veronica Studsgaard.

UNITELLER

Uniteller was founded in 1994 by Eduardo Gutierrez in Rochelle Park, New Jersey. After successfully establishing a money transfer service to Mexico using state-of-the-art technology at the time, its sales rep Arturo Reyes began offering payment services to MTOs in the New York, New Jersey area first. NYFX and VIGO were among the first clients; the highly efficient operation and competitive rates made it an interesting offer. I visited the company's HQ at their small office in Rochelle Park and was very impressed by Eduardo's vision. VIGO's volume to Mexico increased dramatically in a short time.

---

91 Press Release: Coinstar Signs Definitive Agreement to Sell Its Money Transfer Business to Sigue Corporation - August 24, 2010 - https://prn.to/3oVngkI
92 Guillermo de la Viña: Guillermo de la Viña - SIGUE-COINSTAR - IMTC MIAMI 2011 (part 1 of 2); Youtube, November 26, 2011 - https://bit.ly/3BGCAsU
93 Earthport plc; Directorate Change; July 11, 2012 - https://bit.ly/3SkFxFv

Mexico's Grupo Financiero Banorte, the third largest bank in Mexico behind Banamex and Bancomer, began paying remittances in 1999-2000 by acquiring Bancrecer[94], a bank that was already paying remittances at the time. A deal to purchase UniTeller Holdings, Inc. for close to US$20 million was announced by Banorte in April 2006[95]. Luis Peña Kegel, CEO of Grupo Financiero Banorte commented: *Through the acquisition of UniTeller, Banorte gains full presence in the value chain of this important service, as it will be able to capture, transmit, and deliver family remittances on both sides of the border.* At that point, Banorte was already a major player in the payment of remittances in Mexico, processing more than 3.2 million transactions in 2005 (6% market share that year).

At the time, the company had 1,000 agents in 41 states in the US, with more than 4,000 payment points in 19 countries, including Mexico and the Philippines, one of the first non-Philippine firms to be established in Manila to service this corridor. UniTeller processed 1.1 million remittances worth $370 million in 2005; approximately 50% were Mexican transfers.

Alberto Guerra, who was part of Banorte's International Department and was directly involved in acquiring Uniteller, became the General Manager of UniTeller Financial Services. In an interview for this book, Alberto commented:

> A relatively small company, UniTeller was focused on remittance services from the US to Mexico and Latin America, though primarily to Mexico. The company caught our attention because it was small, so the investment level was modest; however, we were most interested in their IT platform. We analyzed and reviewed about 10 MTOs in the US between 2003 and 2006, and UniTeller stood out the most: we wanted to turn UniTeller into a technology processing platform. Since we were not looking to establish branches or collection points but rather to create a hub centered on a technological platform and build a team with an adequate compliance and risk management program, UniTeller was an attractive option. What we liked about this structure and platform was its capacity to support what we had in mind and what we eventually achieved.

---

[94] Press Release: Banco Mercantil del Norte Acquires BanCrecer; September 23, 2001 - https://bit.ly/3S4nXnV
[95] Press Release: Banorte acquires "UniTeller", a US remittances company, April 26, 2006 - https://bit.ly/3BtTB9K

The process at the bank to integrate a remittance company into its operations took almost two years. Many regulatory and procedural steps had to be carried out before we could operate the company. At that time, Bancomer was the leader in remittance payments in Mexico, and they already had a solution in the US that met their needs. This model, Bancomer Transfer Services (BTS) had already proved successful for Bancomer, so it was a logical choice for us to emulate.

We were able to build value with UniTeller by offering our services to other financial institutions in other countries and in other corridors. UniTeller currently manages more than 200 corporate clients in over 80 countries, which is only a snapshot of our client base and portfolio. Through commercial agreements, we have a network of over 2,500 banks and more than 200,000 payment points. We have built a global network and continue to enhance it as part of an exciting expansion plan that we have in place[96].

UniTeller is more than an MTO in the US; it is a global transaction aggregation platform, and it has expanded into providing technology solutions to other financial institutions, both bank and NBFIs, becoming a leading company in the industry.

MONEYGRAM

In the summer of 2022, Rob Ayers and I shared a latte and a croissant in a Baker Street café, reminiscing about his living in London between 1994 and 1996. Known as the *Father of MoneyGram*, Rob had been with the American Express Company since 1987, when the idea came up. At that time, Rob worked for a small AmEx subsidiary called Integrated Payment Systems based in Englewood, Colorado. Through its CEO, Charlie Fote, the company acquired a Nashville, Tennessee firm with two interesting products: a credit and debit card for truckers and a cash advance program offered at casinos, racetracks, etc., for gamblers associated with the Players Club. Rob discovered that casino gamblers were using WU to receive funds when they ran out of money. Why not compete against WU? MGI had been conceived, and its name was chosen at an AmEx executives' meeting in Morocco in 1988.

---

[96] Virtual interview with Alberto Guerra on June 29, 2022, conducted, recorded and transcribed by Lucía Salazar.

MoneyGram was formed as a subsidiary of Integrated Payment Systems Inc., part of First Data Corporation and American Express.

Rob Ayers recalls in the interview for this book[97]: *We had a small team for product development, and it was launched in January 1988. There was an internal campaign where employees entered a contest to come up with the new service's name. Since AmEx owned us, my boss had to consult with the CEO for approval, because we wanted to use the blue American Express logo. And that's how the name American Express Money Gram came about. Soon after, AmEx offices around the world became agents for sending and receiving money transfers; only 300 to 400 initially, but a great start.*

During the process of expanding the presence in the North American domestic market, Rob recalls one of the biggest agent expansion successes, which was dubbed *The Blitz at the Ritz*, a big gala evening organized by the Illinois Check Cashing Association which brought together all of their members to the Ritz, a luxurious downtown hotel, with an unforgettable dinner and a performance by the popular country singer, Louise Mandrell. The agent network expanded.

Rob would arrive in London in 1994 to start a business partnership between American Express and Thomas Cook, since both companies understood that Travelers Cheques faced the risk of becoming obsolete. *Thomas Cook approached us, and that was a big breakthrough. They had banking relationships with financial institutions around the world. One of our major goals was to sign them as agents wherever they had offices. But the two companies decided to work together. This union turned out to be one of the most successful joint ventures in the industry: they owned everything outside of the Americas - the US, Latin America, and the Caribbean. Their financial relationships helped build MoneyGram's international banking network.*

Thus, Rob and Alfredo O'Hagan[98] from MGI in the US and Leon Isaacs and Mohit Davar, on behalf of Thomas Cook, initiated MGI's development in Europe. Ten months later, the four musketeers managed to take over the UK postal service as agents from WU, one of MGI's first victories in the eternal dispute between these two companies over major clients.

---

97 Personal Interview with Rob Ayers on August 26, 2022.
98 Alfredo O'Hagan created the financial and money transfer services division at IDT Corporation, a public US MTO and Communication Company, and has managed it since 2011.

After becoming frustrated with changes in ownership and management structures, Rob left MGI and began working for other large companies, such as Groupex, Coinstar, and Choice, before becoming a consultant. feb

In 1992, Amex spun off First Data Corporation into an independent, publicly-traded company listed on the NYSE, with Henry "Ric" C. Duquès as chairman and CEO of the board. In 1995, First Data Corporation merged with First Financial, the company that owned Western Union. In January 1996, First Data entered into a consent decree with the US Federal Trade Commission (FTC) to spin off MoneyGram, seeking to prevent the creation of a monopoly[99]. On December 11, 1996, MoneyGram became an independent company, and during the first quarter of 1998, it transferred its data processing from First Data to a computer facility provided by IBM. Additionally, licenses had to be issued in its name to complete the separation from First Data.

The twists and turns of MGI's history continued. In April 1998, Viad Corp acquired MoneyGram for $287 million and it was folded into Viad's Travelers Express. In June 2004, Viad sold MoneyGram, and it became a publicly traded individual entity. By 2006, MGI had expanded internationally with over 96,000 agents and had introduced bill payment and online money transfers. But the During the 2007-2008 financial crisis hit the company hard. MGI's shares fell 96% from 2007 to 2009 from a loss of $1.6 billion from investments in securities backed by risky mortgages. Analyst Yakov Kofner, in his analytical blog SaveOnSend, called it *MoneyGram's Suicide*. His blog on MGI, *MoneyGram: whack-a-mole of money transfers?*, is a detailed analysis on the company, and I have used it extensively to write this section[100].

The company had to sell a majority stake to Thomas H. Lee Partners and Goldman Sachs in exchange for a cash infusion and named Pamela Patsley, the CEO, who turned the company around[101].

---

99 Excerpt from a 10-K SEC Filing, filed by Moneygram Payment Systems Inc on 3/31/1998; Edgar Online - https://bit.ly/45TBXsu
100 MoneyGram: whack-a-mole of money transfers?; saveonsend.com blog, updated September 13, 2021 - https://bit.ly/3KDoY4p
101 Moneygram International Company History Timeline; Zippia - https://bit.ly/3EF72UG

In 2014, MoneyGram lost its partnership with Wal-Mart Stores[102] and then began restructuring to cut costs; still, from 2013 until late 2015, shares fell about 70%. In 2017 Ant Financial Services Group, affiliated with eCommerce giant Alibaba Group, announced its intentions to buy MGI, but Trump's administration did not approve the deal[103]. It could have been a new beginning for the company, but US government concerns over China derailed the deal.

In 2018, MGI paid a US$125 Million fine to the US Department of Justice (DOJ) after breaching a settlement that required it to improve its anti-money laundering (AML) controls, and the company faced increasing difficulties in restructuring its loans[104].

On June 17, 2019, MGI announced that they would partner with Ripple, the California blockchain company, to use their technology and cryptocurrency, XRP, and improve their financial situation by relying on this capital. At the same time, they were conducting a joint pilot experiment using this exchange channel in the U.S.-Mexico corridor. Despite being an interesting and valuable project for both firms, MGI did not see significant improvements from the agreement, and it was terminated in 2021[105].

MGI's renewed focus on online and mobile in 2018 began to show results two years later. By Q3 2020, MGI's digital revenue covered the losses of the offline business. For the first time since 2015, MGI was back to growing its cross-border revenue, year-over-year, by 20%.

On February 15, 2022, MGI announced its sale to Madison Dearborn Partners, LLC, a Chicago-based private equity firm, in a transaction valued at $1.8 billion. The sale was completed in June 2023, and the company was delisted from the Nasdaq stock market.

The future for MGI rests on its IT makeover and its focus on competing in the digital space. MGI's CTO Joe Vaughan stated in an interview that he

---

102 On April 17, 2014 Walmart and RIA launched the Walmart-2-Walmart Money Transfer Service, a US domestic money transfer service available at their 4,000 Walmart stores and in 2019 Walmart-2-World added RIA to its international money transfer offering.
103 Greg Roumeliotis: U.S. blocks MoneyGram sale to China's Ant Financial on national security concerns; Reuters, January 8, 2018 - https://reut.rs/3zn1YkL
104 Aaron Weinman and Michelle Sierra: MoneyGram's loan faces performance, money laundering concerns; Reuters, June 7, 2019 - https://reut.rs/462lcee
105 Blockchain firm Ripple to end partnership with MoneyGram; Reuters, March 8, 2021 - https://reut.rs/3RmyaPG

describes the company's drive towards digital: *We'd set a goal to get 50% of our international money transfers onto digital platforms by the end of 2024. We passed that goal at the end of the first quarter [of 2023]*[106]

WESTERN UNION

For WU, its first ten years in the money transfer business were tumultuous - it nearly went bankrupt once in 1993 - and journalists have many times declared its permanent demise. In April 1991, a reporter, Bart Ziegler, wrote a story for the Associated Press with a famous quote: *...a long, sorry decline has left the 140-year-old company a shell of its former self. Today, it is fighting for its very survival. Western Union fell victim to technological advances.* It is a story WU has faced time and again.

Where does WU start as a money transfer provider? At the domestic level, we can go back to the company's beginnings in the 19th century. as a cross-border payment provider, offering remittance services to migrants, first to Mexico and then to other countries, is a fairly recent affair.

Amar Das, a former WU's executive director and a key player in its growth by expanding the company's services to Asia and the Middle East, gave us the following interview for this book:

> I was one of the pioneers of the remittance industry in India, and I feel I made a significant contribution to the industry when I became part of WU. Until 1993, services were mainly domestic, only 10 to 15% of the transfer were sent to Mexico and a few other Latin American countries. WU hired Paul Burnley as the first president of Western Union International. Paul was the former president of American Express in Hong Kong, and he came to the WU headquarters in New Jersey. On his first day, he approached me - we had met a couple of times before - and took me to work with him because I was the only person from India he knew. Paul often repeated that joke. We were to start with my home country and then South Asia (Bangladesh, Pakistan, Sri Lanka, Nepal); I had worked in a bank in New York doing remittances, a tedious process where payments took many days to be executed with lots of paperwork involved.

---

106 Paula Rooney: MoneyGram profits from mainframe move to multicloud; CIO, 16 June, 2023 - https://bit.ly/48h98aY

A few days later, Paul took the globe he had in his office and said to me: You know what? I had an idea last night: look at all these countries very close to each other. I see Saudi Arabia, Qatar, Kuwait, all very close. It's about a 40 to 50-minute flight between each other. I think you can manage it. And just like that, I was also in charge of the Middle East. This is how I became WU's first regional director for South Asia and the Middle East. I started operations in every country in the region; I managed to convince many companies and exchange houses about remittances, using the WU system, the whole package. It was a great success[107].

Following several ownership changes, WU money transfer subsidiary, on a steady growth path, was resurrected as an independent firm in 2006. With volumes, agents, and revenues steadily increasing, WU's performance grew significantly from 2006 to 2014. After this fast initial growth, transfer volumes have been stagnant until the start of the Covid pandemic, picking up in late 2020 as WU's digital channels started to gain scale. However, the lower margin of digital transfers resulted, on balance, in overall static revenue over the last decade.

WU's market share presents a complex picture. Since 2009, it has been gradually declining as the company struggled to keep pace with the growing and increasingly intricate cross-border consumer money transfer market. This graph, taken from an in-depth analysis of Savenonsend.com, shows WU's market share based on estimates of the size of the global market[108].

---

107 Virtual interview with Amar Das on July 8, 2022, conducted, recorded and transcribed by Isabel Cortés.
108 Western Union: the end of permanent leadership in cross-border consumer money transfers; saveonsend.com blog, updates July 26, 2023 —https://bit.ly/3U3aqy6

GRAPH 2: Western Union's Global Market Share (2006-2022)

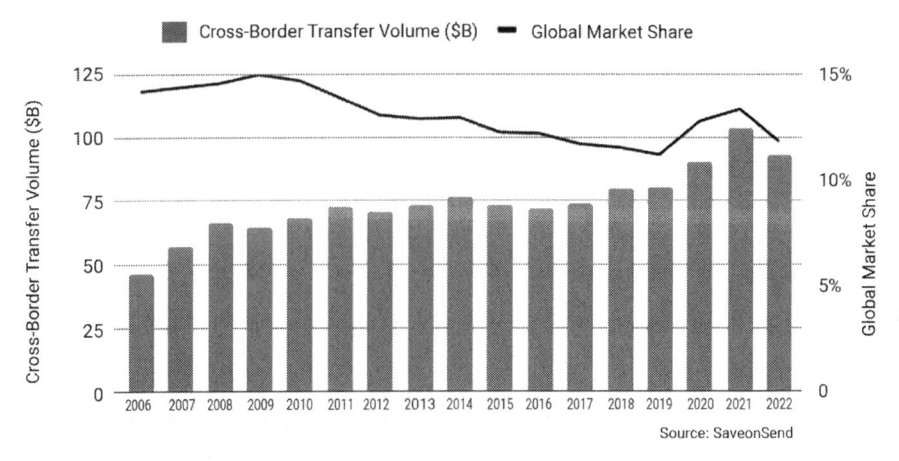

Western Union Cross-Border Consumer: Volume ($B) and Market Share

Source: SaveonSend

Since around 2014, transactions have stagnated despite a 20 to 25% growth in the global remittance market. Volumes increased in the late 2020s as WU's digital channels gained traction in addition to the digital boom resulting from the Covid pandemic.

Quoting from Saveonsend: *In various large corridors, WU's market share is less than 10%, while in some smaller corridors, it approaches 50%. Criticizing Western Union for offering services in places where there is little to no competition would be akin to labeling a single gas station in a small town as a "monopoly".*

WU embraced the online world in 2000, forged mobile partnerships in 2007, and launched a smartphone application in 2011. As of 2023, WU continues to stand as one of the leaders in the digital cross-border consumer business, on par with leading fintech companies. The company has reported that 80% of first-time digital customers are entirely new, showing that it is successfully attracting new customer segments. Graph 23 shows an estimated comparative quarterly revenue between WU and its fintech rivals, Remitly, Wise, and WorldRemit.

GRAPH 3 - Comparative Revenue between WU Digital and its fintech rivals (2017-2023)

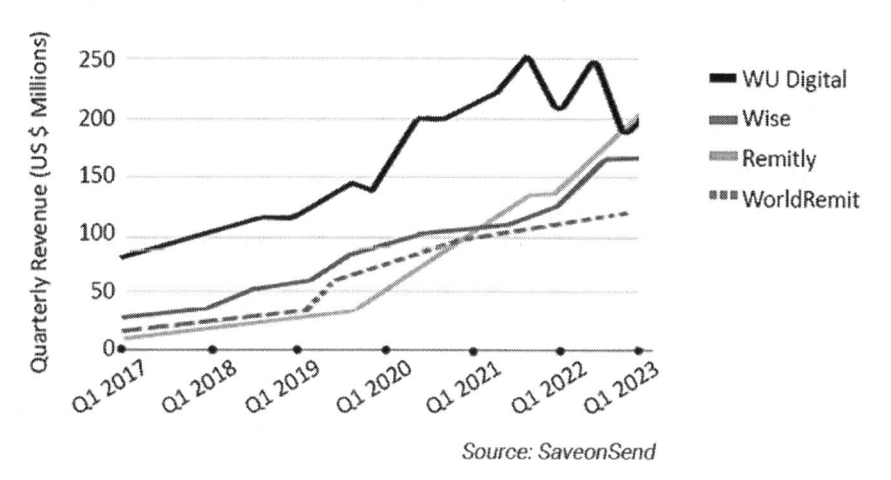

[Line graph showing Quarterly Revenue (US $ Millions) from Q1 2017 to Q1 2023 for WU Digital, Wise, Remitly, and WorldRemit, with values ranging from 0 to 250.]

Source: *SaveonSend*

In the retail P2P market, with MGI deciding not to compete with the large accounts, WU's only competitor is RIA, which has scored a few successes, such as the signing of the Belgian[109], Austrian[110] and Mauritius[111] Post Offices.

COMMERCIAL BANKS AND REMITTANCES

The complex nature of Foreign Exchange and Remittances, in terms of serving retail unbanked clients and their needs, has resulted in a long-standing hesitancy and mistrust by commercial banks, who have always felt in a safer ground in providing conventional banking services to their more affluent clientele and their business clients.

To better understand this hesitancy, I will divide this section into two parts: remittance services provided by banks to direct clients and banking services offered by banks to the industry, such as financial intermediaries and NBFIs as business partners. The issue of financial inclusion is also an essential subject in this discussion, as I will show.

---

109 BPOST teams up with RIA Money Transfer; Post & Parcel, January 20, 2020 - https://bit.ly/46eABs3
110 Ria Money Transfer, Austrian Post sign remittance partnership; The PayPers, February 19, 2020 - https://bit.ly/48eBL8u
111 Mauritius Post Partners With Ria Money Transfer; Ria News, September 13, 2018 - https://bit.ly/3LpmdVF

SERVING REMITTANCE CLIENTS

Historically, commercial banks have offered money remittance services. However, most of them use their Swift wire transfer services, which are not meant for family remittances. Wire transfer services are intended for clients with more significant financial resources sending larger transfers than typical migrants.

Banks can act in the origination of the money transfer or the destination. Banks' participation in the industry varies significantly between the two.

ORIGINATION

In a blog[112] entitled *Banks and Money Transfers: Sleeping Giants?* SaveOnSend compares US banks with MTOs and shows that banks generally dominate cross-border payments. In contrast, their profits in this category are insignificant compared to the rest of their product line.

Based on a comparison of the four largest US banks, JP Morgan, Citigroup, Wells Fargo, and Bank of America, it accounts for only 0.3% to 0.5% of total revenues or 0.7% to 1.3% of consumer banking revenues. It is the same in almost all countries. Is there any point in entering a market with very little revenue?

Just one of the 25 largest banks worldwide is more profitable than all the MTOs combined. Besides being a minor revenue source for banks, cross-border money transfer has become increasingly challenging to manage. Regulations designed to combat terrorism financing, money laundering, corruption, and tax evasion impose significant resource and system investments.

The US accounts for 20% of all cross-border consumer money transfers, yet less than 10% of the 6,000 banks offer this service.

90% of these only offer wire transfers as a method of payment. JP Morgan's personal transfer average is US $14,000, Bank of America's is US $10,000, and Citibank's US $8,000, greatly differing from the US $300 for

---

112 Banks And Money Transfer: Sleeping Giants?; saveonsend blog, updated August 31, 2023 - https://bit.ly/3LNQ8Gc

most MTOs. A few MTOs, such as Wise, reach a maximum average larger than US $1,000 per transaction.

During the 1970s and 1980s, Central American banks opened branches in US cities and neighborhoods to serve their migrants. Although some of them survived for a few years, most of them went out of business. Similar to BanAgricola of El Salvador and Banrural of Guatemala, which sold their US branches to SIGUE, some banks partnered with MTOs to continue serving remittances to their customers.

The turn of the century was equally relevant for banks. Multilateral agencies tried to convince banks to enter the remittance market on two premises. The first one was that they would drive the cost down of remittances by increasing competition —a failed approach— and two, to achieve a broader financial inclusion of migrants and their families —a successful effort in some markets.

With a global presence, some banks, such as Citibank, have offered cross-border payment products to their customers. PayQuik, arguably the first fintech to offer web-based money transfers, was acquired in 2004 by Citibank. Founded in 2000 by Bhairav Trivedi, the company designed a system to help financial institutions offer competitive money transfers in the P2P market. As a result of this acquisition, Bhairav managed Citibank's remittance business and led the launch of QuikRemit[113], a remittance platform that covered more than 90 countries.

QuikRemit was designed to enable financial institutions to offer their customers and employees a solution for sending money. Citibank Global Transfers developed remittance products for Mexican and Indian markets, limited to the bank's customers[114]. Bhairav remained with Citibank until 2010, when he became CEO of Coinstar Money Transfer before it was sold to Sigue. In 2021, he was named the CEO of Crown Agent's Bank, a leading provider of foreign exchange and institutional payment services[115].

---

113 Press Release: Citi Launches New QuikRemit Service; February 06, 2006 - http://citi.us/3SIn2tQ
114 WWB Innovation Brief: Citigroup: Creating Innovative Remittance Products and Services at the Global Level; January 2006 - https://bit.ly/3UQ9bUy
115 Crown Agents Bank names Bhairav Trivedi as CEO Designate; UK-regulated bank appoints fintech-leader to complete its digital transformation; Invest Africa, january 21, 2021 - https://bit.ly/3P34C8x

Despite acquiring banks with specialized remittance services, they closed these units down and developed a remittance service for payments in Central America called Citi Remesas. That was the case in 2006 with the acquisitions of Banco Cuscatlan and Banco Uno. In 2014, Citibank sold Citi Remesas to Transnetwork, a Houston-based B2B electronic domestic and cross-border processing and payment platform[116]. Citi Remesas managed Latin American remittance operations for the bank in El Salvador, Guatemala, Honduras, Nicaragua, Costa Rica, Panama, Ecuador, Peru, and Brazil, where beneficiaries were able to collect remittances at Citi branch locations, retail chains, and financial institutions.

By paying a fine of US $97.4 Million in 2017, Citigroup decided to settle AML charges from the US DOJ. The fine was brought on the investigation that US authorities conducted of Banamex USA, the bank unit that processed remittances from 2007 to 2012. From the more than 30 million transactions processed, the bank generated 18,000 suspicious alerts but only investigated ten, as reported by the DOJ investigation. Citigroup inherited Banamex with the acquisition of Banamex Mexico in 2001[117].

Like Citibank, many US and European commercial banks tried to originate remittances, and the list of failures is more extensive than the list of successes. Latin American, African, and Middle East banks have closed most of their international branches in the US and Europe after failing to attract enough clients to merit the cost of running these branches.

As an example of a successful bank story originating remittances, I would like to mention Wells Fargo in the US. It created a special unit for remittances, ExpressSend International Remittance Service, to the Philippines from its branches in San Francisco in 1994[118]. With Daniel Ayala[119] as head of the *Global Remittance Services Unit*, the service was expanded in 2011 to offer payments in other countries in Asia and Latin America in a partnership with

---

116 Transnetwork acquires Citibank remittance operations; Electronic Payments International, october 7, 2014 - https://bit.ly/3s9SSbd
117 Michael Corkery, Ben Protess: Citigroup pacta pagar 97,4 millones de dólares para cerrar una investigación de lavado; May 22, 2017 - https://nyti.ms/3RqtrN0
118 Press Release: Wells Fargo Celebrates 20 Years of Remittances to the Philippines, November 13, 2014 - https://bwnews.pr/3Qpf7Bh
119 Wells Fargo Celebrates 20 years of Remittances in the Philippines; PNB Philippines - https://bit.ly/3wtxA7R

Uniteller[120]. In 2021, Dani Ayala left Wells Fargo to join a Hispanic-founded fintech, Welcome Tech. Hopefully, Wells Fargo will continue with the provision of remittance services, now headed by Daniela Mounger.

Directo a México is a remittance service that allows sending money from any US bank account subscribed to the service to any Mexican bank account[121]. The idea was conceived In response to the *Partnership for Prosperity* agreement between the Bank of Mexico and the US Federal Reserve Banks, signed in 2003; the system was implemented in 2004. Although many U.S. banks are subscribed (more than 300 in 2022[122]) the service continues to be scarcely used, representing less than 1% of total remittances to Mexico, $368 million in 2020[123].

There are other banks in the US that have been relatively successful in sending remittances to specific corridors, such as the Philippine National Bank (PNB) for The Philippines and its PNB Web Remit service and banks serving India such as ICICI Bank or SBI (State Bank of India). But even originating their remittances to their diasporas and their domestic branding dominance, they do not dominate their international markets and have to compete head-to-head with other MTOs, such as UniTeller, Wise, Remitly, WorldRemit, WU, MGI or RIA.

DESTINATION

There is, however, a significant difference between the role played by banks in sending remittances as opposed to paying them. Payment of remittances is where banks have been most successful, especially in markets where the government, most of the time using discriminatory practices, has set up regulations that tend to favor banks over NBFIs.

Fintechs' entry into the market in the second decade of this century has challenged these discriminatory practices. The fear of quenching innovation in financial services by helping banks remain in control has put regulators and governments in a difficult position.

---

120 Wells Fargo partners UniTeller Financial Services for ExpressSend network expansion; The Paypers, october 12, 2011 - https://bit.ly/3Yv3Q70
121 Directo a México: https://bit.ly/3dlHWQa
122 Directo a México: : Instituciones financieras que ofrecen Directo a México en los Estados Unidos - https://bit.ly/3w5HMTy
123 Panorama Anual de Inclusión Financiera 2021:Comisión Nacional Bancaria y de Valores de México; octubre de 2021 - https://bit.ly/3AnQE9L

Most banks have not targeted remittance-receiving families as bank clients because of their socioeconomic status. The commercial banks' primary interest in entering the remittance business has been gaining access to *cheap dollars*.

At the destination, the profit is not the provision of financial services to clients —the beneficiaries— but the *hard currency* they can get from paying remittances and selling these *cheap dollars* on the market.

With few exceptions, financial inclusion is just part of their PR message; most do not make an honest effort to integrate it as part of the product development and client-serving strategy.

In many countries that receive remittances, banks have been entering the market since the turn of the century, making efforts to persuade remittance beneficiaries —and in many instances coerce— to accept the deposit of the remittance funds into bank accounts instead of collecting cash at the bank's counters. Some bank accounts can act as mobile wallets, which has also been successful in some markets. The deposit of remittances into bank accounts has been claimed as one of the great successes of financial inclusion. Hopefully, as bank customers, these new, underserved clients, can then get access to credit and other bank products.

Banks have been taking over the remittance payment market through advertising, better attention to unbanked clients, an expanded service portfolio aimed at these clients, and loyalty programs. A few entities have succeeded in promoting savings among migrant families, which is not easy, but financial education and digitization of services are key components of their offerings.

In Africa, while banks have attempted to dominate remittance payments in their local markets, MMOs —such as M-Pesa in Kenya, which has 60% of the formal market— are battling such leadership.

With notable exceptions, NBFIs dominate Asia, primarily due to fintechs and MMOs actively operating across the continent. Through the Reserve Bank of India (RBI), the Indian government implemented several policies and protocols to formalize remittances, break exclusive agreements, expand competition, reduce costs, and improve efficiency. RDA[124] (Rupee Drawing Arrangement) is a scheme introduced in 2016 to allow foreign banks and non-banking entities to maintain rupee accounts and credit remittances to Indian bank accounts. The MTSS[125] (Money Transfer Service Scheme) provides a system that authorizes companies outside the country (Overseas Principals) to make agreements with Indian agents directly or through sub-agents.

Similarly, India has sought to convert MMOs into Payment Banks: a law was passed in 2015, and 11 applications out of 41 were approved. Five of these have closed due to limitations in generating income; however, 6 of them are still in operation: Paytm Payments Bank, Airtel Payments Bank, India Post Payments Bank, Fino Payments Bank and Aditya Birla Payments Bank, Jio Payments Bank and NSDL Payments Bank. Paytm has been the leader in Mobile Banking, even ahead of large commercial banks such as SBI, HDFC, Axis, and ICICI[126].

In a country like The Philippines, remittances play a crucial role, and there is an open competition between NBFIs and Banks for remittances. While India, China, and Mexico are the world remittance recipients, this country has been number four for over two decades, hitting a record high of US $36.1 billion in 2022, 3.6% higher than 2021[127]. Competition among NBFIs like M L' Huillier, Cebuana, Palawan, and LBC, with banks such as Banco de Oro (BDO), Metrobank, RCBC, BPI, PNB, Landbank, illustrates the open and comprehensive coexistence of financial services providers.

Around the turn of the century, banks in The Philippines were paying 43% of remittances. At IMTC ASIA 2018 in Manila, the BSP (Bangko Sentral ng Pilipinas or Central Bank of the Philippines) answered industry queries and explained its market policies favoring market openness and fairness. Competition for *Pera Padala*, Tagalog for *Send Money*, is ready to welcome the arrival of the recently approved fintechs and neobanks. Let's keep in mind that technology-wise, a *Filipino* company, G-Cash, is considered the

---

[124] RBI: Master Direction – Opening and Maintenance of Rupee/Foreign Currency Vostro Accounts of Non-resident Exchange Houses - https://bit.ly/3A55ArZ
[125] RBI: Master Direction – Money Transfer Service Scheme (MTSS) - https://bit.ly/3K6rHTG
[126] VARINDIA: Why payment banks in India are struggling?, July 21, 2019 - https://bit.ly/3SZqKR6
[127] Lawrence Agcaoili : Remittances hit record high of $36.1 billion in 2022, The Philippine Star, february 16, 2023 - https://bit.ly/3QxhSTV

world's first company to offer cell phone-based remittance services. The service was launched in 2004, with major improvements in the following years[128].

Some MTOs in sending markets showcase that depositing remittances in bank accounts and mobile wallets is part of their digital growth strategy. Is that an MTO achievement at origination or the growth of banks as remittance payers? Valentina Vitali of FXC Intelligence[129] wrote in 2021: *Transfers sent directly to a bank account or mobile wallet digitally have been a particularly strong growth area for all players. For Ria, digital transfers to a bank account or mobile wallet currently represent almost 30% of the total Money Transfer segment's principal. According to Raj Agrawal, Western Union's CFO, this is also the fastest growing segment of their digital business.*

New digital and technological developments are now prompting banks to consider entering markets where their customers in the diaspora recognize their brand by using White Label products designed by fintechs. These White Label products enable banks to present their brand to clients in many sending countries without the need for large investments or complex regulatory or licensing needs. This way, the diaspora can access a bank-branded application where they live.

BANKING PARTNERSHIPS AND DERISKING

Derisking, De-Risking[130] or Debanking is a phenomenon that has been the subject of many of my articles and countless interviews in newspapers and meetings with regulators.

> Bank accounts are crucial to the industry's operation. The banking partnerships between NBFIs and banks are the best way to provide foreign exchange and remittance services efficiently and transparently.

---

128 When did Gcash start in The Philippines? ; Peso Lab, Money Guide for Filipinos - https://bit.ly/3qji3Yo
129 Valentina Vitali: The rise of digital remittances in 2021; FXC Intelligence, December 21, 2021 - https://bit.ly/3rgIMFn
130 Hugo Cuevas-Mohr: Derisking o Debanking; Llegaremos a una solución?- Crosstech Blog, junio 16, 2021 - https://bit.ly/3bS9psy

A small NBFI can temporarily operate without a bank account, and many have managed to do so while they lose one account and find another. There are many ways for an NBFI to use different methods to settle funds with other NBFIs and continue operating, such as Hawala, or by transporting physical money, striking deals with third parties, or, in recent times, with the help of cryptocurrencies. But, although the use of cryptocurrencies is real, it is still a complex path when the value of operations is relatively large.

Professionals in the industry refer to derisking as a *never-ending issue*. It is part of the industry's history, and it will continue to be so in the future. It seems that the situation is improving for certain NBFIs, especially digital fintechs, which have a greater ability to deal with banking institutions due to their use of technology and the digitization of transactions. For ethnic remittance companies is very difficult to build the trust of commercial banks not willing to take the risk. For banks, the profits they earn from serving MTOs do not offset the additional investment requirements and legal exposure created by regulations.

The term *derisking* first appeared in 1987, and its use has grown exponentially since 2011-2012, as Graph 24 shows. There is even now a dictionary entry for the word: *to make something safer by reducing the possibility that something bad will happen and that money will be lost*. The use of the word debanking is even more remarkable: it peaked in the 1920s, its use fell sharply to peak again in 1997 and again in 2020[131].

GRAPH 4: Use of the word "derisking" (1997-2019) -
Graph was made using Google's ngram viewer

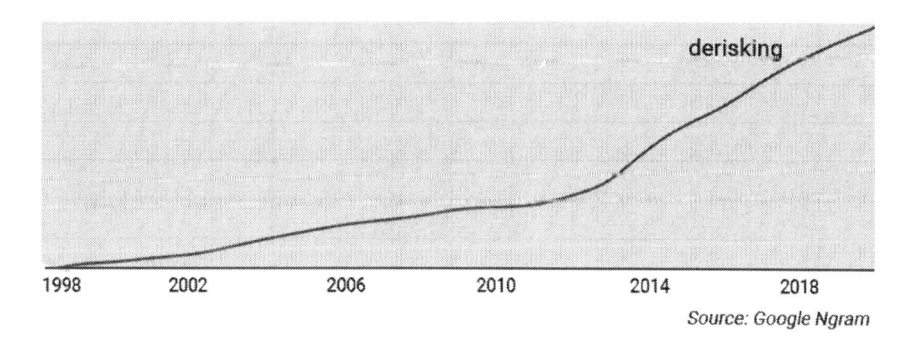

Source: Google Ngram

---

131 Ngram: Use of the word "debanking" (1900 - 2019) - https://bit.ly/2UYnCeP

The first derisking alarm was sounded off on June 21, 2006, at a hearing of the House Financial Services Committee of the U.S. Congress entitled *Bank Secrecy Act's Impact On Money Services Businesses*, chaired by Ohio Congressman Michael G. Oxley as Chairman and attended by more than 70 of his colleagues in Congress. David Landsman, on behalf of the NMTA representing the Money Transmitters, presented the problem in great detail, as did Michael Goldman, on behalf of the Financial Service Centers of America (FISCA), representing other MSBs. In describing the problem, the message could not have been clearer or more alarming. I quote some of Mr. Goldman's remarks at this hearing:

> I would like to make two observations. One is that we have not heard from the banks that have terminated [...] I think there is a wealth of knowledge that we could get from the banks that have terminated, and I suspect that they would agree that there is no clarity. They are being asked to be the regulators. Two, [...] there is nobody who is prepared or willing in the regulatory system to take the bull by the horns ...[if you reread] the testimony of the regulators, and you know, they do not have all the answers, they do not have any direction... nobody has taken it by the horns, and that is why I have said that I really believe, genuinely, that it has come time for the legislative body to make a statement, a legislative body to pass legislation and say, you know, "no more blanket high risk and no more banks being asked to regulate the industry", and until that happens, we are having a lot of meetings, we are having a lot of conferences, we are having a lot of hearings, but nothing is happening[132].

Nothing happened. And nothing happened afterward. A decade later, Mr. Goldman's words are still as relevant as ever. The problem is systemic, and almost no country cares enough to solve it —except Australia, as we will analyze.

Banks send closing letters with very vague explanations: *due to our internal risk policy; it is a business decision of the head office; due to large deposits (incoming or outgoing); due to high amounts of cash managed in your account; after a strategic review, we are not in a position to provide you with banking services.* In most cases, banks do not provide a deserved explanation.

---

132 Michael Goldman (FISCA) & David Landsman (NMTA); Bank Secrecy Act's Impact on Money Services Businesses: Congressional Hearing of the Financial Services Committee, US House of Representatives; June 21, 2006 - https://bit.ly/3zvINVW

In response to this hearing, FinCEN requested comments on the issue[133]. I will use as an example extracts from a couple of letters FinCEN received that illustrate the situation clearly. In one of them, Ronald Schwartzman, a compliance expert who worked for many years with Uniteller, writes[134]:

> Banks continue to choose to ignore the responsibilities that come with the privileges granted to them in their licenses by the federal banking authorities [...] it would be a derogation of duty if federal authorities with power over the national banks do not categorize bank access for LRC's [Licensed Remittance Companies] as critical and necessary assistance to underprivileged neighborhoods which have the largest number of persons using LRC services.

Julieann M. Thurlow of Reading Co-operative Bank, a small Massachusetts bank, commented on the same call for feedback[135]:

> Maintaining accounts for MSBs require increased costs and deteriorates [our bank's] earnings even further. These are not consumer accounts, therefore, we can opt not to allow MSBs to be our customers. In the event an existing customer adds this service, the bank can opt to close the account. No additional rulemaking will reduce the operational burden, alleviate the customer risk or lessen the regulatory scrutiny for these accounts.

The FATF first addressed the issue in 2014 when President Roger Wilkins, reacted to an op-ed in The Economist, stating that *some of the stronger regulatory practices in the area of AML and CTF threatened to de-bank significant regions or sections of the public*[136].

The op-ed was published in response to Barclays Bank's wave of bank account closures in the UK that year, which sparked public outrage, meetings, and debate. The impact of Barclay's decision on Somali remittances was widely discussed. However, very little changed. The FATF kept mentioning

---

133 FinCEN published what is known as a *Pre-rule* (RIN: 1506-AA85 - Spring 2008 - Provision of Banking Services to Money Services Businesses) to receive comments from the industry and from banks - https://bit.ly/3bQiAK8
134 Ronald Schwartzman: Uniteller Financial Services; Response to FinCEN RIN: 1506-AA85 - https://bit.ly/3w26kNu
135 Julieann M. Thurlow: Reading Co-operative Bank; Response to FinCEN RIN: 1506-AA85, May 4, 2006 - https://bit.ly/3SQ9sFR
136 FATF: The danger of driving both illicit markets and financial exclusion; FATF President Roger Wilkins remarks at the 6th Annual International Conference on Financial Crime and Terrorism Financing, Kuala Lumpur, 8 October 2014 – https://bit.ly/3gx4kWg

"derisking" for about three years but eventually stopped doing so, either because it believed the problem had been resolved or could not do much about it.

In February 2021, the FATF launched a project to study and mitigate the unintended consequences resulting from the incorrect implementation of the FATF Standards, including de-risking, financial exclusion, and human rights restrictions[137].

The list of organizations, NGOs, associations, and think-tanks denouncing derisking has clearly demonstrated the harm this practice brings to the poorest and most vulnerable individuals who are left without financial services provided by NBFIs. Over the years, I have analyzed and written about many of these reports. In 2015, OXFAM published a detailed study by Tracey Durner and Liat Shetret of the Global Center on Cooperative Security[138]. The termination of Correspondent Banking Relationships (CBRs) has affected many banks in small countries, including those in the Caribbean, such as Belize[139]. Derisking also affects charities and humanitarian aid organizations that provide services to countries devastated by war or natural disasters. In the same year, 2015, the Center for Global Development in Washington published a series of recommendations[140] based on an analysis conducted by Jim Woodsome, Vijaya Ramachandran, Clay Lowery, and Jody Myers.

In 2015, the US Treasury Department convened a meeting in Washington. Outside the building, Alexander Hamilton welcomed us. The monument was designed by James Earle Fraser in 1923. It was a cold January morning, and we all took pictures in front of this impressive bronze sculpture. On December 15, 1790, Hamilton proposed the Bank of the United States, a central bank for the new country. His effort ultimately failed. Hamilton did help found The Bank of New York, which still exists today (as BNY Mellon). This bank helped mark New York City as a financial center.

---

137 FATF: Mitigating the Unintended Consequences of the FATF Standards – https://bit.ly/3iEG4Ru
138 Tracey Durner & Liat Shetret: Understanding Bank Derisking And Its Effects On Financial Inclusion, an exploratory study; OXFAM -Global Center on Cooperative Security, November 2015 - https://bit.ly/3C1YGWY
139 Gustavo M. Vasquez: Assessing the Impact of the De-risking on Remittances and Trade Finance in Belize; dic 2017 – https://bit.ly/2Ve90rt
140 Jim Woodsome, Vijaya Ramachandran, Clay Lowery y Jody Myers: Policy Responses to De-risking Progress Report on the CGD Working Group's 2015 RecommendationsCenter for Global Development; 2015 - https://bit.ly/3dQwX1j

About a hundred attendees gathered that day at the Cash Room to participate in the roundtable for an in-depth discussion on derisking[141]. There were interventions from Leslie Caldwell, Melissa Koide, Alexia Latortue, and Jennifer Fowler, who were all very aware of the problem. Treasury preferred to use the term *Bank Discontinuance* rather than Derisking. After them, the next speaker was Jamal El-Hindi, whom I met at this event and whom I would share the stage several times in later FISCA, IMTC, and MTRA conferences. Jamal was clear and direct: the problem had to be solved. We left with a sense of satisfaction that the issue would be resolved. Sadly, we were wrong. Again.

In 2016, The Treasury Dept. and four US federal regulators issued a *Joint Fact Sheet on Foreign Correspondent Banking* stating that US institutions had overreacted to AML/BSA compliance concerns by unnecessarily terminating correspondent relationships with foreign banks[142]. They pointed out how crucial these relationships were to the global economy and that derisking could destabilize or disrupt access to US financing, hinder international trade, cross-border business, and charitable activities, as well as complicate remittance transactions. While it was well written, it didn't yield any positive results.

Daniel Trias, a Uruguayan consultant and ex-banker, who helped in the constitution of CIASEFIM, a southern cone association to face the problem of derisking of NBFIs, explained at the time: *De-risking is characterized by an overreaction to risk, adopted by many international banking institutions. They are simply abdicating their institutional and social responsibility for managing risk, as recommended by FATF and international regulators as part of the fight against money laundering and terrorist financing, thus interrupting commercial relations with other financial institutions without any justification*[143].

I would like to draw attention to Marco Nicoli's article[144] on the World Bank blog entitled *De-risking and remittances: the myth of the "underlying transaction" debunked*, containing this crucial statement: *Any argument based*

---

141 Hugo Cuevas-Mohr: US TREASURY ROUNDTABLE ON FINANCIAL ACCESS FOR MONEY SERVICE BUSINESSES; January 13, 2015 - https://bit.ly/3dSjUNa
142 US Department of the Treasury: Joint Fact Sheet on Foreign Correspondent Banking; October 30, 2016 – https://bit.ly/3QFC7LX
143 Daniel Trias: Reunión Internacional en Madrid de las Asociaciones de Entidades de Pago y de Servicios Financieros; July 13, 2018 - https://bit.ly/3vZSDP2
144 Marco Nicoli: De-risking and remittances: the myth of the "underlying transaction" debunked; World Bank Blog, June 13, 2018 – https://bit.ly/3BC47cC

on the bank's lack of visibility to the underlying transactions performed by MTOs should be dismissed in principle. Instead, it should be a requirement of the banks to ensure that MTOs have adequate AML/CFT checks and processes in place to avoid being exploited.

I am no stranger to this problem. In early 2010, Serviexpreso, a company founded with my business partner Roger Sanchez, had five bank accounts closed in Costa Rica when regulators forced us to get a foreign exchange license - before that we were a remittance company. As soon as the news of having obtained the foreign exchange license was published, the banks began sending the closing letters. Two state-owned banks were required to continue servicing the company, and we could continue operating. By 2015, derisking and the regulator's view that the remittance sector had to be dismantled —after the closure of over 15 remittance companies in 10 years— Serviexpreso was sold to the only remaining local competitor.

Erick Schneider, a former executive at American Express, Citibank, Intermex, WorldRemit and a specialist in cross-border payments, believes that banks, seeking to avoid regulatory and compliance risks, are putting remittance companies up against the wall and abusing their position:

> The word derisking by itself means absolutely nothing. However, it causes fear because it means that a bank is trying to reduce risk, which means it is no longer offering services to remittance companies, claiming it is too risky. In my opinion, this is an entirely misleading term: banks need to understand that most, if not all of these companies, have a solid compliance platform. For example, WorldRemit is a digital platform for sending remittances whose compliance system automates and simplifies control. However, banks don't want to hear about this, or if they do, it is under a very punitive approach, either from a financial standpoint, demanding minimum volumes and charging more for services, or punitive in the fact that there are constant reviews and more requirements up to the point of no return. I think derisking is the biggest problem the industry faces[145].

The World Bank conducted a survey and published a report on derisking in CRBs issued in June 2018[146], and found that *de-risking ultimately is a busi-*

---

145 Entrevista virtual, grabada y transcrita, realizada a Erick Schneider, el 14 de junio de 2022, por Isabel Cortés.
146 World Bank: Are Global Banks Cutting Off Customers in Developing and Emerging Economies?; May 1, 2018 - https://bit.ly/3Qkov8Z

ness decision, since global banks consider CBRs to be a low-margin but high-risk activity[147]. The findings imply that if the cost of CBRs could be lowered through fintech or other tools, or if risk could be reduced through effective anti-money laundering (AML) regimes, CBRs would be a more attractive business line for global banks[148]. In other words: there is nothing to do. The World Bank ruled that the effects of derisking were minimal, shocking, and upsetting to most companies that contributed to the study.

In February 2020, Pavel Kuskowski, CEO and co-founder of Coinfirm, told Forbes: *Anyone doing business in the crypto space knows it's not regulations that are the biggest obstacle to getting off the ground. Rather, it's the widespread lack of access to basic financial necessities -- like a bank account. This is killing crypto businesses by shutting them out of the mainstream economy.* Further in his article, Kuskowski discusses the new actions being tried in Europe[149].

After the *Crypto Winter*[150] in 2022-2023 —a term loosely based on *Winter is Coming* from the series Game of Thrones— several banks feel vindicated of having derisked crypto companies.

Derisking of fintech, blockchain, and crypto businesses is a global issue.

As Kroll's Malin Nilsson and Ed Shorrock discussed in their May 2019 article *Debanking and the Law of Unintended Consequences*[151]: *When "Risk Management" becomes "Risk Avoidance," there is not much to say except that the system is broken.* Dr. Ellen R. Wald of the Atlantic Council, in a blog written in Barron's[152], makes it clear: *Debanking hurts everyone*. She questions in her

---

147 World Bank: The decline in access to correspondent banking services in emerging markets : trends, impacts, and solutions - lessons learned from eight country case studies; (2018) - https://bit.ly/3QltNkR
148 World Bank: https://bit.ly/3QXi8Zt
149 Pavel Kuskowski: "Europe's New AML Directive Means Banks Can No Longer Shut Crypto Out"; Forbes, February 20, 2020 - https://bit.ly/3eSdBXi
150 Sean Michael Kerner: What is crypto winter? Everything you need to know; WhatIs by TechTarget - https://bit.ly/48oaTD6
151 Malin Nilsson and Ed Shorrock: "Debanking and the Law of Unintended Consequences", Kroll; May 28 2019 - https://bit.ly/3zNcqjU
152 Ellen R. Wald (Atlantic Council): "Debanking Hurts Everyone"; Barron's, January 8, 2021 - https://bit.ly/2WlZ8wq

article whether the US OCC's *Fair Access to Financial Services Rule* is the right measure to stop debanking[153].

In her speech at the 26th Egmont Group Plenary held in The Hague in July 2019, Queen Maxima of The Netherlands raised the issue of derisking:

The issue of de-risking still threatens these crucial financial flows. The number of active correspondent banks declined by 3.8% in 2018 —a decline that has been continuous since 2009. And of course the situation varies regionally. Each region has lost at least 10% of their correspondent banking relationships between 2011 and 2018. During that period, South America, Northern Africa, Polynesia, Micronesia, Melanesia, and the Caribbean have all lost more than 30% of these relationships. The decline of correspondent banks and money transfer operators has negative consequences for individuals, businesses, and non-profit organizations that send or receive money abroad. With less channels and actors in the market, we run two risks: First, the reduced number of correspondents and the concentration of the market could increase the price of remittances and prevent us from reaching the target price of 3%, as set in the UN Sustainable Development Goal 10 with an aim to reduce inequality. Second, by closing down smaller actors, especially money transfer operators, customers might move to informal money transfer services, which are opaque and less reliable—a loss for financial integrity and a loss for financial inclusion.

The loss by derisking or debanking of ethnic remittance companies and smaller MTOs, even the impact on financial inclusion, seems to create little concern for governments and regulators.

When derisking impacts innovation or large business sectors is when we see the media coverage increase.

In May 2020, the European Banking Authority (EBA) made a public consultation to learn more about the reasons, scale and impact of derisking. In March 2021, as explained in the article[154] published by consultants

---

153 OCC: Fair Access to Financial Services Rule; February 5, 2021 - https://bit.ly/3i9hEk7
154 IMTC: Payments in Europe: Latest derisking developments; Pascale-Marie Brien; Nina Huelsken: interview, June 21,2021 - https://bit.ly/3pddcUe

Pascale-Marie Brien and Nina Huelsken, the EBA issued three regulatory instruments to address these practices:

- An Opinion in which it concluded that de-risking is a continuing trend that has substantial implications from a ML/TF risk, consumer protection and financial stability point of view;
- The publication of revised ML/Risk Factor Guidelines which clarify that the application of a risk-based approach To AML/CFT does not require financial institutions to *refuse or terminate business relationships with entire categories of customers that are considered to present higher ML/TF risk*;
- EBA launched a public consultation on potential changes to its existing guidelines on risk-based AML/CFT supervision to request European competent authorities (in each Member State) to address de-risking in their own risk assessments.

EBA policies have stimulated the growth of fintechs, especially EMIs that have reached agreements with banks to provide domestic and cross-border services.

The UK Federation of Small Businesses in July 2023 expressed its concern: *Business chiefs have accused banks of being overzealous and taking a "blunt and sweeping approach" to risk management – with appearing to close accounts on arbitrary grounds, including on the grounds of a holder having a "Russian-sounding" name and as a result of transactions with countries deemed at high risk of corruption*[155].

To illustrate that derisking affects the industry globally, let's look at how it has impacted the industry in Australia, The Philippines, and Spain.

AUSTRALIA

Derisking and debanking in Australia has been so challenging that the country has made a great effort —the world's most comprehensive analysis of the problem— to hear as many voices as possible and compile the confronting views of banks and NBFIs. But it did not reach the level it did until innovation was threatened.

---

155 Cahal Milmo: Banks must be reined in over 'thousands' of account closures, say business chiefs; inews, July 26, 2023 - https://bit.ly/46cNp1T

In 2015 AUSTRAC published the *Strategic Analysis Brief Bank De-risking of Remittance Businesses*[156]. Even if the conclusion of the analysis based on remittance volumes states that *Bank de-risking activities do not appear to have had a significant impact on international funds flows through the remittance sector*, the Australian Parliament continued to hear complaints from fintechs and other NBFIs.

An article written in 2021 by Denham Sadler, senior reporter for InnovationAus[157] exemplifies how the issue of derisking is affecting innovation in this country. The article titled *Debanking risks 'undermining' local tech sector* explains: *The seriousness of debanking cannot be understated. Technology and financial businesses who have been debanked must allocate precious capacity to correcting the operational damage caused by a loss of financial services.*

The Australian Parliament convened *The Senate Select Committee on Australia as a Technology and Financial Centre*, which delivered its recommendations to the parliament in a final report in October 2021[158]. This final report in *Chapter 4: De-banking*[159], provides the best examples of the many points of view surrounding this contentious issue. The chapter analyzes examples of debanking, sectors affected, effects, reasons, bank response, competition, regulatory landscape, and suggestions to improve the framework governing debanking practices.

Two of its final twelve recommendations:

The committee recommends that in order to increase certainty and transparency around de-banking, the Australian Government develop a clear process for businesses that have been de-banked. This should be anchored around the Australian Financial Complaints Authority (AFCA) which services licensed entities.

The committee recommends that [...] common access requirements for the New Payments Platform should be developed by the Reserve Bank of

---

156 Strategic Analysis Brief Bank De-risking of Remittance Businesses; AUSTRAC, Commonwealth of Australia, 2015.- https://bit.ly/3r6u4Rn
157 Denham Sadler: Debanking risks 'undermining' local tech sector;InnovationAus,July 26, 2021 - https://bit.ly/3K5DT7b
158 The Senate Select Committee on Australia as a Technology and Financial Centre, Final Report, October 2021 - https://bit.ly/3PGvrj9
159 The Senate Select Committee on Australia as a Technology and Financial Centre, Final Report, Chapter 4: De-banking, 2021 - https://bit.ly/46eodIe

Australia, in order to reduce the reliance of payments businesses on the major banks for the provision of banking services.

The first recommendation has created a need for the regulator to be notified when a bank decides not to open or close the bank account of a licensed entity. The second deals with the access of NBFIs to the Payments Platform, a way to allow NBFIs to have access to settlement and clearing facilities reserved by banks. Allowing fintechs to access bank rails has been gaining acceptance in many countries to increase competition and transparency.

Another recommendation was establishing a market licensing regime for Digital Currency Exchanges, including capital adequacy, auditing, and responsible person tests.

THE PHILIPPINES

In October 2017, George Inocencio, President of ABROI (Association of Bank Remittance Officers Inc.), a Philippine guild, reported at a World Bank Roundtable on Access to Correspondent Banking and Other Cross-Border Financial Services in Washington[160], that, as a result of a survey conducted by this association, 52 Australian accounts had been closed in the previous year, 15 from Philippine companies and banks and 36 from entities licensed and supervised by AUSTRAC. A follow-up report was presented by Mr. Inocencio at IMTC ASIA 2018 in Manila, further showing how derisking was advancing inexorably.

The new "de-coupling"or "de-risking" policies from Europe, Australia and the US towards Russia and China, has involved many meetings and state visits involving The Philippines. By accelerating cooperation with the Philippines, the aim is to *derisk trade relations* with China and Russia, by helping all business sectors remove the trade barriers that exist[161]. Debanking of Filipino banks and fintechs in Europe, Australia and the US is a subject that is on the list and we hope it is addressed, not only for this Asian country, but also for countries in Africa and The Americas.

---

160 George Inocencio: Addressing The Issue Of De-Risking Through Financial Inclusion; Association Of Bank Remittance Officers (ABROI), Manila, Philippines; World Bank Roundtable on Access to Correspondent Banking and Other Cross-Border Financial Services; Washington, D.C; October 13, 2017- https://bit.ly/3Ahuw0x
161 Samuel P. Medenilla: PHL sees economic gains as EU 'derisking' goes on; Business Mirror, August 1, 2023 - https://bit.ly/48HDofj

SPAIN

Derisking in Spain has seen a different outcome than almost any country in the world, as payment institutions have successfully sued the banks to stop the closure of their accounts. According to a report by consultant Lourdes Soto[162], two Spanish banks, Santander and BBVA, started offering remittance services to migrants in 2005, followed by Sabadell, Caixabank, and Banco Popular. Several days later, the bank accounts of their competing payment institutions were closed. The Court of Justice of the European Union found Spain guilty of violating the fundamental rights of its citizens with its *Law on the Prevention of Money Laundering and Terrorist Financing* in a ground-setting case settled in 2016[163]. Attorney Antonio Selas —who was key in obtaining the 2016 judgment— has been fighting for the right of the industry to maintain its bank accounts.

Many payment institutions have successfully used this 2016 court ruling to defend their right to use the banking system every time a new wave of closures flares up.

The Bank of Spain and other European Regulators require safeguard accounts, which means that client funds must be kept in separate bank accounts - administrative and operational - for their protection. If the regulations demand a bank account to hold client funds, the banks are responsible for opening these bank accounts for NBFIs. Even though the rules are in the books, the regulator does not seem to have the tools —or the political power— to intervene.

ARE THERE SOLUTIONS FOR DERISKING AND DEBANKING?

In essence, banks' profits from serving MTOs do not offset the additional investment requirements in compliance and the legal and reputational exposure created by regulations. I have consulted for financial institutions, and there are many ways to manage the revenue generated by serving MTOs using improved monitoring systems and a deep understanding of each client's risk management.

---

162 Lourdes Soto Morales: Cierre de cuentas a Entidades de Pago por Bancos Comerciales en España - CrossTech Blog, July 23, 2021 - https://bit.ly/3zSoTEP
163 Money Transfer Companies Win a Match Against Banks in Brussels, CrossTech, February 7, 2016 - https://bit.ly/3RxyQlH

The few banks that have succeeded in developing or continue to serve the industry know that offering these specialized services will increase the appetite for regulatory audits and examinations. The fear of an overzealous examination is always present, and regulatory agencies believe these high-strung audits are necessary. My question has always been: *Are these audits fair comparatively? Is there a bias lurking behind?*

Regulators need to be notified when a bank decides not to open or close the bank account of a licensed entity, similar to what the Australian Parliament recommended its regulator to do. The decision should be notified by both the bank and by the licensed entity on a form where the reasons and details of the decision are presented.

Some have argued, when I have voiced this idea, that the form might sit in a regulator's desk without any measures taken or any action carried out as a result of the report. That is a legitimate argument, but it might at least give the regulator a direct view of the problem —not hearsay— and create a database that can be used to bring numbers and information to the table.

Access of fintechs to settlement and clearing entities reserved for banks is a way to give the industry a more competitive playing field. Some fintechs can become the de-facto providers of bank services if they are given access to the banking rails.

Of course, other solutions should come from willing banks in close alliance with NBFI organizations. MSB-friendly banks should work together to develop better practices that can give them, as a group, a way to lower the perceived risks of providing bank services to the industry.

FINANCIAL INCLUSION VS. BANCARIZATION

Dominican entrepreneur Ernesto Armenteros, former Vice President of Remesas Quisqueyana and member of the Banco Union Board in the Dominican Republic, has dedicated much of his career to financial inclusion. In his view, migrants are not well regarded by the banking sector, excluding them from the benefits of having a banking relationship.

During an interview for this book, he stated: *Banks in Manhattan, for example, are all located south of 125th, while immigrants who send remittances live north of 125th. Banks are culturally hostile to undocumented immigrants. They are not able to open a bank account. Furthermore, they work irregular hours and live far away; a gap is created and then companies like ours emerge to serve these marginalized people.*

In Ernesto's view, exclusion from the banking system has prevented immigrants from accessing digital money services, resulting in further segregation and disadvantages for them and their families. The system keeps the cash economy in place:

> Remittances have two sides: origination and delivery. During the origination, a payment order can be digitized through a website, an application, a digital wallet, etc. However, migrants — the service users— need to be able to digitize their income, a big challenge since most of them are paid with cash or checks. As long as immigrants are demonized and condemned to low wages, they have no choice but to pay for utilities, energy, and water, buy air time, and send money home from cash counters.
>
> We now move on to the delivery side. Migrants leave their countries of origin in search of a better life because they have not been able to protect and provide for their families.

In other words, they and their families have been marginalized, unbanked, and excluded from the mainstream economy. In the end, it's the same on both sides: marginalizing a community means forcing it to carry operations in cash anonymously. There's nothing illegal about that. It's just that they have had no bank branches to turn to, no cards, no recognition of their income history, so they have to make their deals in cash[164].

It is this attitude of banks that fintechs are taking advantage of to offer inclusive solutions to migrants in many countries. Most fintechs have developed products for millennials catering mainly to them. But some of them have brought services to migrants and their families. A Belgian MTO, MoneyTrans, has been successful with the introduction in 2020 of their Smile account serviced with a Debit Mastercard, allowing remittance families access to the digital economy[165].

In the US, Latin American consulates have provided their citizens with Consular Identification Cards (Matricula Consular) so they can open bank

---

164 Virtual Interview with Ernesto Armenteros on June 28, 2022, conducted, recorded and transcribed by Lucía Salazar.
165 Amandine Servotte: Moneytrans partners with Mastercard to include close to 1 million people into the financial system; Mastercard, March 5, 2020 - https://mstr.cd/4505Juj

accounts regardless of residency status, so they can have access to debit cards and other digital payment solutions. In remittance destination countries, digital solutions and virtual wallets are opening up new possibilities too.

The term financial inclusion was developed at the turn of the century, and even if initially it meant the ability for individuals to have a bank account, the term is now used on a broader sense: the power of an individual to access digital financial services with accounts, not only with banks but with NBFIs such as fintechs and Mobile Money Operators.

In Spanish, the term bancarización was used originally. The term has declined in favor of *inclusión financiera,* even if sometimes banks use it as they were synonyms. Graph 5 shows us the use of both terms from 1990 to 2019.

GRAPH 5: Use of the Spanish term bancarización vs inclusión financiera (1990-2019)

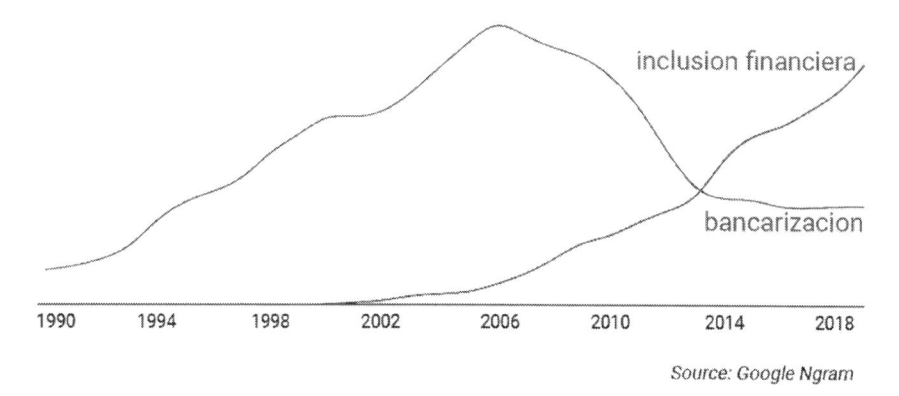

Source: Google Ngram

Note: The graph for financial inclusion, the English term, is almost identical to the line for inclusión financiera, above, climbing from 2005 until today.

The World Bank's website clearly reflects this new vision of financial inclusion without using the term bank anymore: *Financial inclusion means that individuals and businesses have access to useful and affordable financial products and services that meet their needs –transactions, payments, savings, credit, and insurance– delivered in a responsible and sustainable way.*

> **Commercial banks have objected to some *financial inclusion* measures, especially when they are forced to open no-cost or very low-cost accounts that cause them to lose money.**

Governments have sometimes imposed these measures to democratize the financial system. The issue becomes political, as it is in Latin America, with the arrival of governments that want to change the financial system to democratize the sector. It is evident from Uruguay's 2019-2020 discussion of the Financial Inclusion Law[166] that government measures can generate conflicts with banks when these measures aim to serve the common good and a broader spectrum of individuals.

Piero P. Coen, president of AirPak, WU's master agent in Central America, a financial services provider for migrants and unbanked consumers, believes that financial inclusion can be achieved through more appropriate means: *I don't believe much in banks and the future of the current banking model. What I do believe in is financial inclusion, and that is what we want to do: financially include. We want to be the best provider of financial services for the neediest population, together with all the services a bank provides, all of them, from financing your motorcycle to financing your house, or, in other words, developing all financial services without the paperwork and costs associated with banks. As a fintech, that is what we want to do*[167].

> **Changing the concept of financial inclusion is also crucial for the future of fintechs, as it challenges politicians and public officials to approach state intervention differently compared to previous decades.**

The Dominican Central Bank's Director of Payments System, Fabiola Herrera[168] and the Mexican Central Bank's Payments Director Miguel Díaz

---
166 Mathías da Silva: La LUC y la inclusión financiera: lo político, la libertad y una tendencia irreversible; La Diaria, November 10, 2021 - https://bit.ly/3flrMY1
167 Virtual Interview with Piero P. Coen on July 5, 2022, conducted, recorded and transcribed by Lucía Salazar.
168 Jairon Severino: Inclusión financiera difiere del concepto de bancarización; Dinero, October 30, 2017 - https://bit.ly/3K4dg2b

are aware of this. Díaz stated[169] that financial inclusion *will not necessarily imply opening an account and a formal relationship with a bank*. He points out that *the payment may even be made through a prepaid card associated with the mobile phone*. NBFIs might find government support for promoting financial inclusion, which had previously been denied to them.

THE WAR ON CASH

The *war on cash* refers to a set of policies by governments around the world, with incentives from banks, card companies, and the *digital intelligentsia* to suppress the use of paper currency. The principal aim is to shift transactions from untraceable cash to an electronic data trail that is a win-win for governments, LEAs, tax authorities and all the payment providers that make a revenue from managing the electronic data. It is excellent for all the financial services providers; the controversy lies with everyone that believes that it goes against privacy and constrains the liberty of individuals in society[170].

> **The War on Cash has created challenges for migrants, the underserved and the elderly and the companies that serve them.**

As writer Malcolm Harris in The Intelligencer[171] commented: *Cash doesn't discriminate, but Mastercard might*, pointing to the problems that many individuals are facing in a cashless world.

Derisking and Debanking challenges are major problems for traditional MTOs and FECs with branches and agents that handle cash. Commercial banks no longer want to handle physical money although some continue to do so, usually through outsourcing. Banks are limiting cash management services or they become so expensive that it is almost impossible to provide services when you cannot dispose of cash easily.

---

169 Armando Jurado Arellano: ¿Es lo mismo inclusión financiera y bancarización? Inclusión financiera y bancarización, aunque sean términos parecidos, no necesariamente significan lo mismo; September 23, 2020 - https://bit.ly/3ArrU09
170 David McRee: The War on Cash: How Banks and a Power-Hungry Government Want to Confiscate your Cash, Steal Your Liberty and Track Every Dollar You Spend. And How to Fight Back, Humanix Books, 2020 - https://bit.ly/48EbFw9
171 Malcolm Harris: The War on Cash; The Intelligencer, June 22, 2022 - https://nym.ag/45pfna3

In Europe, cash management and transport companies belong to ETA[172] (European Security Transport Association), while in Asia, Africa, and Oceania, they belong to ACMA (Asian Cash Management Association). The group has advocated for regulations that allow them to operate as *cash banks* and thus manage the *cash cycle* in a more efficient and less costly way for the users. Additionally, they advocate for government and business actions to be restricted to avoid users being forced into adopting digital solutions and having a choice.

Currency Research[173] (CR) is an international organization that specializes in studies, reports and events on payments and cash management, as has Cash Matters[174], funded by the International Currency Association[175] (ICA), a forum that supports the existence and relevance of physical money as a key component of payments in the future and now. ATM associations, such as the ATM Industry Association[176] (ATMIA), are also playing an increasing role as independent ATMs become more common.

I have actively participated in some of these unions and advocacy groups' events as I share the same concerns as many analysts: cash management is vital to migrants' economies, both at the origin and destination, and denying them access to it will only make their lives more challenging. Financial education not necessarily mean digitizing payments. I have also seen how MMOs in some countries such as M-Pesa in Kenya, have managed to responsibly *combine physical and electronic money* for the sake of society and the most disadvantaged strata. The Better than Cash Alliance[177] (BTCA) has earned the support of the United Nations by engaging governments, businesses and international organizations to speed up the transition to digital payments.

Bills are becoming extinct, according to all the supporters of digitization. Several countries have drastically reduced their cash use, while others have found it difficult to completely remove them from circulation. Using cash in a country like Germany, which defends the privacy of citizens' usage of cash is one way to limit government oversight, a freedomist attitude that will

---

172 European Security Transport Association - https://bit.ly/3A7pP8v
173 Currency Research: https://currencyresearch.com/
174 Cash Matters: https://www.cashmatters.org/
175 International Currency Association: https://currencyassociation.org/
176 ATM Industry Association: https://www.atmia.com/
177 Better than Cash Alliance: https://www.betterthancash.org/

persist and may, at some point, thrive again for political reasons. In the face of totalitarian governments, cash may be a way to maintain the freedom of people and their activities.

Cash has been very important in conflict and when natural disasters occur. When the earthquake struck Haiti in 2010, the US Navy assisted NBFIs and banks[178] with the transportation of millions of dollars in cash from the US to Haiti so that remittances could be disbursed while conditions returned to normal. In Somalia, transporting cash from other countries has been a way to support migrant families, especially when government institutions have been unable to bring stability to the country. Remittances delivered to Syrian refugee camps in Jordan are yet another example of the need for cash to provide basic services to families in need. In countries with undocumented migrants, who rely almost exclusively on cash for survival, restricting payments or remittances is certainly a major concern.

> Despite the steady advance of digitization, the number of remittances that originate and end digitally is still very low, roughly between 5% and 10%. I have no doubt that the percentage will continue to grow.

AGGREGATORS EVOLVE

In the industry, the term aggregator refers to companies that develop back-office interconnection systems between MTOs, banks, fintechs, and payment providers for system integration, treasury, and expanding remittance distribution. By integrating correspondent networks at origin and destination, they create a value chain to scale cross-border payment services with lower costs and faster delivery. As the industry becomes more complex, it takes time and resources - both technological and compliance related to add a new correspondent, a new destination, and a new channel, and these B2B crosstechs are gaining increasing relevance. The use of state-of-the-art APIs makes integration much more efficient. From domestic to regional and worldwide aggregators, they have transformed the industry from top to bottom.

---

[178] Manuel Orozco: Las repercusiones del terremoto sobre las remesas; Interamerican Dialogue, ene 18 2010 - https://bit.ly/3KdUANv

In 1992, we founded Titan Payment Center (TPC) in Colombia, a payment aggregator to serve the MTOs that were working with TITAN in the U.S. and Europe for payments in Venezuela, Panama, Costa Rica, Nicaragua, El Salvador, Honduras, and Guatemala. As TITAN's correspondents sent remittances to Colombia in large quantities, they could aggregate transactions to the countries offered by TPC and reconcile accounts without having to establish direct relationships. In 1994, TPC was forced to cease operations after the Colombian Financial Superintendency made a ruling that local regulations only allowed remittances to and from Colombia. Following the closing of TPC, we tried to move the operation to Costa Rica, and again, SUGEF, the local regulator, ruled that the regulations only allowed remittances to and from the country. French writer Jean Cocteau said: *When a work appears to be ahead of its time, it is only the time that is behind the work*. It took almost a decade before regulators understood and accepted the role of aggregators as part of the *remittance market payment value chain*.

In 2003 More Money Transfers, based in Zonamerica —a Free Zone Business and Technology Park— outside Montevideo, began offering payment aggregation for Uruguay, Paraguay, Argentina, Chile, and Bolivia and then added countries in South and Central America. A similar strategy has been followed by Transnetwork, founded in 2002, which has been acquiring MTOs and other aggregators in the region.

Uniteller has also become one of the main payment aggregators in Latin America. MFS Africa and AZA Finance have become important aggregators on the African continent. In Asia, notable aggregators include Tranglo —acquired by TNG, a Hong Kong ewallet, for US $28 million in 2018 from Malaysian National Private Equity Fund Ekuinas[179]— and EMQ, founded by Max Liu in 2014 in Hong Kong.

Thunes, founded in 2019 when Transfer-To split its phone recharge service (now DTOne) from its money transfer service, has been steadily growing in the sector with its payment services that interconnect MTOs worldwide. With Peter De Caluwe as CEO —previously the CEO of Naspers and Ogone (Ingenico)— the company has completed many successful investment rounds and hired well-known industry executives to become a leading

---

179 TNG Acquires Global Cross-border Payment Gateway Company Tranglo from Malaysian National Private Equity Fund Ekuinas at US$28 Million; Press Release, 15 October 2018 - https://bit.ly/445uJjd

worldwide aggregator. With the purchase of Limonetik[180], renamed Thunes Collections, its Director, Aik Boon Tan, assumes leadership of this B2B fintech service.

Nium is an aggregator that markets itself as an industry newcomer that can instantly collect, convert, and disburse funds around the world to accounts, cards, and wallets. Nium's origins lie in InstaRem, an MTO co-founded in 2014 by Prajit Nanu and Michael Bermingham. After securing its first license in Australia in 2014, the company set-up offices in India, Singapore, and Australia, and in 2015 it obtained its license in Canada. In 2019 InstaReM rebranded[181] to become part of Nium and launched the new vision as an *Open Money Network*.

Another aggregator, Bancomer Transfer Services (BTS), was a B2B fintech founded by BBVA in the US, initially to route remittances from US MTOs to the group's Mexican bank Bancomer, and later on to other BBVA-owned banks in Latin America. This way, BTS *filtered* the remittances paid by its banks in the region. In 2020 PNC Financial Services, based in Pittsburgh, Pennsylvania, one of the ten largest banks in the US, acquired BBVA's North American operations for $11.6 billion[182]. BTS was merged with PNC Global Transfers (PNCGT), the group's cross-border payment processor. Aurora Garza Hagan, who has been part of BTS since 2011, is now heading PNCGT. Aurora has also been Chairman of the MSBA, the association of US NBFIs.

POSTAL SERVICES

All over the world, Postal Services face complex survival challenges as government-run mail courier services. Postal Services (PSs) have developed banking products in many countries, and in most countries, PSs have become agents of the larger MTOs. WU was probably the company that first convinced many postal administrators in Europe and elsewhere to use their payment services. WU provided the IT needed —in some cases hardware and software— to develop the service. Most of these partnerships became

---

180 Thunes acquires Limonetik to accelerate rollout of global payment collections; Press Release, July 21, 2021 - https://bit.ly/444T4Ww
181 InstaReM rebrands to Nium, world's first global enterprise payments platform; PRess Release, October 28, 2019 - https://bit.ly/3KFIiip
182 BBVA: BBVA sells US subsidiary to PNC for $11.6 billion, November 16, 2010 - https://bbva.info/3AYhHbQ

exclusive. Now, under five-year contracts that include substantial bonuses, WU has managed to keep these relationships. MGI and RIA have challenged WU to become PSs partners with relatively low success.

Mark J. Scher commented in 2001 in a UNDESA (United Nations Department of Economic and Social Affairs) paper[183]: *Generally, the success of these companies derives from their cost-effective use of the postal system's extensive network. For example, a majority of Western Union's more than 100,000 worldwide agency locations are post offices. [...] Nevertheless, despite their use of the postal infrastructure, Western Union and Moneygram's fees are disproportionately high in relation to the amounts remitted, and an extremely disadvantageous exchange rate may be charged in markets that lack competing services.*

PSs have been able to negotiate better rates and conditions over time. In some cases, these partnerships have deepened. In April 2022, the UK Post Office and WU announced[184] an expansion in their partnership with a minimum of 4,000 of its 11,500 branches offering cross-border money transfers at their counters for the first time in an effort to increase foot traffic. The UK Post Office only offered WU services online. The new in-branch service will double WU's UK retail network.

The World Bank and IFAD have supported projects to improve conditions for PSs. One such project was APFSI (African Postal Financial Services Initiative), a partnership led by FFR (Financial Facility for Remittances) that brought together the World Bank, the Universal Postal Union (UPU), WSBI (World Savings and Retail Banking Institution) and UNCDF (United Nations Capital Development Fund), and was co-financed by the EU. This regional program aimed to increase competition in the African remittance market by enabling African Post Offices to offer financial services. It aimed to promote cheaper, faster, more convenient, and customer-friendly remittances, especially in rural areas, while fostering dialogue between regulators and policymakers. A report on this project[185], was written by Hans Boon and

---

183 Postal Savings and the Provision of FinancialServices: Policy Issues and Asian Experiences in the Use of the Postal Infrastructure for Savings Mobilization; DESA Discussion Paper No. 22, December 2001 - https://bit.ly/47mJFMG
184 Post Office announces partnership expansion with Western Union; Press Release, April 29, 2022 - https://bit.ly/3OVfcOP
185 Hans Boon, Mauro Martini: The African Postal Financial Services Initiative: A success story on remittances at the post office in Africa; march 2018 - https://bit.ly/3YwvBw4

Mauro Martini. Improving the quality of services and the competitiveness of these institutions will benefit migrant families in the destination countries.

The IOM, in collaboration with UPU, has also carried out similar projects, as it did in 2014 with Burundi Post[186], and projects with PSs in Tanzania and Uganda, in addition to projects related to remittances in Albania, Georgia, Moldova, and Tajikistan[187].

Scandinavian fintech Eurogiro, founded in 1993 by fourteen European PSs, provides PSs with a digital financial services platform that includes remittances and international connections with correspondents in several corridors. In 2018, it merged with Inpay[188], a Danish crosstech with a unique history. Founder Jacob Tackmann Thomsen wanted to donate funds to help a center for orphaned children in Myanmar after Cyclone Nargis in 2008. He was annoyed by the fees and the long wait for his payment to arrive. Frustrated, he pledged to create a solution and founded Inpay that same year.

By 2022, the company employs more than 120 people from more than 33 nationalities and performs millions of transactions annually. Through its partnership with PSs, Inpay customers can make payments to post offices in hard-to-reach rural areas like Bangladesh, Sri Lanka, Vietnam and Bhutan[189].

---

186 IOM Partners for Remittance Reform with Universal Postal Union; October 17, 2014 - https://bit.ly/3KFGqGt
187 IOM and Remittances: https://bit.ly/3qukPtK
188 Inpay acquires Eurogiro; Press Statement, Copenhagen, 21 February 2018 - https://bit.ly/3QEh8fS
189 Tilly Kenyon: Fintech Inpay named fastest growing company in Denmark, Fintech Magazine, March 2, 2022 - https://bit.ly/45pv4OL

CHAPTER 3

THE DIGITAL AGE TAKES HOLD

On June 15, 2017, I arrived at the United Nations headquarters in New York to participate in the Sixth Global Forum on Remittances, Investment and Development (GFRID). It was an extraordinary moment for me. IMTC had been invited to the GFRID after we had discussed with the organizers, Pedro Vasconcelos and his team at IFAD, the presentation of the first Remittance Innovations Awards (Remtech Awards). Many times, coming from the Queens-Midtown Tunnel, I had seen the tall, flat UN building, built in 1950 on the edge of the East River in Manhattan, but I had never stepped inside, not even when I lived in New York or went on sightseeing tours around the Big Apple.

While passing through the security gates on a beautiful sunny summer day, I felt the pleasant breeze from the East River, swaying the flags from around the world that were greeting us. Our cameraman, Luis, saw how excited I was and asked me to go back outside the reception area and come back in to record a video. It was not the right time to pretend to be an actor, but the occasion called for it. I was overwhelmed by the vast halls where the great world political leaders held conferences and speeches to prevent war and conflict. Sharing with industry colleagues the panels that IFAD had organized and then getting on stage and presenting the RemTech award winners was a memorable experience. We wanted all the winners and some nominees to be present to receive the crystal trophy we had ready for them to take proudly home. We had convened several members of the independent jury, and we had the pleasure of having them on stage: Leon Isaacs, Greta Geankopolis, and Luis Buenaventura.

This first edition had 36 participants[190], eleven prizes awarded, and ten mentions from the judges. Azimo, a UK crosstech, won the *Judges Overall Favorite Award*, while Safaricom M-Pesa received the *Mobile Creativity Award* and another crosstech, Xoom, won the *Digital Pioneer Award*. Regtech Trulioo was recognized for its customer insight, and EcoCashDiaspora received the *Visionary Award*. The *Innovative Service for Compliance Award* went to ComplyAdvantage, another regtech, while fintechs Moneytis, Airpocket, and Everex received honorable mentions. Crypto company Bitso received the award for its *Pioneering Spirit* in its innovative quest to offer cryptocurrency solutions to the industry.

That afternoon ended with a boat ride to see the city's skyscrapers, and we enjoyed a pleasant evening with colleagues and friends. The following day, June 16, we celebrated IDFR, the International Day of Family Remittances[191], a universally recognized observance adopted by the United Nations General Assembly. It is a tribute to migrants supporting their families that IFAD managed to put on the world calendar. The Day recognizes the contribution of over 200 million migrants to improve the lives of their 800 million family members back home and to create a future of hope for their children.

A second edition of the RemTech Awards[192] was held at the Seventh GFRID 2018 in Kuala Lumpur, Malaysia. On May 8, with coordinator Olivia Chow, we presented the awards to the winners: RemitONE, Trulioo, Paykii, ValYou, Koibanx, Mahindra Comviva, TransferTo (Thunes), Rewire and Afbit. Due to the COVID pandemic, the GFRID paused, and the Remtech Awards were presented at IMTC WORLD in Miami in 2019 and CROSSTECH WORLD in November 2022. The Eight GFRID took place in Nairobi, Kenya, in June 2023, and we were present again with

---

190 IMTC-CrossTech: Presentation of the 2017 Remtech Awards, United Nations, New York, June 15, 2017 - https://bit.ly/3Rc6Rog
191 International Day of Family Remittances: 16 June; United Nations - https://bit.ly/3PnY7Ms
192 GFRID2018 Report; International Fund for Agricultural Development (IFAD); Global Forum on Remittances, Investment and Development 2018, 8-10 May 2018 p.36 - https://bit.ly/3Qbgxyr

the RemTech Awards[193], this time under the management of CrossTech's Priscilla Doliveira-Friedman.

REGULATING INNOVATION

Many researchers and academics have analyzed the evolution of regulations and their enforcement, the impact on the industries affected, the sanctions imposed by regulators against what they perceive as violations, and the industry's response. The financial services industry is one of the sectors amid this regulatory evolution brought by NBFIs, especially the new fintechs, and the challenge they place on banks and the overall *status quo* of the financial world. Regulatory forces' role in driving or delaying innovation is critical to any country. Competition, cooperation, and regulation affect industry-specific innovation patterns.

Regulating Innovation is a topic with a vast amount of literature that is important to mention.

> The innovative nature of new challengers is normally met by a hostile environment reluctant to change.

Regulatory systems have enormous difficulty understanding and objectively analyzing new products and services. The pressure of the incumbents to maintain their benefits and place barriers to entry is sometimes high-handed.

Parma Bains, a researcher at the IMF, has been publishing reports and documents analyzing fintech regulation and taking on the complex subjects of Cryptocurrencies and Blockchain regulation. In a June 2023 document[194] co-authored with Caroline Wu, they state:

> Depending on the effect of fintech, authorities may adopt a passive approach of monitoring fintech, try and capture new business models in existing regulatory frameworks, develop bespoke regulation, or adopt test and learn policies through institutional arrangements like innovation hubs and sandboxes. The test and learn approach is relatively unique to

---

193 Global Forum on Remittances, Investment and Development Summit 2023 Africa; 14–16 June 2023 p.14 - https://bit.ly/45nF8YC
194 Parma Bains and Caroline Wu: Institutional Arrangements for Fintech Regulation: Supervisory Monitoring, IMF, 26 June 2023, eISBN: 9798400245664 - https://bit.ly/452DvQx

fintech in financial regulation and supervision and has advantages and disadvantages. While it can help authorities monitor and respond to the challenges of fintech in some scenarios, in others it could lead to risks to consumers and markets, particularly when designed poorly or with an unclear use case.

Regulating Fintechs, as Bains and Wu discuss, shows how complex the subject is and how expansive the controversies are worldwide. The situation is much more complicated in the US due to the role of State and Federal regulators and the diverse viewpoints of the different agencies willing to excerpt their own controls. The US Securities and Exchange Commission (SEC) sued Ripple Labs[195], Coinbase[196], and Binance[197], three of the largest cryptocurrency firms in the world. The legal battle started in 2020 when the SEC accused Ripple of breaching laws and using the alleged unregistered security XRP to raise funds. The SEC believes cryptocurrencies are speculative investments, similar to a stock, and their sale and management should be perceived and treated as such. In July 2023, a US Judge ruled that most of its XRP sales did not constitute an offer of unregistered securities[198]. The legal battle continues.

Korean author Junghoon Kim[199], based on the analysis of Robert Kagan and colleagues[200], explains that deterrence-oriented regulation may penalize a well-meaning citizen for a minor infraction that does not threaten the regulatory objective, resulting in an antagonistic and uncooperative attitude toward imposed measures.

On the other hand, compliance-oriented implementation improves rationality. In this approach, compliance and non-compliance do not have absolute

---

195 Connor Sephton: What is XRP? Your simple guide to Ripple's cryptocurrency, Legal battle with the SEC, currency.com, July 18, 2022 - https://bit.ly/3Pwybw7
196 SEC Charges Coinbase for Operating as an Unregistered Securities Exchange, Broker, and Clearing Agency; SEC Press Release, Washington D.C., June 6, 2023 - https://bit.ly/3OipjeM
197 Under court deal with SEC, Binance can continue U.S. operations amid fraud suit; PBS Economy, June 17, 2023 - https://to.pbs.org/3KmEcM9
198 Dimitar Dzhondzhorov: Ripple v SEC Lawsuit; CryptoPotato, Last Updated September 18, 2023 - https://bit.ly/46kpvS6
199 Junghoon Kim: Strategies of Financial Regulation: Divergent Approaches in Conduct of Business Regulation of Mis-Selling in the UK and South Korea; Springer Verlag, 2021, Singapore, ISBN: 9789811573316 - https://bit.ly/3K2ysFH
200 Robert A. Kagan, Neil Gunningham & Dorothy Thornton: Fear, Duty, and Regulatory Compliance: Lessons from Three Research Projects; in Nielsen and Parker "Explaining Regulatory Compliance", 2011, Edward Elgar, UK pp 37-58 - https://bit.ly/3Pvhj8P

boundaries because the objective of implementing a measure is to make the regulated party aware and understand the function of the regulation and its role within this mechanism. Enforcers can choose from various options, from education and persuasion to sanctions and the *policy of the stick*. *Regulation by Fear* (RBF[201]) conspires against innovation, prevents open competition, and harms market stability, among other consequences.

There is a big gap between restrictive regulation and consensus regulation. Public enforcement of a regulation is effective when there is a balance between compliance and deterrence-oriented approaches based on the motivation of the regulated community. I have always advocated dialogue and cooperation among industry and regulators to promote understanding and cooperation.

While sanctions can be useful in many cases, they lose meaning when they are the only goal. Policing for Profit creates a tainted pattern that is difficult to restrain.

When news headlines accompany sanctions and lawsuits, as they typically are in the US, most small companies have to close down. Only large companies can pay the fines or face the regulator in court. Negotiating to avoid facing a court is a game only the larger institutions can take on. The small ones and the most vulnerable usually disappear.

Regulatory consistency across jurisdictions is essential for NBFIs, especially those offering cross-border payment services. It is an industry requirement. The *regulatory consistency* of banking regulation is much more apparent since they have been building and solidifying their presence in the market for years. The banks, seen as the *pillars of the economy* and with their close relationships with government officials, strength as a group, and organizational and lobbying abilities, have acquired the accepted *regulatory consistency* needed. NBFIs and Fintechs still have a difficult road ahead.

---

201 Los antropólogos Susana Narotzky y Gavin Smith posiblemente usaron este término por primera vez para describir las políticas del dictador español Francisco Franco. Usado por muchos críticos, se podría traducir por "Regulación por Temor" o "Regulación por Miedo". Ciertos periodistas usan el término "regulación por las malas" en contraposición a "regulación por las buenas".

NBFIs have historically faced the dilemma of offering a service in one country where their financial activity is regulated and, simultaneously, in another country where this activity is either unregulated or provided *informally* —or as part of a parallel market. Making a commercial agreement with another NBFI offering payment services in a jurisdiction where there is a gray area in the regulation or a lack of regulatory clarity is always a risk that must be faced.

As a result of NBFIs' innovative mindset throughout history, they have always faced regulations that barely protect them. Also, due to their innovative or alternative nature in terms of markets, products, or services, they often do not fit into the existing framework.

Farhana Draine, former head of compliance at a UK fintech company, wrote: *New technology will always be the driver of evolving regulatory requirements – if something is truly innovative, it rarely fits into existing regulatory frameworks*[202].

I am familiar with the effort regulators in many countries make to understand the new technologies and the financial products and services they generate. I have given seminars in several countries and answered their questions, trying to contribute my viewpoint to a rational search for better financial services regulation. I have participated in advisory councils too. Additionally, I recognize that regulators and LEAs have significant internal differences in their points of view, which are not usually resolved behind closed doors. Without consensus among the actors and companies in the market, outdated laws that need to be rewritten or new ones that need to be created, fail to achieve their intended purpose: transparency.

I agree with Farhana Draine, who states: *To avoid historic scary headlines [...] regulation must be agile and continue to evolve alongside the technology industry, and we must embrace regulation as a friend, not fear it*[203].

NEW KIDS ON THE BLOCK

When Gene Nigro, an industry colleague, told me in August 2017 that he was joining Remitly, I was happy for him as I had seen his work at Xoom

---

[202] Farhana Draine: Is regulation the enemy of innovation? Leading Fintech entrepreneurs respond!; February 10, 2020, Silicon Roundabout - https://bit.ly/3g6G7YN
[203] Farhana Draine: Is regulation the enemy of innovation? Leading Fintech entrepreneurs respond!; February 10, 2020, Silicon Roundabout - https://bit.ly/3g6G7YN

next to Zory Muñoz, and the company seemed to have a promising future. Besides, at IMTC WORLD in Miami in 2015, I had its founder and CEO, Matt Oppenheimer, in a panel, and I was convinced that he had the *X Factor* that would lead him to success. Remitly relied on its digital app development and concentrated initially on the Philippine corridor. In his interview at that event[204], he showed a keen eye for developing a customer service approach that would get his app promoted among migrants through *word of mouth*.

I had the same feeling when I met Nabil Kabbani, another visionary from WU, at one of our conferences in 2010; we became friends, and I admired his technical vision and ability to synthesize complex ideas. Known for his entrepreneurial creativity, he has conceived numerous projects, including his new fintech, Neofie, a Banking-As-A-Service (BAAS) mobile wallet interconnector[205].

I want to provide an overview of the fintechs developed as digital solutions for P2P money transfers in the last two decades, beginning with the digital pioneer XOOM, founded in 2001. Fintechs have been categorized within specialized fields.

Regtechs was a term first promoted by the UK's regulator, the FCA, stating in 2015: *RegTech is a sub-set of FinTech that focuses on technologies that may facilitate the delivery of regulatory requirements more efficiently and effectively than existing capabilities.* Regtechs are now providing compliance solutions to banks and NBFIs, in a continuous race to develop better products and services.

Another sub-set is Insuretechs, referring to the technological innovations created and implemented to improve the efficiency of the insurance industry. There is no widespread term for fintechs that are developed to serve the cross-border payments market. We decided to call this sub-set Crosstechs when we rebranded IMTC and chose CrossTech.

A crosstech's *Front End* is digital: an app —or a website— at its origin. At the destination, payments are made *digitally* by depositing the remitted funds in an account —bank, card, or mobile wallet— or *cash-reliant*, using the thousands of cash counters set up by MTOs, banks, MMOs, retail chains, postal offices, etc.

---

204 IMTC WORLD 2015 Interviews - Matt Oppenheimer (Remitly) - https://bit.ly/3pMNKW4
205 Neofie and the future of BAAS - https://bit.ly/48kWVly

The sender can choose to have payments done to accounts or cash over the counter as desired. Beneficiaries can also withdraw cash from their accounts at ATMs or agents —a choice many take— mostly when the local digital ecosystem is not very developed and cash is needed for daily activities. These hybrid *digital-analog systems* are tailored to the needs of clients in each receiving country. Many crosstech firms have evolved their P2P money transfer services to target customers besides migrants, such as luxury migrants, millennials, or international remote workers.

Analysts estimate that the global digital remittance market is worth about US$1.5 billion and growing at a fast pace. The total remittance market was estimated at $15.27 billion in 2021 and is expected to reach US $36.54 billion by 2028, at a CAGR of approximately 14.6% between 2022 and 2028[206].

HOW FAST IS THE MARKET CHANGING?

THE US

In the US, the NMLS report for the second half of 2022[207] shows interesting facts about the growth of NBFIs (MSBs) and fintechs. The report shows that most of the 2,748 MSBs in this country provide check cashing services: 44.6% of all NBFIs, while MSBs offering money transmitting services accounted for 15.5%. But with most check cashers providing services in only one state, their share of all the state licenses is minimal. From 10,256 state licenses, Money Transmitters account for 77% or 7,915.

Among the 577 money transmitters in the US reported, 354 had no agents (61%), an increasing percentage since digital companies do not use them. About 300,000 agents were reported, one-third having multiple contracts with different MTOs. Only 23 MTOs had over 1,000 agents and held an average of 11 licenses. MTOs processed 66% of the total volume in the US, $1,821 billion in 2020; 15% were cross-border transactions. This gives us an idea of how massive the domestic money transfer market in the US is and explains why fintech companies have been mainly focused on this part of the market. The average transaction managed by MTOs, domestic and cross-border, was US $303.

---

206 Industry Trends & Forecast Report by Facts & Factors: 2022 - https://bit.ly/3ddH0h2
207 NMLS Resource Center; Annual and Quarterly Industry Reports - https://bit.ly/3S6ntOW

Based on an analysis of four states in terms of licenses issued in the last five years compared to all licenses standing, the top ones are Florida with 60%, Texas with 47%, New York with 45%, and California with 32%. These numbers reflect the decisive entry of fintechs into the industry since 2017 and the dynamism of NBFIs within the US market. California has a surprisingly low number of new licenses for a state with Silicon Valley at its core: from 120 active licenses since 1979 (up to 2022), only 32% have been granted in the last five years. Perhaps the reason for this is the same as in New York: the high cost and lengthy application process.

Florida, as Miami Mayor Francis Suarez has been proclaiming, has intentions to become the US's innovation hub[208], and Governor Ron Di Santis has also made an effort to attract fintechs to the state[209] despite his policies to discourage migration and make it harder for foreigners to reside in the state. Graph 25 compares these percentages across the four states.

GRAPH 6: Percentages of Licenses awarded in the last five years in 4 US States (2017-2022)

Money Transmitter Licenses

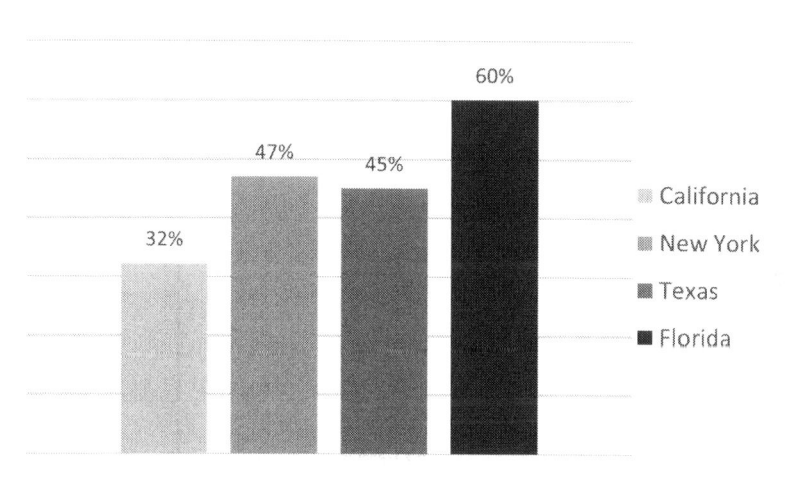

- California: 32%
- New York: 45%
- Texas: 47%
- Florida: 60%

% of active Licenses granted 2017-2022

---

208 Leeor Shimron: Miami Mayor Francis Suarez Talks Bitcoin & Building A Tech Innovation Hub; Forbes, February 7, 2021 - https://bit.ly/3dj9xlz
209 Governor Ron DeSantis Announces FinTech Priority Initiatives; Enterprise Florida, September 16, 2019 - https://bit.ly/3KC1zkV

Airbnb, CoinX, Adyen, Transfermate, Chime, Stripe, Coinbase, Wise, Apple, WorldRemit (ZEPZ), Earthport (acquired by VISA), VISA, Alipay, eBay, YapStone, Robinhood Crypto, Sofi Digital Assets, and Veem are among the fintechs licensed in the last five years. The list of new licensees includes companies in business for years, such as Viamericas, Maxitransfers, Golden Money, Atlantic Exchange, and IDT, all of which have become licensed in states where they did not hold licenses before 2017.

EUROPE

As for Europe, Table 3 shows the number of licenses granted in the EU between 2019 and 2021, which reflects a significant increase in the last few years due to the numerous fintechs seeking licenses. Despite the UK's past leadership as Europe's hub, it is important to note that, due to Brexit, companies with licenses in other EU countries had to apply in the UK and vice versa, to be allowed to operate in both markets, a fact reflected in these figures as well.

TABLE 3: Number of licenses (PIs & EMIs) issued per country (2019-2020-2021)[210]

País	PI 2019	EMI 2019	PI 2020	EMI 2020	PI 2021	EMI 2021	TOTAL
UK	48	52	33	38	107	45	323
Netherlands	52	11	4	3	11	3	84
Spain	50	6	5	3	5	2	71
Sweden	41	7	3	0	8	2	61
Lithuania	7	5	20	15	3	10	60
Germany	24	8	2	0	10	2	46
France	12	3	4	1	6	2	28
Ireland	5	1	10	5	2	0	23
Italy	5	5	1	1	4	2	18
Belgium	7	4	2	0	2	0	15

---

210 Advapay Blog: Industry Outlook 2020-2021: EEA and UK registered E-money and Payment Institutions - https://bit.ly/3dmzgte

The following Table shows the major crosstechs to give you a bird's eye view of how they compare before analyzing each one of them.

TABLE 4 - Comparing the main crosstechs in the market as of September 2022 (Crunchbase)

Name	Founded	Investment USD	IPO	Apptopia*
XOOM	2001	$104.3M	Feb. 15, 2013	49,056
FLYWIRE	2009	$323.2M	-	
ZEPZ	2010	$699.7M	-	127,900
WISE	2010	$1300M	Jul. 7, 2021	1,095,434
REMITLY	2011	$505M	Sep. 23, 2021	575,594
TRANSFERGO	2012	$126.5M	-	170,275
AZIMO	2012	$88.1M	-	20,821
BITSO	2014	$314.5M	-	
PAYSEND	2016	$157.6M	-	169,350
PAPAYA GLOBAL	2016	$444.5M	-	

Apptopia measures the number of times per month that an application is downloaded (Android and Apple). Information obtained in September 2022.

Most of these crosstechs focus is on P2P, P2B, and B2P. After acquiring AZIMO, Papaya Global, a payroll (B2P) fintech, now integrates B2P and P2P services. Flywire, formerly PeerTransfer, aimed to solve the challenge of individual payments —international students— to universities and is mainly a P2B company. Bitso is a B2B payment provider, and as a cryptocurrency exchange, it also provides foreign and crypto exchange services for MTOs. It is the only cryptocurrency analyzed here for its role in the US-Mexico corridor.

Other digital companies, including Revolut, an overall financial product and services provider, have been breaking into the cross-border market. It is more akin to a NeoBank and holds a European Banking license granted by Lithuania in 2018. With a $ 1.7 Billion Investment from 2014 to its latest round in 2021, it rivals Wise in products and services. In terms of money transfer, comparison site Monito states[211]: *Because of its excellent exchange rates and ease of use, we think Revolut Money Transfer makes the most sense for regular users of Revolut who want to send money abroad or for new users who'd also like to take advantage of Revolut's wider range of services in addition to money transfers. However, if you're simply looking for low-cost international money transfers, Revolut isn't always the cheapest option and will probably offer more than you need.* It is not a service that most migrants use, who prefer a simple way to send money and are not attracted by all the financial services Revolut provides.

> **Be mindful that much of the information I provide in this chapter might soon become outdated in such a dynamic industry.**

THE DIGITAL DILEMMA

Before we analyze the new crosstechs in the market, the digital-first MTOs, it is important to understand that every MTO that has agents, from WU down to the last MTO has faced —or is facing— the digital dilemma: How much resources should I spend going digital? As a consultant, many clients come to us with the same question. At every CROSSTECH Conference, we discuss the issue with companies successfully managing the transition.

Amar Das, who served as one of the executive directors of Western Union —achieving the company's expansion in Asia and the Middle East— believes that traditional companies have to make difficult choices in the leap towards the digital world:

> Money transfers today, globally, but especially in South Asia and India, are moving to digital. When you are a traditional organization with a network of agents, how can you transform into a digital company? Well, there are two ways to do it: either you leave your agent network and go 100% digital, or you focus on your agents adapting your technology to improve the agent offer. But most companies want to do both. And this is a challenging and complicated problem to solve. Let's look at the case of WU: if someone has the best digital money transfer system in the world, it is probably WU. They have invested hundreds of millions of dollars in

---

211 Byron Mühlberg: Revolut Money Transfer Review: Exchange Rates, Safety, Alternatives, and Monito's Verdict; Monito.com, May 26, 2023 - https://bit.ly/3PsZeKR

creating a digital platform so that people anywhere in the world have access to their website or their app. WU.com is still the number one digital company. We also know that WU has the largest agent network.

Then why do we hear about Remitly, WorldRemit, and Wise, but never hear much about WU digital? Compare the valuations of these companies against WU. Investors know that WU is constantly facing this strategic dilemma: if they focus too much on the digital product, they will cannibalize the agent business at some point. At some point the agents are going to rebel; the agent will start to question: *I am definitely not interested, WU is taking my clients so I will go with any company of the competition.* But any other choice for agents won't change much since MGI, RIA, and others are facing the same problem.

The challenge for a traditional company is to achieve a good hybrid strategy or an omnichannel strategy, trying to find the balance, and that is where the marketing tactics, strategies, the position of the brand, everything needs to fall into place. It is difficult, and sometimes you need outside intervention to *rock the boat*[212].

As consultants, we must force them to confront the issue and define a hybrid or omnichannel strategy tailored to each case. No strategy is perfect for everyone. Some companies have had to split their company into two: two divisions working independently to reach this balance.

In several public scenarios, I have raised this question: *What about developing a digital strategy so agents can become part of the digital world and draw their remittance clients in?* Maybe that digital agent solution will come from a fintech that will be creative enough to find a cost-effective option that can be marketed successfully to cash agents.

The remittance market continues to grow for cash agents and digital companies; the collapse of the cash component is much slower than predicted. The *new kids on the block*, the crosstech companies that I am going to describe in this chapter, did not have to face these types of decisions.

---

212 Virtual interview with Amar Das on July 8, 2022, conducted, recorded and transcribed by Isabel Cortés.

XOOM

Xoom's fifteen-plus year history is full of missed opportunities and second chances, according to the article in Saveonsend by analyst Yakov Kofner[213]. Xoom emerged from the so-called *PayPal Mafia* under the protection of Sequoia Capital, a well-known financial investment firm founded by Don Valentine in 1972 in Menlo Park, California. Valentine, the *grandfather of Silicon Valley venture capital*, born in 1932, passed away in October 2019. The *PayPal Mafia* is a group of former PayPal employees who founded companies such as Tesla, LinkedIn, Palantir Technologies, SpaceX, Affirm, Slide, Kiva, YouTube, Yelp, Yammer, and Xoom. Their nickname became even more popular when everyone, including Peter Thiel from Xoom, appeared in Fortune magazine on November 13, 2007, dressed as mobsters[214]. Elon Musk, a clan member, was the only one who missed the photo.

Xoom was founded in 2001 as the first digital money transfer company and the first to provide an efficient web-based money transfer portal. WU already had a website where customers could initiate money transfers, but its operation was deplorable.

Xoom's website was formally launched in 2003. It deployed an excellent marketing campaign using the brand of the paying companies, banks, and institutions, both on the web and in the app, leading migrants to believe they were "connecting" with their preferred payer abroad.

To create a great first experience for the sender, XOOM provided transaction processing information to the sender —and recipient— step-by-step, from start to finish, with simple SMS messages, a strategy that was later copied —and improved— by competitors. In the early days, fraud control was challenging because very little sender information was available, making it a lengthy and costly process for Xoom, which spent millions on fraud control. Later on, regtech firms were able to offer fraud control and KYC services at a reduced price compared to the new crosstechs. XOOM had to start its fraud control system from scratch.

By 2007, six years and five funding rounds later, Xoom had created a service aimed exclusively at the digital consumer with instant money transfers.

---

213 Yakov Kofner; XOOM Money Transfer: The Disruptor That Wasn't; Saveonsend, August 3, 2021 (The blog is updated frequently) - https://bit.ly/3zivDLU
214 Jeffrey M. O'brien: The PayPal Mafia; Fortune, November 13, 2007 - https://bit.ly/3YuO4ct

In those early days, Xoom was still a small company with less than US $20 million in revenue —WU was making US $3.5 billion per year— managing to accelerate growth by tripling revenue from $26 million in 2009 to $80 million in 2012. With this strong performance, Xoom had a great start to its Initial Public Offering (IPO), and on the first day in February 2013, Xoom shares rose almost 60%.

From then on, Xoom began to show weaknesses, and its growth and strength faltered, according to market analysts[215]. In 2015, the fintech hit the wall. Its competitors could provide better exchange rates. As a public company, Xoom preferred to keep its margins. While criticizing the competition for its irrational exchange rate behavior, Xoom held its position until it had to back down and lower its prices; it was too late. After an internal fraud that caused a larger loss, the company was acquired by PayPal in July 2015 at a very profitable price for Xoom's shareholders. In spite of the stock rising from US $17 to US $22 —over acquisition rumors, PayPal purchased it for US $32 per share[216].

Xoom's performance was then diluted among Paypal's reports; however, despite its high volume of transactions, the company lost much of its prominence in the digital remittance market compared to its digital competitors. After integrating all of XOOM clients into PayPal, and all of its transactions, the company announced the intention of selling XOOM in May 2023. The question in everyone's mind is: What is PayPal selling?[217]

ZEPZ (WORLDREMIT - SENDWAVE)

Upon buying Sendwave in 2020, WorldRemit kept these two brands in the market; in August 2021, the company changed its name to ZEPZ, after a US $292 million funding round and a valuation of US $5 billion[218]. This crosstech started in 2010 when three entrepreneurs, Ismail Ahmed, Catherine

---

215 Yakov Kofner; XOOM Money Transfer: The Disruptor That Wasn't; Saveonsend, August 3, 2021 (The blog is updated frequently) - https://bit.ly/3zivDLU
216 Connie Loizos: PayPal Agrees to Buy XOOM for $890 Million; TechCrunch, July 1, 2015 - https://tcrn.ch/3fNpYqW
217 Lucy Ingham, Callum Tyndall: Xoom at PayPal: A deep-dive into the brand inside the payments giant, and why it might sell; FXC Intelligence, May 25th, 2023 - https://bit.ly/3OwG9Xu
218 Paul Hindle: WorldRemit Group rebrands as Zepz, raises $292m Series E funding; Fintech Futures, August 25, 2021 - https://bit.ly/3LgHakA

Wines, and Richard Igoe, decided to develop a web-based system in the UK to encourage migrants to send money home using debit cards.

Ismail, originally from Somaliland, used his knowledge acquired working for international agencies to develop a system for paying money orders in Somalia. Catherine joined from First Remit, a company acquired by Travelex Money Transfer, and with Richard's support, the three started this venture. In 2011, I visited their small London office when they had only been open for a few months. During that time, one of the biggest challenges was obtaining information from the senders to verify that the transaction was feasible and legitimate. Senders were required to give very little information when using agents, and it was an enormous task to convince remitters to give their personal information over the phone to confirm the transaction.

In response to the UK business growth, they started operations in Canada and then Australia in 2013. As shown in Table 13, they received their first capital injection of US $40 million from Accel Partners in 2014, followed by several funding rounds. They opened subsidiaries in South Africa, Japan, Singapore, the Philippines, and New Zealand in 2017. Upon entry into the US, the development of their Latin American corridors followed, led by Erick Schneider, until it closed most of their regional centers.

In 2020, the company lost Catherine Wines, who sadly passed away; Catherine was a well-loved and respected person in the industry. The company had four CEOs and three marketing chiefs in 2021, and the CTO and CFO left in December of that year. ZEPZ was hoping to go public in the US in 2022 at a valuation estimated at US $6 billion following the August 2021 investment of $292 million. Those plans were scrapped[219].

---

219 WorldRemit Parent Zepz Reportedly Shelves IPO Plans to Focus on Profits; PYMNTS, July 13, 2022 - https://bit.ly/3DYRtXm

TABLE 5: ZEPZ Investment Rounds (2014-2021)[220]

Year	Series	Investment (Millions US)	Investors	Valuation (Millions US)
2014	Series A[221]	$40	Accel	
2015	Series B[222]	$100	TCV, Accel	
2017	Series C[223]	$40	TCV, Accel, Leapfrog	$538-670
2019	Series D[224]	$175	TCV, Accel, Leapfrog	$900
2021	Series E[225]	$292	Farallon Capital, TCV, Accel, Leapfrog	$5,000

The company bought SendWave, another digital remittance company specializing in Africa, in 2020 for approximately US $500 million, informing that it would keep the app and marketing as a separate brand[226]. SendWave was founded in 2011 by Drew Durbin and Lincoln Quirk, classmates at Brown University. SendWave has focused on African markets from the very beginning. Right before the sale, I conducted a study for their entry into Latin America, the next corridor they wanted to explore.

WISE (TRANSFERWISE)

Wise was founded by Kristo Käärmann and Taavet Hinrikus, London-based Estonians, searching to create a digital Hawala where money could be paid at the destination with locally generated funds, reducing customer costs. Founded as Transferwise in 2010, it is known for its TV commercials and management of social channels, as well as its sauna and ping pong and foosball tables at the office, features that immediately distinguished it as the market's coolest company. With investors such as Peter Thiel, Richard Branson,

---

220 ZEPZ: Crunchbase; accessed in September 2023 - https://bit.ly/3Pnf1e1
221 Ingrid Lunden: Money Transfer Startup WorldRemit Collects Its First Investment, $40M From Accel; TechCrunch, March 12, 2014 - https://bit.ly/3QCHZIT
222 Press Release: WorldRemit Raises $100M Funding Round to Drive Global Growth, February 18, 2015 - https://bwnews.pr/3RSwMl1
223 WorldRemit Raises $40m in Series C Funding; Finsmes, December 7, 2017 - https://bit.ly/3BGAqJH
224 Ingrid Lunden: WorldRemit raises $175M at $900M+ valuation to help users send money to contacts in emerging markets, TechCrunch, June 3, 2019 - https://tcrn.ch/3RTzGWD
225 WorldRemit Hits $5B Valuation, Rebrands As Zepz; Pymnts, August 23, 2021 - https://bit.ly/3RCyya7
226 WorldRemit to acquire Sendwave; Finextra, August 26, 2020 - https://bit.ly/3RS2HC8

Ben Horowitz, and others who believed in the company's ability to be innovative, it became the first unicorn in cross-border transfers.

While offering lower prices and better exchange rates than competitors have been essential to its success, focusing on providing excellent customer service and being the highest-rated mobile app has helped it grow its user base.

At times, the company has been scrutinized by regulators and criticized by competitors for seeking alternative expansion methods. Upon entering the US and to avoid obtaining licenses in all 50 states, a process that takes one and a half to two years, it partnered with PreCash, which already had the licenses in place. As a result of this *authorized delegate/rent-a-license set up* deal, the State of Texas fined the company $150,000[227]. Wise then began working under the umbrella of CFSB (Community Federal Savings Bank). Only one year after entering the US market, Wise had operations worth US $2 billion in 2015.

The company ranked #3 worldwide for monthly transaction volume in 2017, transferring US $1.5 billion. The same year, it raised the largest Series E funding round for a crosstech, with US $280 million[228]. After this, it obtained its own licenses in each US state. In Canada, the company's success was much greater; a year after launch, in the spring of 2016, it had already transferred $2 billion, 10% of Canada's outbound remittances.

TABLE 6: Wise investment Rounds (2013-2021)[229]

Year	Series	# of investors	Investment	Investment Leader
2013	Series A	9	US $6M	Valar Ventures
2014	Series B	7	US $25M	Valar Ventures
2015	Series C	8	US $58M	Andreessen Horowitz
2016	Series D	2	US $26M	Baillie Gifford
2017	Series E	9	US $280M	IVP, Merian Global

227 Kadhim Shubber: Transferwise meets US money transmitter laws, Financial Times, April 5, 2016 - https://on.ft.com/45rhn1L
228 Marco della Cava: Banks not keeping up with tech times, fintech CEO says; USA TODAY, November 1, 2016 - https://bit.ly/3xeJGSD
229 Wise: Crunchbase; accessed in September 2023 - https://bit.ly/3qt2VUr

Year	Series	# of investors	Investment	Investment Leader
2018	Debt Financing	3	£65M	JP Morgan, LHV Ventures, NatWest
2019	Secondary Market	8	US $292M	Lead Edge, Lone Pine, Vitruvian
2020	Secondary Market	7	US $319M	D1 Capital, Lone Pine
2021	Debt Financing	1	£160M	Silicon Valley Bank

Wise announced that it held 15% of the UK market in January 2018. It was valued at US $3.5 billion in May 2019 and prepared for its IPO, which took place in mid-2021 and went public with a value of more than US $10 billion[230]. As of 2022, Apptopia reports the App has been downloaded over 1 million times per month, a record in the industry, and is expected to surpass WU.com's download volume, the market's leading online remittance option.

Analysts anticipate that its significant growth will come not from its cross-border volumes but its virtual wallets and companion cards, becoming a *leading international neobank*[231].

REMITLY

This crosstech was founded in Seattle, Washington, in 2011 under the name BeamIt Mobile by Matthew Oppenheimer, Josh Hug, and Shivaas Gulati. Initially, the company was a search engine for remittance services. In August 2012, it changed its name to Remitly and started operating in the US-Philippines corridor, developing a mobile app that gained wide acceptance. They added services to countries in Latin America, Africa, and Asia, with the incorporation of Gene Nigro, as their international rep. Gene had developed the payment network for Xoom.

---

230 Yakov Kofner: TransferWise (aka Wise): Rebel, What is Your Cause?; Saveonsend, September 14, 2021 - https://bit.ly/3xcxxO4
231 Wise: Why The Undervalued FinTech Is More Than A Money Transfer App; September 12, 2022; Seeking Alpha, ThinkValue - https://bit.ly/3CAbAvo

TABLE 7: Remitly Investment Rounds (2014-2021)[232]

Year	Series	# of investors	Investment	Investment Leader
2014	Series A	6	$5.5M	QED Investors
2015	Series B	4	$12.5M	Threshold
2016	Series C	2	$23.5M	–
2016	Series C	6	$38.5M	Stripes
2017	Series D	4	$115M	PayU
2019	Series E	9	$135M	Generation Investment
2019	Debt Financing	3	$85M	–
2020	Series F	8	$85M	PayU
2021	Corporate Round	1	–	VISA

The shares at its IPO on September 23, 2021, opened at US $43 with a US $6.9 billion valuation. In 2022, Apptopia reported over 575,000 downloads per month.

In August 2022, Remitly announced the acquisition of Rewire, a crosstech that has designed a novel cross-border financial services platform. Founded by Guy Kashtan, Adi Ben Dayan, Saar Yahalom, and Or Benoz, Remitly acquired it for approximately $80 million with a mix of cash and stock. Founded in 2015 with offices in Amsterdam and Tel Aviv, Rewire's remittance platform builds deep customer relationships with debit cards, local payment accounts (IBANs), insurance products, and bill payment services and is geographically complementary to Remitly[233].

TRANSFERGO

This fintech was founded in 2012 by four young Lithuanian entrepreneurs, its CEO Daumantas Dvilinskas, along with Arnas Lukosevicius, Edvinas Sersniovas, and Justinas Lasevicius. They began with an office in Vilnius before moving the headquarters to fintech accelerator Level 39 in London a year later.

---

232 Remitly: Crunchbase; accessed in September 2023 -https://bit.ly/3d6RL4W
233 The Paypers: Remitly to buy Rewire for around USD 80 mln; August 17, 2022 - https://bit.ly/3U5vvZY

As with any new company, getting off the ground was difficult. Derisking initially affected it, but by securing continuous growth in Eastern Europe and the Baltic states, it consolidated and prospered[234]. VEF, a Swedish investment fund, has supported the company from the start[235]. By 2021, they served 3.5 million customers. In March 2022, Francesco Fulcoli, the company's Compliance Officer, announced[236] the suspension of money transfers to and from Russia, likely affecting the company's operations volume. However, the reported rise in payments to Ukraine might benefit the company.

TABLE 8: TRANSFERGO Investment Rounds (2016-2022)[237]

Year	Series	# of investors	Investment	Investment Leader
2016	Series A	1	$3.4M	VEF
2017	Series B	2	$2.9M	VEF
2018	Series B	5	$17.6M	Hard Yaka, VEF
2018	Equity Crowdfunding	–	€11.3M	–
2018	Series B	3	$10M	–
2019	Series B	6	£2.6M	VEF
2020	Debt Financing	1	£4M	Silicon Valley Bank
2020	Venture Round	5	$10M	Seventure, VEF
2021	Series C	7	$50M	Black River, Elbrus, Unlimint
2022	Secondary Market	2	£5M	Nordic Secondary Fund, Siena Secondary Fund

The company has reached many agreements with banks and companies such as Mastercard to send transactions to any card in more than 20 countries. In its 2022 secondary market round, TransferGo said it had 3.5 M

---

234 TransferGo: Necessity: The Mother of Invention - https://bit.ly/3xmUEpf
235 VEF portfolio company TransferGo announces USD 50 mln Series C financing round; IPO Hub, September 30, 2021 - https://bit.ly/3LeVFoJ
236 LinkedIn: Francesco Fulcoli's Post - https://bit.ly/3qHqEjO
237 TRANSFERGO: Crunchbase; accessed in September 2023 - https://bit.ly/48kg9rt

customers across 160 markets and achieved consistent 80% year-on-year growth since its launch[238].

AZIMO

In 2012, Michael Kent, Marta Krupinska, Ricky Knox, and Marek Wawro founded this crosstech company in London. Micheal had been one of the founders of Small World, a traditional money transfer company, and Tandem, a digital bank. Marta, a leading woman in fintech, originally from Poland and based in the UK, has been widely recognized for her innovative spirit, which she now uses to develop novel technology solutions in different sectors. She describes herself as a startup founder who completed the *big three*: failed one start-up, scaled one, and sold one, enjoying and learning along the way. With Ricky's background in Tandem and SmallWorld and Marek's great technological expertise, AZIMO became a digital competitor in constant competition with its digital rivals and received the first overall RemTech Award in 2017 in New York. In many panels I moderated, Michael was always one of the best panelists due to his harsh honesty and critical thinking coupled with his British irony.

In 2019, Richard Ambrose was appointed CEO, and Michael became Executive Chairman as the company announced its first profit for the second quarter of that year[239]. Three years later, the company was acquired by Papaya Global.

TABLE 9: AZIMO Investment Rounds (2013-2020)[240]

Year	Series	# of investors	Investment	Investment Leader
2013	Seed Round	6	$1M	–
2014	Series A	9	$10M	Greycroft
2015	Series B	7	$20M	Frog Capital
2016	Venture Round	2	$15M	Rakuten

---

238 TransferGo Welcomes New Investors as Rapid Expansion Continues; Fintech Finance News, February 16 2022 - https://bit.ly/3s8UmT3
239 Steve O'Hear: Azimo appoints new CEO as money transfer service reaches profitability, TechCrunch, August 28, 2019 - https://tcrn.ch/3xfWbNF
240 Crunchbase: AZIMO - https://bit.ly/3B754tV

Year	Series	# of investors	Investment	Investment Leader
2017	Non Equity Assistance	1	–	Future Fifty
2018	Series C	8	$20M	Rakuten
2020	Debt Financing	1	€20M	European Inv. Bank

PAPAYA GLOBAL

This B2P company was founded in 2016 by Israeli entrepreneurs Eynat Guez, Ruben Drong and Ofer Herman to develop a platform for cross-border labor management and payments, such as payroll, contractor and third-party payments, thus removing barriers to global sourcing. With the highest levels of security, privacy, and speed, the solution begins with hiring, continues through ongoing employee management, and ends with payment. The company has grown tremendously since its first investment in 2016, achieving US $250 million in 2021 in its Series D investments and a US $3.7 billion valuation[241].

TABLE 10: Papaya Global Investment Rounds (2016-2021)[242]

Year	Series	# of investors	Investment	Investment Leader
2016	Seed Round	–	$1.5M	
2018	Venture Round	2	$3M	New Era
2019	Series A	4	$45M	Insight
2020	Series B	9	$40M	Scale
2020	Secondary Market	1	$5M	Group 11
2021	Series D	10	$250M	Insight, Tiger
2021	Series C	11	$100M	Greenoaks

---

241 Ricky Ben-David: Israeli payroll management startup triples valuation after $250m investment Papaya Global, founded in 2016, is said to be eyeing an IPO following multiple funding rounds; The Israel Times, September 12, 2021 - https://bit.ly/3B0IiUE
242 Papaya Global: Crunchbase; accessed in September 2023 - https://bit.ly/44Z8w74

Its founders combined their expertise: Eynat in personnel management and the communications industry, while Ruben and Ofer brought their expertise in technology development and innovation. Eynat has been honored multiple times as a female role model, in addition to being Israel's CEO of the Year by the Geek Awards[243]. Together with Rapyd, Tipalti, Payoneer, and MoneyNet, these companies have been great examples of fintech entrepreneurship in Israel.

Papaya's cloud platform provides a white-label solution that supports companies such as Fiverr, where more than 3.4 million individuals and businesses can find services from freelancers worldwide. Upwork is the leading remote hiring platform. Its revenue is expected to grow to $665-$675 million in 2023, with 822,000 active clients.

Fiverr and Upwork have transformed the job market by providing income to thousands of people working from anywhere in the world without the need to migrate to provide for themselves and their families.

In 2022, Papaya announced the acquisition of AZIMO with the goal[244] of building *an innovative new payments and finance offering for clients in cash advance, credit-related products, and cryptocurrency*. Newspapers in Israel estimated the purchase to have been between US $150 to $200 million. However, Papaya's CEO, Eynat Guez, indicated in an interview with Daniel Webber from FXC Intelligence that this is incorrect. In the same interview, Eynat explained: *We were looking for someone with the expertise, with the ability to have strong compliance and who already has a global footprint and global money transfer licenses, which are key. [Remittances] is definitely not going to be our main business. We did not [buy Azimo] in order to set up a new line of business. We're probably going to retain the current business on a low scale.*

The merger confirms the trend of cross-border service integration, which will certainly increase in the coming years, as I will discuss further in the last chapter of this book.

---

243 Israeli high-tech voted: These are the big winners of the 9th annual GeekAwards: CEO of the year: Eynat Guez, Papaya Global, Geektime, February 18, 2021 - https://bit.ly/3RCDAUd
244 Money transfer app Azimo acquired by payroll and payments firm Papaya Global; FinTech Futures. April 4, 2022 - https://bit.ly/3d4sBUC

PAYSEND

PAYSEND was established in the UK in 2016 by Abdul Abdulkerimov and Ronnie Millar. As one of the fastest-growing companies in the market, it provides money storage, payment, and sending services to over 150 countries via a multi-currency wallet, reportedly reaching more than 6.5 million customers. Raised and educated in Russia, Abdul earned degrees in financial and technology fields, then went on to study in the UK and the US, before launching this company. Ronnie, a serial entrepreneur, having co-founded and run many companies, including Paywizard and MGt Plc, comes from an accountancy and investment background and was formerly Finance Director for Argent Group.

The first objective of PAYSEND is to make cross-border payments as easy as sending a text message. The company offers services to help users manage their credit and a link to a growing network of cross-border payments available in the market, such as those being developed by Mastercard, VISA, and UnionPay[245].

TABLE 11: Paysend investment Rounds (2016-2021)[246]

Year	Series	# of investors	Investment	Investment Leader
2016	Seed Round	1	–	
2018	Series A	1	$26.3M	MARCorp Financial
2019	Series B	3	$10.7M	Digital Space, GVA, Plug & Play
2021	Venture Round	1	–	Global PayTech
2021	Series B	4	$125M	One Peak, Intravia, Hermes, Plug & Play

Note that Paysend in 2019 raised funds through Seedrs, offering a wide variety of investment options receiving £4.6M from 926 investors and launched its digital currency Pays XDR, a stablecoin using the Stellar blockchain, backed by five currencies: GBP, EUR, USD, JPY and CNY[247].

---

245 Paysend CEO: Cross-Border Payments Have Failed Consumers and SMBs; PYMNTS, April 25, 2022 - https://bit.ly/3UHzsEb
246 Paysend: Crunchbase; accessed in September 2023 - https://bit.ly/3PkxCHA
247 PaySend Review: Becoming a Leader Money Transfer App - https://bit.ly/3s2GWoc

FLYWIRE

This P2B company was founded in 2009 as peerTransfer by Spaniard Iker Marcaide after studying in Boston and noticing the difficulty international students faced in paying US university fees. With this idea in mind, he developed this service and received financial support to begin, and then he raised $1.1 million in an initial funding round led by Spark Capital.

The company processed $1 billion in cross-border payments in the 2014-15 academic year and adopted the Flywire name, expanding into China, the world's largest market for young people studying abroad. Nearly 1,000 educational institutions used its platform.

TABLE 12: Flywire Investment Rounds (2010-2021)[248]

Year	Series	# of investors	Investment	Investment Leader
2010	Grant	1	–	–
2010	Seed Round	11	$1.1M	Spark Capital
2011	Series A	4	$7.5M	Spark Capital
2013	Series B	6	$6.4M	QED Investors
2014	Series B	5	$6.2M	–
2015	Series C	6	$22M	Bain
2018	Series D	3	$100M	Temasek
2020	Series E	4	$120M	Goldman Sachs
2021	Series F	8	$60M	Marshall Wace, Sunley House Capital, Whale Rock

In 2018, Flywire acquired OnPlan Health[249], a company providing payments for patients seeking treatment outside their home countries. Following its 2020 investment round, the company acquired Simplee[250], a fintech that provides payment services to hospitals and healthcare institutions. The

---

248 Flywire: Crunchbase; accessed in September 2023 - https://bit.ly/3t4ax4A
249 Julie Muhn: Flywire Acquires OnPlan Holdings; Finovate Blog, January 18, 2018 - https://bit.ly/3KES04R
250 Flywire Acquires Simplee to Transform Healthcare Payments Experience; Press Release, February 13, 2020 - https://bit.ly/3OAYEKi

health payment industry is valued at $4 to $5 billion with a yearly growth rate of 10-15%.

In 2021, Flywire made its IPO, and its shares were first listed on NASDAQ at US $34 each, above its IPO price of US $24. With a rise of approximately 4% on its first day of trading, the fintech was valued at approximately US $3.5 billion[251].

BITSO - B2B

The company was founded in 2014 in Mexico City by Pablo Gonzalez and Ben Peters, shortly joined by Daniel Vogel. Pablo, a Mexican student in Vancouver, Canada, became interested in cryptocurrencies, and being aware that the remittance corridor from the US to Mexico is the largest remittance corridor in the world, he thought bitcoin could be used effectively to offer better exchange rates.

Pablo came to the IMTC conferences to explore the cross-border payment market and came out convinced that his mission could be accomplished. Ben, a British native with vast experience in technology, had met Pablo in Vancouver, and both founded the company together. After studying at Stanford and Harvard and working for Quantcast in Silicon Valley from 2009 to 2013, Daniel had already experimented with using Bitcoin for sending remittances. He was also looking for ways to adopt blockchain technology in his country[252].

Despite Bitso's wide acceptance in the Mexican market, it was a challenging start due to the continued regulatory challenges and difficulties in obtaining bank accounts. It is ranked second among the eight unicorn companies in the Mexican market after Kavak, a fintech business that sells used cars[253]. On October 9, 2019, Gibraltar's regulator, the Gibraltar Financial Services Commission (GFSC), granted the company a DLT (Distributed Ledger Technology License) after a lengthy application process[254].

---

251 Eliza Haverstock, Margherita Beale: Flywire Hits $3.5 Billion Valuation After First Day Of Trading As Fintech IPO Frenzy Continues; Forbes, May 27, 2021 - https://bit.ly/3L6Oi2V
252 Miguel Ángel Martínez: ¿Quién es Daniel Vogel? El CEO de Bitso, primer unicornio de Criptomonedas mexicano; El Heraldo Binario, June 25,2021 - https://bit.ly/3U0ZSAC
253 The 8 Unicorns Founded in Mexico; Faylory; Updated: May 18, 2023 - https://bit.ly/45YQjHM
254 Mexican Crypto Exchange Bitso Awarded DLT Licence by Gibraltar Financial Services Commission - 729/2019; Bitso becomes first Latin-American company to receive DLT licence in Gibraltar; October 9, 2019 - https://bit.ly/3U3ybHu

It then obtained two major funding rounds in 2020 and 2021, expanding to Argentina in February 2020, Brazil in April 2021, and El Salvador in the same year, where it collaborated with Silvergate to facilitate dollar transactions for El Salvador's official Bitcoin (BTC) wallet, the Chivo wallet[255].

TABLE 13: BITSO Investment Rounds (2014-2021)[256]

Year	Series	# of investors	Investment	Investment Leader
2014	Seed Round	1	–	–
2015	Seed Round	3	–	–
2016	Non Equity Assistance	1	–	MassChallenge
2016	Series A	7	$2.5M	MONEX group
2020	Series B	7	$62M	Kaszek, QED Investors
2021	Series C	8	$250M	Coatue, Tiger

In 2021 Bitso acquired Quedex[257], a Gibraltar-licensed exchange, which developed innovative technological solutions to make a qualitative leap in the company's technology infrastructure.

Bitso announced its entry into Colombia as Nvio Pagos Colombia in 2022[258]. It is one of the companies approved by the country's Financial Superintendency under its new *sandbox* regulation. Banco de Bogotá and Bitso have announced their partnership to offer cryptocurrencies to their local users[259].

By providing financial intermediation for MTOs and using cryptocurrencies as a medium of exchange, Bitso reportedly handled 4% of remittances

---

255 Helen Partz: Bitso to assist the launch of El Salvador's official Bitcoin wallet Chivo; Cointelegraph, September 07, 2021 - https://bit.ly/3DeQdAx
256 BITSO: Crunchbase; accessed in September 2023 - https://bit.ly/3RZbwdd
257 Ian Allison: Bitso Buys Gibraltar-Based Crypto Derivatives Platform Quedex; Mexico City-based Bitso plans to incorporate Quedex's high-performance trading engine across the exchange; Coindesk, February 11, 2021 https://bit.ly/3d7Jmhy
258 BITSO: Colombia (Alianza BdB - Nvio Colombia); September 12, 2022 - https://bit.ly/3qyGAFk
259 Helen Partz: Top Latin American exchange Bitso officially expands to Colombia; Cointelegraph, February 10, 2022 - https://bit.ly/3xjwH22

from the US to Mexico in the first half of 2022, more than $1 billion in total, four times its 2021 volume, aiming to surpass 10% of the market by 2023[260].

MMOS - COMMUNICATION & PAYMENTS

Mobile Money (MM), or digital money, refers to a payment service that uses mobile phones to access financial services and conducts transfers within a relatively closed ecosystem. Value is transferred from one digital wallet associated with the phone number to another. Technically, the device handles only data and balances since funds are stored in a bank account. Funds are protected even if the user loses the device as long as it is password-secured. Some systems operate on cell phones with only the most basic functions; the operator, the MMO, maintains traceability of the ecosystem and provides a cash-in/cash-out network so users can deposit or withdraw cash. Regulators now require interoperability of different networks and wallets, thus expanding the digital ecosystem reach.

Most MMOs are mobile network operators offering mobile wallets that transfer funds, pay bills, and send or receive international money transfers. These NBFIs are not usually considered fintechs, even if they are. Several aggregators have entered the market to successfully provide the interconnection between MTOs, banks, fintechs, and MMOs.

> In Africa and Asia, the success of NBFIs providing mobile solutions has dramatically changed the picture of financial services.

People outside these markets are unaware of the dramatic changes, especially in countries where mobile wallets are not widely adopted. In North America and Europe, for example, the availability of different payment methods, mostly bank card-based, is the norm. Regulators in Latin America have favored banking institutions in the development of mobile wallets and have, therefore, slowed the evolution of these digital ecosystems.

Although MM originated in the Philippines (Smart and Globe were already active in 2002), M-Pesa stands out as the world's first mobile wallet

---

260 Andrés Engler: Bitso Processed $1B in Crypto Remittances Between Mexico and the US so far in 2022; Coindesk, June 16, 2022 - https://yhoo.it/3r6BUGT

deployment, thanks to its success. M-Pesa (M for mobile and pesa, money in Swahili) was launched on March 6, 2007, by UK-based Vodafone and Safaricom[261], Kenya's leading mobile network operator, after receiving a grant from the UK Department for International Development. This partnership was designed to support financial inclusion efforts, and Vodafone and Safaricom applied for the grant to create a microfinance service. It was intended to allow rural residents of Kenya to access loans and make payments without visiting bank branches, which are nonexistent in the countryside. Tests on the outskirts of Nairobi revealed that the payment model was being used for a very different purpose. On M-Pesa's 10th anniversary, then-CEO of Safaricom, Michael Joseph, wrote in a blog post: *What we found in practice was that people who received the loans were sending the money to other people hundreds of miles away. In hindsight, we had inadvertently identified one of Kenya's biggest financial challenges.*

Everyone was surprised at M-Pesa's rapid growth, from the operator to the banks to the regulator and people in government. It reached 10 million users in 2010 and 25 million in 2017. A strategy inherited from MTOs included the use of agents, small establishments located across the country that served as points for users to upload and download cash from their mobile wallets. M-Pesa reached more than 140,000 agents in 2017 and 80,000 Lipa na M-Pesa merchants that accept M-Pesa payments, creating a truly unique digital ecosystem[262]. The technological solution met the great need of a community ready to adapt to change.

M-Pesa has been deployed in Congo (Democratic Republic of Congo - DRC), Egypt, Ghana, Lesotho, Mozambique, and Tanzania, where, together with Kenya, the number of agents has exceeded 600,000. Safaricom announced at the end of 2017 the release of an M-Pesa app, which includes QR code-enabled payments and in-phone NFC capabilities, rather than typing in lengthy strings of characters on a USSD interface. QR code stickers are now deployed to M-Pesa's agents and Lipa na M-Pesa merchants[263].

---

261 M-Pesa: https://bit.ly/3QPwnji
262 Addisu Lashitew, Rob van Tulder & Yann Liasse: Mobile Phones for Financial Inclusion: What Explains the Diffusion of Mobile Money Innovations?; Research Policy 48(5):1201-1215 , January 2019 - https://bit.ly/3PQMagf
263 Greta Bull: Financial Inclusion in 2018: BigTech Hits Its Stride; CGAP Blog, 9 January 2018 - https://bit.ly/47uTwA8

As a result of this expansion, M-Pesa began receiving international remittances directly to mobile wallets, reaching US $1.5 billion in 2020, equivalent to 60% of formal remittances in Kenya and 20% in Tanzania.

Following the success of M-Pesa, other MMOs have been developed in many other countries. The GSMA, the umbrella organization for mobile phone companies, through their *Mobile Money Programme*, aimed at supporting and promoting the provision of MMO services, celebrated 10 years of its annual publication (SOTIR - *State of the Industry Report on Mobile Money*) in 2022. According to its annual report, there were 1.35 billion registered accounts worldwide, with more than 500 million active (in the last 90 days).

Regarding remittances, 126 corridors worldwide allowed mobile wallets to receive remittances in 2017, but only 53 allowed sending and receiving. By 2021, only 3% of global remittances were sent or received via mobile wallets[264]. This number will surely continue to rise with the success of mobile and digital wallets and the increased number of operators in the market.

When traditional companies, such as WU, buy a Brazilian fintech, like digital wallet fintech Te Enviei[265], the percentage of money transfers from or to digital wallets will rise exponentially. It is all about changing the mindset of senders and beneficiaries from transactional to relationship-based customers.

Sergio Pérez, Co-founder of MORE Money Transfers, comments on the importance of Africa for the industry:

> African immigrants are growing and will continue to grow in numbers, and the question is: *What are they coming here for?* Individuals do not realize that in Africa, you might have to walk up to 20 km to fetch water every day. There are thousands of people moving because of floods or drought. So, even sleeping on top of cardboard, in a square, or under a bridge, they have a better life than the one back home. We forget that. And that person, sleeping under a bridge, ends up becoming the patriarch of the family, being able to send 100 euros to the family every month, which he gets as a street vendor in Salamanca, in Madrid, in London, selling counterfeit Michael Kors or Louis Vuitton bags for 10 euros, provided by a Chinese

---

264 Sherillyn Raga: More action is required to lower the costs of remittances through mobile money - ODI, May 20, 2022 - https://bit.ly/3RdHkuP
265 Western Union Acquires Te Enviei to Speed Digital Wallet Launch in Brazil; PYMNTS, September 12, 2022 - https://bit.ly/3SLnxny

merchant... this is the business we are in, serving these individuals wherever they are.

The immigrant from Latin America or Asia leaves their country with more tools than Africans. It is part of the reality we face. So, if we are aware that this is our client, we have to be mindful of the service we provide, how we provide it, what processes we implement, etc. The flow of each transaction is directly related to that person's life story and why he is where he is.

As payment methods in Africa expand, costs will come down, and the easier it will be to provide the services we provide. New African migrants used to mobile wallets will probably arrive with a new attitude toward mobile solutions that can transform the industry too. That is Africa, the new frontier, that is why we have to look at Africa and what is happening in the continent, where most of our migrant clients will be coming in the next few decades[266].

PUBLIC COMPANIES

Until 2006, the only publicly traded companies in the industry were WU and MGI, when Euronet acquires RIA. Then, in 2013, Xoom went public before being acquired in 2015 by PayPal, making it the fourth public company involved in cross-border payments. Many other public companies provide cross-border payments, and a few fintechs have successfully gone public, too.

One of the most knowledgeable firms analyzing our industry with its frequent publications is FXC Intelligence, founded in 2010 by Daniel Webber, a British ex-pat, in Washington, DC. In addition to providing industry data to its growing list of clients, the organization selected the top 100 companies in cross-border payments in March 2022, including 30 Publicly Traded Companies, based on the publication's chart[267]. The publication lists seven categories: VC-backed (growth-stage), private equity-backed, independently owned, crypto and blockchain, banks, mobile and public companies. The variety and diversity of the industry in the graph published by FXC Intelligence clearly indicates the dynamic evolution we are experiencing.

---

[266] Virtual Interview with Sergio Pérez on April 12, 2022, conducted, recorded and transcribed by Lucía Salazar.
[267] Daniel Webber, Joe Baker, Lucy Ingham: The Top 100 Cross-Border Payment Companies; FXC Intelligence, March 24, 2022 - https://bit.ly/3xjO82g

The public companies in the chart are shown here:

adyen · AL ANSARI EXCHANGE · A · ARGENTEX · fiserv. · flywire · globalpayments

Corpay FLEETCOR · d·local · EBIX · intermex · Mastercard · MONEX

EQUALS Group · Euronet ria xe · FIS · OFX · Payoneer · PayPal xoom

StoneX · VISA · Western Union · WISE · WORLDLINE · Paysafe · Remitly

We find companies such as VISA, Mastercard, FIS, fiserv, Tencent, (WeChat owner), Monex, OFX, Fleetcor, dlocal, and Paysafe, to name a few that I did not include in Table 22 below.

The Table compares the performance of a few of these public company stocks. Compared to new fintech companies, investors value traditional companies less.

TABLE 14: Selected Public Company Financial Information (companies involved in cross-border payments) - *as of August 2023*[268]

Name	Market Cap (USD billion)	Change (last year)	Stock Price (lowest-highest)	Stock Price (August 15, 2023)	Revenue 2022 (US B)
PayPal PYPL	$68.66	-15.44%	$30.63 - $308.53	$61.50	$27.51
WISE	$9.29	+33.65%	$3.61 - $15.71	$9.08	$0.73
WU	$4.44	-16.34%	$10.34 - $28.35	$11.90	$4.47
Remitly RELY	$4.23	+116.64%	$6.88 - $48.45	$23.80	$0.65
Euronet EEFT	$4.20	-10.17%	$84.79 - $149.92	$84.70	$3.35
Flywire FLYW	$3.39	+27.19%	$15.24 - $53.96	$30.60	$0.28
PAYO**	$2.09	+9.29%	$3.45 - $14.40	$5.82	$0.74

[268] information source: https://companiesmarketcap.com/

Name	Market Cap (USD billion)	Change (last year)	Stock Price (lowest-highest)	Stock Price (August 15, 2023)	Revenue 2022 (US B)
IMXI*	$0.65	-27.7%	$7.16 - $27.03	$17.90	$0.61
IDT	$0.74	+3.72%	$0.61 - $66.40	$24.36	$1.26
MGI[269]	$1.07	+2.16%	$1.18 - $289.60	$11.00	$1.31

*IMXI: International Money Express (Intermex) - **PAYO: Payoneer - Information from companiesmarketcap.com

I want to comment on International Money Express (IMXI), IDT Corporation (IDT) and Payoneer (PAYO):

International Money Express (IMXI) was formed from the merger of FinTech Acquisition Corporation (FNTE) and Intermex, a pioneer in the remittance market to Mexico and Guatemala, founded in 1994 by Colombian entrepreneurs John and César Rincón in Miami. Lindsay, Goldberg, & Bessemer, a New York firm, invested in the company in 2006. Its rapid growth continued with the hiring of CEO Bob Lisy and executives Eduardo Azcárate and Robert Dinkins. Eduardo would later move on to Elektra, one of Mexico's leading remittance payment companies, and Robert would join MoneyGram, responsible for the Caribbean region. Stella Point Capital acquired the company in May 2016 and merged it with International Money Express (IMXI) in July 2018, creating International Money Express (IMXI)[270]. On April 05, 2023, the company announced the acquisition of LAN Holdings, Corp., the owner of La Nacional Envio de Dolores, one of the traditional Dominican MTOs in the market. Through the purchase of LAN Holdings[271], it also acquired I-Transfer Global Payments, a payment institution with presence in Spain and Italy. The expansion of IMXI in Europe will be an interesting challenge for this US company.

---

[269] MGI announced on June 1, 2023 the all-cash acquisition of the company by Madison Dearborn Partners (MDP), a Chicago private equity investment firm, for $11.00 per share. MGI ceased trading and has been delisted from the Nasdaq stock market; MGI Press Release - https://prn.to/3KGwKvj
[270] SEC: FinTech Acquisition Corp. II Stockholders Approve Definitive Merger Agreement with Intermex Holdings II, Inc.; July 23, 2018 - https://bit.ly/3Dlmx4v
[271] Intermex Press Release; MIAMI, April 5, 2023; Globe Newswire - https://bit.ly/461NqGe

IDT Corporation was founded in 1990 as International Discount Telecommunications (IDT), by Howard S. Jonas, a businessman and telecom entrepreneur from New York who has been involved with many companies, as a founder, as well as participating in different executive roles. Some of these companies are Genie Energy —spun off from IDT in 2011—, Starz Media, Straight Path Communications —sold to Verizon in 2017—, Net2Phone, a subsidiary of IDT and Rafael Holdings[272]. Mr. Jonas is also a published author. One of IDT's flagship products in the industry is IDT's BOSS Revolution, a well-known international calling service used by many migrants. Its subsidiary, IDT Payment Services, began offering remittance services in 2014 after acquiring its state licenses in the US. The new brand for IDT's money transfer services, BOSS Money, was unveiled in 2021. In March 2022, IDT acquired Leaf Global Fintech Corporation[273]. Leaf is an award-winning provider of digital wallet services in emerging markets with presence in Rwanda, Uganda, and Kenya. Leaf leverages the Stellar network for storing and managing transaction data using stablecoins. IDT's subsidiary, IDT Financial Services Ltd is a regulated bank, licensed by the Financial Services Commission in Gibraltar, which provides settlement and foreign currency exchange services for mobile network operators using the International Remittance Clearinghouse (RCH) brand[274].

Payoneer (PAYO) is another fintech that emerged from Israel's technological innovation hub. It was founded by Israeli businessman Yuval Tal in 2005. From its beginning, it has specialized in international B2B payments. As the company grew, it received over $245 million in funding from firms including Viola Group, Greylock Partners, TCV, Susquehanna, Vintage, Wellington, and Chinese company Ping An Insurance. With over 1,500 employees worldwide and over 900 in Israel, it serves clients, including Amazon, Airbnb, Google, etc. Payoneer held its IPO in June 2021, merging with FTAC Olympus Acquisition (a company known in the stock world as a SPAC or Special Purpose Acquisition Company) in a transaction worth about US $300 million.

---

[272] IDT Corporation: Form 10-K (2013) - https://bit.ly/46PNR7f
[273] Press Release: IDT Corporation Acquires Leaf Global Fintech, March 14, 2022 - https://bit.ly/3FnRPrm
[274] Press Release: IDT Launches Remittance Clearinghouse for International Mobile Money Transfer - https://bit.ly/3rZpbtK

There are two rival public companies Mastercard (MC) and VISA, which are not only competing in the provision of cards and card-related services, but have been very active in the cross-border payment industry in the last few years.

MC acquired an ethnic MTO, Trans-Fast, in 2019, founded in 1988 by Brazilian entrepreneur Francisco Manoel Rodrigues De Matos in the US In 2007 this MTO was part of the consolidation with New York Bay Remittance, under the mentorship of Samish Kumar, receiving financial backing from Greenhill Capital Partners for US $37 million[275] and additional investments from Apis Partners in 2016 and 2017599, then launching Transpay[276]. Upon acquisition, MTO's remaining agencies were closed to allow MC to focus solely on digital transactions.

In 2015, MasterCard Send was launched to allow users to send money between debit cards and bank accounts, domestically and internationally. It has steadily grown its partnerships with banks and MTOs. A deal between MC and WU, first announced in 2017[277], and still under development, involves payment of funds to any US debit card, then expanding to other countries, initially in Europe[278].

Upon the sale of the MTO in the US, Francisco De Matos continued to run Trans-Fast Financial Services S.A. in Madrid, Spain, while his partner Jenny Ortiz Ruiz, moved on to operate as an independent entity.

In 2020 VISA acquired Earthport for US $257 million to gain access to the cross-border bill payment service the fintech had developed[279]. Using a network of local bank accounts, they've created a virtual international ACH network powered by the speed of domestic ACH payments. Then, in 2021, it announced the acquisition of CurrencyCloud for US $925 million, a currency management firm with more than 500 bank and non-bank clients and

---

[275] SEC Form 10K: Annual report for fiscal year 2009 - https://bit.ly/3S8Wan2
[276] The Nielsen Report: Transpay Mass Payment Platform; May 2015, Issue 1064 - https://bit.ly/3r2xOz
[277] Press Release: Mastercard and Western Union Team Up on Transfers to US Debit Cards; October 23, 2017 - https://mstr.cd/3DOouGT
[278] Press Release: Western Union and Mastercard Expand Global Partnership; November 12, 2021 - https://bit.ly/3DJTKqJ
[279] Amber Donovan-Stevens: VISA acquires Earthport for US$257mn; Fintech Magazine, May 16, 2020 - https://bit.ly/3SrhbZW

operations in 180 countries[280]. In 2022 it acquires Tink, a Swedish fintech, for US $2.15 billion, after failing to purchase Plaid[281]. Through a single API, Tink enables customers to move money, access aggregated financial data and use smart financial services, such as risk information and account verification.

Tink is affiliated with more than 3,400 banks and financial institutions. With its strong brand presence in most local markets all over the world, VISA is preparing to be a highly recognized cross-border payment processor. VISA Direct has stepped in to provide merchant partners with a global payment solution that will open up new opportunities for crosstechs and fintechs conducting domestic transactions. Currently, the service is available in over 200 countries and territories, with immediate or same-day crediting on 75 of them and supporting more than 160 currencies.

In the Crosstech World 2022 event in Miami I moderated a panel where VISA Direct's Head, Richard Meszaros, presented the cross-border payments industry with its new service[282]. The service allows remittances to be sent to VISA cards around the world and businesses to make payouts to VISA cards in minutes. Many fintechs are partnering with VISA to enable VISA Direct payments to their customers[283]. In the business front, VISA has unveiled Visa B2B Connect[284], a multilateral network that aims to compete with SWIFT for interbank cross-border B2B payments.

The Chinese rival UnionPay has continued to grow thanks to the size of the local economy and not only at the domestic level but also at the international level due to Chinese tourists and shoppers expanding into markets throughout Asia, Europe, and North America. The company has launched Moneyexpress[285], a cross-border remittance service available in more than 57 countries through local agreements with banks such as Canada's CIBC, South Korea's Woori Bank, BOC Hong Kong, Singapore's HSBC, Russia's

---

[280] Press Release: VISA Completes Acquisition of Currencycloud; December 20, 2021 - https://vi.sa/3xLm8Vy
[281] CB insights: After Its Scrapped Plaid Deal, VISA Acquired This Open Banking Platform For $2.15B. June 28, 2021 - https://bit.ly/3LCf6Z3
[282] Crosstech World 2022: The Fireside Chat, November 16, 2022, FXC Intelligence - https://bit.ly/45hKbcI
[283] Visa Direct is a global real-time[1] money movement network for individuals - https://bit.ly/46AOf8M
[284] Visa B2B Connect's multilateral network delivers B2B cross-border payments - https://vi.sa/3BAzbLB
[285] UnionPay International: Cross-border Remittance - https://bit.ly/3f5cuqe

Russian Standard Bank, and an extensive network of MTOs such as MGI, Wise, Paysend and Omnipay.

GOING PUBLIC: THE COLLAPSE OF UAE EXCHANGE

The UAE EXCHANGE group collapsed rapidly after 40 years of growth and consolidation due to circumstances unrelated to its foreign exchange and remittance operations. Internal financial irregularities were alleged to have caused the sudden collapse in 2020.

UAE EXCHANGE was founded in 1980, the same year that Abu Dhabi's first money exchange and remittance office opened. The company was acquired by Dr. Bavaguthu Raghuram Shetty (Dr. Shetty), although its founder, Daniel Borghese, alleges fraud led to the loss of his rights over the company he founded. Dr. Shetty was born in Udupi, a coastal city in western India. After graduating as a pharmacist and being involved in local politics, he moved to Abu Dhabi.

Through Dr. Shetty's leadership and the efforts of a growing team of executives, the company expanded across the region, opening branches in Oman, Kuwait, India, and Sri Lanka. Between 2005 and 2009, it expanded to Hong Kong, Uganda, Qatar, Jordan, Canada, New Zealand, and China and acquired MoneyDart Global Services in the US. The company began online transfers with its Money2anywhere.com website and received its UK license to operate via their Xpress Money brand. It announced the opening of its 100th office in one of Dubai's new metro stations in 2012.

The purchase of Travelex[286] from its founder, Lloyd Dorfman, was announced in 2014. With Peter Jackson as its CEO, the firm remained a separate entity. The firm Centurion Investments, owned by Saeed Bin Butti Al Qebaisi, and another UAE Exchange shareholder, Khalifa Bin Butti Al Muhairi, both related to the Abu Dhabi royal family, participated in acquiring Travelex[287].

---

286 Smith Square Partners advises Travelex Holdings Limited: agreement to acquire Travelex; May 23, 2014 - https://bit.ly/3bGIaB1
287 Investegate: Irish Stock Exchange Announcement; Acquisition of Travelex Completed, January 29, 2015 - https://bit.ly/3dbrd20

In 2015, at the GFRID in Milan that year[288], I met Dr. Shetty, a tall man who used to always walk surrounded by assistants and guards. He complimented me on my contributions to the industry, and from the wink given to me by Xpress Money's CEO Sudhesh Giriyan, I imagined that he had told Dr. Shetty who I was. At the time, Dr. Shetty was an award-winning –and millionaire– businessman revered by all.

An article from 2017[289] reported that The UAE Exchange Group ranked second in the world with US $27 billion in money transfer volume, behind WU and ahead of MGI. The group, which generated US $114.5 billion in revenue in 2018, operating in 32 countries with 700 branches and a vast worldwide network, was preparing to become a public company as Finablr[290].

Finablr's 2019 IPO started poorly, losing value within days of going public. Travelex suffered a cyber-attack in December of that year, which crippled company operations. The cyber-attack occurred on December 31, 2019, and hackers perpetrated the attack using a virus called Sodinokibi, demanding a payment of $ 3 million to return files and system functionality. Some cyber-security companies have used this distressing incident to warn other companies in our industry to step up IT security measures.

Months later, airports began closing down due to Covid, and tourism collapsed, which, coupled with other internal accounting and administrative problems, led to Finablr's downfall[291].

In December 2020, a consortium of Israeli and Emirati firms acquired Finablr for US $1, effectively acquiring its debts. The company was renamed Wizz Financial. Then, Wizz Financial acquired BFC, a holding company that included Bahrain Financing Company, Bahrain Exchange Company, and Bahrain Forex & Financial Services in India. As one of the strongest industry groups in the Middle East, BFC had branches in Bahrain, Kuwait, and India. Wizz kept Xpress Money and Unimoni, UAE EXCHANGE brands.

---

288 See Appendix A for details on the Global Forums on Remittances, Investment and Development (GFRID)
289 Mauro F. Romaldini: How Is the International Money Transfer Market Evolving? Toptal, 2017 - https://bit.ly/3zALuFL
290 Simeon Kerr: Travelex parent plans $200m London initial public offering; Finablr looks to tap strong investor demand for financial technology flotations; Financial Times, Dubai, 9 April 2019 - https://on.ft.com/3C67Z8D
291 Oscar Williams-Grut: Thousands of jobs at risk as Travelex-owner on brink of collapse; Yahoo Finance UK, March 17, 2020 - https://yhoo.it/3zHAXsh

Taking control of UAE EXCHANGE in September 2021, the UAE Central Bank approved the acquisition[292]. In 2022, the UK authorities approved the purchase of the company's local operations.

With more than 5,000 employees, Wizz Financial, based in Zug, Switzerland, is rebuilding its team and consolidating its presence in the industry.

Travelex remained a separate entity, and in April 2022, Richard Wazacz was appointed as its new CEO[293]. In June 2022, it announced the creation of more than 1,200 new jobs worldwide, in the UK, Australia, New Zealand, Brazil, 60 jobs across Europe, and 180 new jobs across the Middle East[294].

Dr. Shetty's legal issues are part of a complicated process with no clear answers regarding what happened inside the companies he managed, where the money went, and whether he will face charges outside of his home country, India.

---

292 UAE central bank approves WizzFinancial's acquisition of UAE Exchange; Reuters, September 26, 2001 - https://reut.rs/3RQ2z6F
293 Emily Hawkins: Travelex recruits BrickVest boss Richard Wazacz as new CEO; City AM, april 19, 2022 - https://bit.ly/45t8WDn
294 Travelex creates 1,200 jobs globally in expansion spree; Gulf News Report, June 28, 2022 - https://bit.ly/3OQYTSR

CHAPTER 4

CRYPTOCURRENCY AND MONEY TRANSFERS

At IMTC Miami in November 2012, I organized a debate between Roger Ver, the *Bitcoin Jesus*, and University of Miami professor Arun Sharma, who openly questioned the future of cryptocurrencies based on political economy arguments. In preparation for moderating this debate, I downloaded my first wallet and acquired my first bitcoins, which I still own, to gain a deeper understanding of blockchain theory and Bitcoin. Professor Sharma had invited me to his favorite Indian restaurant in South Miami, where I have returned many times since our meeting. I would lie if I said I fully understood his macroeconomic approaches, but, as a good teacher, he explained them with confidence and authority.

Having discovered Bitcoin a year earlier, Roger became very vocal and shouted from the roof-tops how important it was for society. He repeated his *mantra* in Miami: *Bitcoin is one of the most important inventions in the history of humankind. For the first time, anyone can send or receive any amount of money with anyone else, anywhere on the planet, conveniently and without restriction. It's the dawn of a better, more free world.* This motto is at the top of his website.

At the time of the debate, apart from his big cryptocurrency premonitions and anarchist rants, Roger's only argument was to show real-time Bitcoin transactions on the big screen. On the other hand, very circumspectly, Dr. Sharma explained his theories with a PowerPoint where he presented his graphs until a US$500,000 transaction appeared on the screen, and Roger mockingly rebuked the professor to the laughter of the audience. If someone was willing to buy half a million dollars worth of bitcoin, for Roger, there was nothing more to discuss. As best I could do at that moment, I decided to end the session, and we went into a break.

People who witnessed this debate remember it as the first time they heard about Bitcoin. Roger Ver, a committed libertarian and anarchist, made a fortune buying cryptocurrencies and investing in many fintechs in their initial rounds, such as Bitpay, Kraken, and Ripple. He has also funded many foundations, NGOs, and campaigns promoting cryptocurrency adoption. He renounced his US citizenship in 2014 to become a citizen of St. Kitts and Nevis; he was denied a visa to enter the US in 2015 but got it a year later. Lately, he has been bullish about Ethereum, the decentralized blockchain platform known for its native cryptocurrency, ether (ETH), and its smart contract capabilities.

> **My analysis of cryptocurrencies is at the end of this book since it is a fact that they are impacting the financial services sector today.**

However, it is not necessarily because it has provided remarkably successful solutions for delivering domestic and international financial services. Its merits can partly be attributed to challenging the status quo and creating a fiercely competitive environment to improve the current system. It has made the vision behind cryptocurrencies, and to some extent, its idealism, change paradigms and foster competition at all levels. Additionally, it has inspired thousands of people to create solutions and many investors to provide the funds to support them. Money has been lost in terms of returns on investment, but many people have also become millionaires.

Implementing the advantages of cryptocurrencies is underway, but in the third decade of this millennium, crypto's integration into the cross-border payments industry has been slower than expected despite the advantages of the solutions developed by many fintech companies.

It was always enlightening for me. and attendees to have in my lectures and courses the presence of Luis Buenaventura explaining the simple scheme used to develop ventures in corridors from Asian countries to the Philippines using Bitcoin. Luis, a creative entrepreneur with first-hand experience in the sector, wrote two books: the first one, *Reinventing Remittances with Bitcoin: Stories from the Startups on the Front Lines*, which compiles strategies on remittance development using cryptocurrencies, and the second, *The Little Bitcoin Book: Why Bitcoin Matters for Your Freedom, Finances, and Future* in 2019, with other authors[295].

Bloom Solutions, the fintech founded by Israel Keys, Ramon Tayag, and Justin David in 2014, where Luis contributed for many years, exemplifies creativity and perseverance. Many fintechs are developing bridges between traditional rails and crypto —crypto2fiat and fiat2crypto networks— in addition to those developing crypto ATMs.

Cryptocurrencies still have their enthusiastic supporters and their fierce critics. Jeff Mazer, an attorney and financial consultant, summarized it in 2017[296] as follows: *For every person declaring that cryptocurrencies are in a bubble, another is insisting that they are the next wave of the democratization of finance. At their simplest, they are merely the newest fintech fad, yet at the most complex level, they're a revolutionary technology challenging the political, economic, and social underpinnings of society.*

Supporters claim, and they are right, that the current technological revolution resulting from the confrontation of Crypto and Blockchain with the status quo has driven remarkable advances in data management, payment speed, transparency, and financial democracy. Stablecoins and CBDCs are clear examples of the impact of Crypto and Blockchain on the payments landscape.

Blockchain, as a decentralized data processing technology, and its potential as a technology for the financial services industry is a tool that, besides being at the heart of cryptocurrencies, is a technology that provides a low cost and low-maintenance alternative to existing processes. It has the potential to disrupt finance, but I am more inclined to think it can help —and is helping— fix some of our industry's challenges. Some examples are using blockchain in compliance and audits, configuring automation around risk

---

295 Luis Buenaventura: Amazon Marketplace - https://amzn.to/3rP3WH3
296 Elizabeth Howell Hanano: Demystifying Cryptocurrencies, Blockchain, and ICOs; Medium, Dec 18, 2017 - https://bit.ly/46CnKA5

policies, and streamlining payment and remittance processes while significantly speeding settlement times and costs.

Experts have predicted that the blockchain market is set to reach $1.4tn by 2030 and will enable banks to save $27 billion on cross-border settlement transactions by the end of the decade, reducing costs by 11%[297].

BASIC CRYPTO ADVANTAGES

Understanding the advantages of using cryptocurrencies is relatively straightforward. I will simplify my explanation while acknowledging that crypto fintechs are experiencing growing pains. The *crypto winter* of 2022-2023 is part of the evolution of this sector and is *akin to the growing pains experienced in the traditional/centralized financial services industry during the Crash of 1929 that preceded the Great Depression and the financial crisis of 2007–2008 that resulted in the failure of a handful of major banks, mortgage lenders and insurance companies*[298].

Here are some advantages in a nutshell:

1. They are digital currencies that can be bought and sold instantly.
2. There is no government or regulatory intervention in determining the exchange rate.
3. They are based on a decentralized, widely distributed technology that is less susceptible to hacking or tampering. Each transaction is recorded and immutable.
4. There are no intermediaries, such as banking institutions, resulting in greater financial democracy and less friction and interference.
5. The industry does not need working capital to make quick payments, eliminating credit, advances, or complex trade-offs.

There is still a long way to go concerning regulations and what products and services crypto initiatives can offer the public. Recent developments exist in major regional financial centers such as the UK, Singapore, the United Arab Emirates, and Bahrain. These and other countries are revising their

---

[297] The benefits of blockchain in financial services; Moody's Analytics, December 13, 2022 - https://bit.ly/3PZGPqo
[298] Hunt S. Ricker and Robert N. Holup: Nascent cryptocurrency industry continues to experience growing pains; ROI NJ Op-Ed, November 18, 2022 - https://bit.ly/48FHCnK

regulations to give more transparency and security to crypto companies and boost innovation by attracting investment.

US regulatory transparency is key in defining the pace of cryptocurrency adoption globally. In 2023, the US demonstrated ambiguity at best towards crypto adoption with restrictive regulation towards crypto firms and their financial partners, as Silvergate & Signature banks found out. The debate over regulations will continue in the US for quite some time. States rely on existing regulations —although some have been more creative— while the federal government seeks to centralize licensing and control. Rather than a freely circulating digital currency, some governments see a cryptocurrency as a financial asset, similar to publicly traded company shares. Financial assets, or legal assets that provide future profits for the investor once invested, are governed by federal authorities in the US. It will take time for the states and the federal government to settle these debates, as well as what the interests of regulated companies and lobbyists are.

A crypto asset advisor, Nic Basson, commented: *The problem is regulatory certainty. This element of people trying to retrofit crypto into existing structures and product ranges is difficult. Existing systems and services just don't fit*[299].

The pace of integrating the advantages of using cryptocurrencies by the cross-border payment industry will depend on regulators and the use of existing —and evolving— crypto payment rails.

The financial sector is already realizing some of the benefits of cryptocurrencies, shaping its use in many different ways to suit the infrastructure in place, the need for control of governments, the changing political landscape, the pressure of NGOs, think tanks and multilateral agencies, and the role that banks want to play in the new ecosystem being built. If banks realize the potential of partnering with crypto-rail fintechs and the cross-border payment industry, we might see a new ecosystem fast developing.

The new ecosystem is also being shaped by the development of domestic fast payment systems, the rise of stablecoins, CBDCs, and the monetary unions in the works.

---

299 Maya Sibul: Cryptocurrency demand means growing pains for fund operators; Fund Operator, December 15, 2022 - https://bit.ly/3rB5tEo

Industry executives have many doubts about the role that cryptocurrencies can play. Salvador Velázquez, who was part of DOLEX and is currently developing a digital bank in Mexico, believes cryptocurrencies still present many challenges and governments won't accept decentralization. He also highlights that banking institutions are doing everything they can to prevent their integration into the market: *Central banks continue to distrust cryptocurrencies, at least the ones outside their area of control. Furthermore, remittances using cryptocurrencies are not as cost-effective as they can be; there are still too many bumps on the road*[300].

However, hard-core cryptocurrency enthusiasts defend decentralization; they consider that the freedom of market forces and the control algorithms that have been developed will always be better than the centralization that exists or the one central banks want to have with the use of central bank money. With this in mind, the discussion becomes more philosophical and policy-oriented than economic or political. Renowned thinkers have debated questions that go to the roots of money and its control. I recommend two works; the first is *Philosophy, Politics and Economics of Cryptocurrency: Money without state*[301] by Andrew M. Bailey, Bradley Rettler, and Craig Warmke. The second is Simon Butler's *The Philosophy of Bitcoin and the Question of Money*[302]. Butler considers that the control of the money supply and the power it grants is ultimately the root of the dispute, outside of the practical value of cryptocurrencies as a payment solution.

CRYPTO AND REMITTANCES

Do cryptocurrencies make sense for sending money internationally? In his SaveOnSend blog, Yakov Kofner, the analyst we cited above, elaborates on the pillars upon which many cryptocurrency ventures have relied to obtain funding and promote themselves as a solution to the international money transfer sector's inefficiencies. Yakov identifies the following pillars:

---

300 Virtual interview with Salvador Velasquez, May 4, 2022, recorded and transcribed by Lucía Salazar.
301 Andrew M. Bailey, Bradley Rettler, Craig Warmke: Philosophy, politics, and economics of cryptocurrency: Money without state; Philosophy Compass, Volume16, Issue11; November 2021 - https://bit.ly/3fhsQwm
302 Simon Butler: The Philosophy of Bitcoin and the Question of Money; Theory, Culture & Society, Volume 39, Issue 5 (2021) - https://bit.ly/3szO2Rm

1. Remittance disbursements are slow, typically taking days, but with cryptocurrency, they are immediate. *The argument is based on antiquated studies; most remittance payments are executed in under 5 minutes, and only a few take longer than 24 hours (payments to bank accounts, for example).*

2. Sending remittances is extremely expensive; using a cryptocurrency is almost free. *Despite lower remittance costs in recent years, migrants no longer consider remittance costs a significant concern, as reported in most surveys. Costly corridors exist, especially in Africa, but they are different from the ones where cryptocurrency pilots have developed due to the same challenges faced when operating in many of these zones: no electricity supply, a lack of internet access, geographical isolation, etc.*

3. Remittance customers are highly dissatisfied and complain about the existing deficiencies: *This is not true either. Complaints to financial services supervisory authorities in several countries (US, Mexico) and surveys show high customer satisfaction with traditional and digital distribution channels.*

Cryptocurrency enthusiasts have made two predictions. The first one is that they are the solution to providing access to financial services to the poor and vulnerable worldwide, including migrants. Considering cryptocurrencies' complexity and how they are used, this seems unlikely. The use of crypto by certain migrant groups and the grassroots adoption in some LMI countries is an interesting fact worth noting.

The second one is that they can solve the interoperability issues in the global correspondent banking system and the access to banking rails by MTOs. Numerous companies and fintechs across the industry would like this promise to be fulfilled due to derisking and debanking. Despite this not happening soon enough, the mere possibility of using crypto to bypass banking barriers and banking rails inefficiencies is forcing some regulators and banks to react and come up with real solutions.

The war in Ukraine has awakened solidarity, and the use of cryptocurrencies has been part of the funds that have helped Ukrainians deal with the Russian invasion. Eric Barbier highlights the role of remittance companies and cryptocurrencies as two key tools to provide humanitarian aid in Ukraine:

Payment companies are doing their best to continue providing remittance services to Ukraine. We are seeing a lot of donations in cryptocurrency; it seems that people who use cryptocurrencies are more generous, or they simply have more means than others, or because of their youth, I don't know, but it seems that cryptocurrencies have been a line of support for Ukrainians[303].

Humanitarian and Relief Programs, a subject I will be covering in the next chapter, are full of initiatives using crypto-rails and blockchain solutions, and some of these use cases, which involve cross-border payments, might be more widely adopted to many remittance corridors that will benefit from these solutions.

USE OF CRYPTO BY CONSUMERS

As processes and systems are being developed to realize the advantages of cryptocurrencies to improve financial services, we must remember that a growing number of individuals are figuring out how to use crypto to send money between countries. Millennials or young people with tech skills are not the only ones; an increasing number of migrant communities are also utilizing cryptocurrencies for remittances and trading and at the same time, spreading their use through word-of-mouth marketing (WOM marketing).

It has been reported that Latin America has become one of the fastest-growing regions for crypto adoption. Mastercard's New Payments Index 2022[304] revealed that at least 51% of Latin Americans have used crypto to make a purchase, while 54% are optimistic about their use as an investment; 66% express a need for greater flexibility to use crypto and traditional payment methods interchangeably.

Chainalysis' Global Cryptocurrency Adoption Index found that the total crypto inflows to Latin America topped $562 billion during 2021–2022, a 40% jump from 2020. Chainalysis ranked Venezuela number three in 2021 but dropped out of the top twenty in 2023: India, Nigeria, Vietnam, the Philippines, Ukraine, Indonesia, and Pakistan are at the top of the Overall

---

303 Virtual interview with Eric Barbier, April 11, 2022, recorded and transcribed by Isabel Cortés.
304 Mastercard Latin America & the Caribbean Press Release: Latin America's crypto conquest is driven by consumers needs; June 22, 2022 - https://prn.to/3S5Zkuv

Index Ranking[305]. Argentina ranked 13th. Chainalysis reports for 2023 that cryptocurrency grassroots adoption remains well off its all-time highs. Still, there's one crucial segment of countries where grassroots adoption has seen a more robust recovery than anywhere else: Lower Middle Income (LMI) countries[306]. LMIs have seen the most remarkable recovery in grassroots crypto adoption over the last year, remaining above where it was just before the most recent bull market (Q3 2020)[307].

A preview of the 2023 Chainanalysis reports states: *If LMI countries are the future, then the data indicates that crypto is going to be a big part of that future. That, combined with the fact that institutional adoption — primarily driven by organizations in high-income countries — continues to gain steam even during the ongoing crypto winter, paints a promising picture of the future. We could see a combination of bottom-up and top-down cryptocurrency adoption in the near future if these trends hold, as digital assets fulfill the unique needs of individuals in both segments.*

Despite being banned in countries like China, Algeria, and Bolivia, Bitcoin is still widely used. In Venezuela, for instance, authorities blocked Coinbase access in September 2020, along with Mercadolar, a company set up by Venezuelan entrepreneurs to offer their fellow citizens a way to buy and sell dollars[308].

In response to Venezuela's economic crisis, the remittance market migrated to Bitcoin to facilitate money transfers in both directions. A Venezuelan leaving the country sells their house; payment is made, and the seller buys Bitcoin locally, sends it to someone outside the country who sells it, and the funds are now available abroad in local currency. The Bitcoin seller in Venezuela pays remittances or makes payments, closing the buying and

---

305 The 2022 Global Crypto Adoption Index: Emerging Markets Lead in Grassroots Adoption, China Remains Active Despite Ban, and Crypto Fundamentals Appear Healthy, Chainalysis, oct 14, 2022 - https://bit.ly/3MzFVO9 - *The Global Crypto Adoption Index Report is published yearly in October.*
306 LMI is one of four designations used by the World Bank to classify countries based on gross national income (GNI) per capita. For the current 2024 fiscal year, LMIs are those with a GNI per capita between $1,136 and $4,465. 40% of the world's population live in LMI countries - https://bit.ly/3PIjwjB
307 The 2023 Global Crypto Adoption Index: Central & Southern Asia Are Leading the Way in Grassroots Crypto Adoption; Chainalysis Blog, September 12, 2023 - https://bit.ly/3Q2C6nN
308 Sebastian Sinclair: Venezuela Blocks Access to Coinbase and Remittance Service MercaDolar; Coindesk, September 9, 2020 - https://bit.ly/3SLWNTU

selling cycle. This is how informal buying and selling have happened in this country and in many other countries where this alternative fund transfer system is more accessible, cheaper, or presents fewer barriers than formal cross-border systems. In the US and other countries, these crypto sellers and buyers might be considered illegal when helping others to use this system — or any other alternative system— without a proper license. As I mention in my seminars, it is a risk not worth taking.

The Argentina inflation crisis has made individuals aware of the possibility of using cryptocurrencies to preserve the value of their money, a refuge from high local inflation[309]. Americas Market Intelligence (AMI) infographic[310] drawn from a survey of 520 Argentine smartphone owners, found that 27% bought crypto regularly in 2022, increasing 15% from 2021. AMI also found that 98% of Argentines know about cryptocurrency, and one in five residents plans to buy crypto in the future. Stablecoin adoption in Argentina is exceptionally high, and Tether (USDT) and USDC seem to be their best choice. Wallets such as Vibrant, built over the Stellar network using Circle USDC, seem to be one of the most popular wallets used in the country.

Most cryptocurrency buying and selling is informal in the majority of developing countries. Some online services connect buyers and sellers. One of the most popular is LocalBitcoins[311], founded in Helsinki, Finland, by two brothers in 2012 and has been expanding ever since. Buyers and sellers connect and post ads specifying how many bitcoins they wish to sell or buy, the payment method, and commissions. Communication and contact through this medium allow users to meet, online or in person, within and outside their own countries or cities, to conduct transactions. These Bitcoin *personal* exchanges don't involve intermediaries; real people backed by community reviews make it possible to verify users' trustworthiness. Some authorities have attempted to limit or regulate this activity to prevent illegal usage. Transaction values and frequency are limited as part of the company's efforts to establish a *Know Your Customer* program.

---

[309] What is Argentina's Relationship with Cryptocurrency?; worldcoin.org, September 4, 2023 - https://bit.ly/3Sd3vom
[310] Ignacio Carballo: Infographic: 2022 Crypto Landscape in Argentina; Americas Market Intelligence (AMI), August 29, 2022 - https://bit.ly/46BPntc
[311] LocalBitcoins - https://bit.ly/3w92m5E

Khashayar Abbasi of Bankless Times has written a detailed analysis of this company in 2022, commenting[312]: *There is conflicting information about where LocalBitcoins is available. According to some sources, it is banned in the US, China, Syria, Indonesia, and North Korea. However, when using the app you can find many listings for the US. You can also find listings in China in CYN accepting Alipay. Russia, Colombia, and Venezuela are the largest markets for LocalBitcoins, and together makeup 41% of the total volume of transactions.* The highest weekly turnover for LocalBitcoins was reported in December 2017, with over $129 Million; In October 2023 the weekly volume was over $7M[313]. The charts per country provided by coin.dance for LocalBitcoins weekly usage in Latin American countries shows an upsurge that began in 2017 with ups and downs that reflect each country's socioeconomic situation. As an example, Egypt shows an upsurge since 2020 with a weekly average of over 1.5 Million Egyptian Pounds (US $0.5 Million).

Eric Barbier, CEO of TripleA, a crypto payment gateway licensed by the Central Bank of Singapore, considers that the direct advantages for users of cryptocurrencies, especially stablecoins, are enormous, such as avoiding devaluation, among others:

> I think stablecoins are the fairest way to keep the value of the money earned. Let's take the example of a person who works in Argentina doing freelance design work, and their payment is international. This person might receive Argentine pesos, which in a short time will lose their value. Keeping the money in stablecoins is similar to having an offshore bank account. The possibility of receiving and sending money without going through traditional banking channels harnesses the freedom of using money anywhere, at any time[314].

Facilitating B2C payments using cryptocurrencies and providing the choice to consumers will be crucial for the industry and solve many pain points and complaints of users. As eCommerce and P2P MTOs are providing an increasing number of payment choices to consumers, B2C fintechs must do the same, especially to workers in developing countries. International employment platforms, such as Upwork, Fiverr, and its competitors, should

---

312 Khashayar Abbasi: An Honest LocalBitcoins Review in 2022; Bankless Times, may 16, 2022 - https://bit.ly/3A2l3ca
313 LocalBitcoins Weekly Volume (Global); coin.dance - https://bit.ly/3QnR9IM
314 Virtual interview with Eric Barbier, April 11, 2022, recorded and transcribed by Isabel Cortés.

begin piloting cryptocurrency wallets as an optional payment mechanism for the workers who offer their work internationally to achieve better payment conditions than they currently receive at a lesser cost. In chat rooms and community boards[315], members are increasingly demanding their use.

INDUSTRY PARTNERSHIPS

The California-based company Ripple first attended IMTC, sponsoring the Miami WORLD conference in 2013 as Open Coin, then Ripple Labs, and has been an active participant ever since. This B2B firm created a blockchain with restricted access to trade its cryptocurrency, XRP. During the first events, this innovative company explained how the system worked, trying to convince companies in the sector to become *gateways* of their private ecosystem to compensate for the funds sent using their digital currency. Ripple continued to improve its products and services to meet its customers' needs. Commercial agreements with companies in the sector are constantly being announced, showing the industry's interest in this technology.

Brendan Berry from Ripple explained[316] how efficient and low-cost XRP settlement can be. The system compensates *both ends of the transaction for an immediate sale and purchase. Berry explains: When you think about cross-border payments, one of the most important factors is settlement (when funds actually clear). The traditional manner of preemptively parking funds, which can be incredibly expensive, is an estimated $10T market, but through using a digital currency, one can settle these transactions instantaneously in real-time.*

Since Ripple's beginnings, regulatory challenges have been a constant burden for the company. It was fined US $700,000 in 2015 for acting as an MSB without a license; the fine was relatively small, and FINCEN referred to as *the first civil enforcement action against a virtual currency exchanger*[317]. In making the announcement, Jennifer Shasky Calvery's statement carried a warning, which I found very interesting: *Innovation is laudable, but only as long as it does not unreasonably expose our financial system to tech-smart criminals eager to abuse the latest and most complex products.* This is another example of US regulation through advertised sanctions.

---

315 Upwork Community Forums - https://bit.ly/3M9pVTJ
316 Loren Straub Gabe Hawkes: The Future of Cross-Border Payments with Brendan Berry (Ripple); Bowery Capital, jun 8, 2022 - https://bit.ly/3PDcXwI
317 FinCEN Fines Ripple Labs Inc. in First Civil Enforcement Action Against a Virtual Currency Exchanger; may 5, 2015 - https://bit.ly/3QxOWYW

The legal wrangling Ripple has been facing with the SEC has occupied the media since 2020. What the courts decide after rulings and appeals is a discussion that will continue for some time. The legal dispute is of great interest[318] to the financial services industry. Hopefully, some *light at the end of the tunnel* might come after the legal battle ends or an agreement is reached.

An operational test for Ripple was its pilot with MGI announced in 2018[319] and the $50 million it invested in MGI in 2019[320] to generate liquidity for the US-Mexico remittance corridor. However, the partnership came to a halt in 2021[321]. Industry analyst Yakov Kofner, on his saveonsend[322] blog, explained: It is not that Ripple's superior technology made the MoneyGram business model fundamentally more effective against Western Union or Transferwise. *It is that MoneyGram transfer flows made XRP more valuable, and Ripple was willing to pay for it $50 million per year (Ripple made similar deals with smaller providers like Intermex, TransferGo, Azimo, etc., but less than $20 million annually in total).* Still, MGI CEO Alex Holmes believes it was successful[323], arguing that the cancellation resulted from the SEC investigation.

MGI turned to Ripple's rival, cross-border crypto payments network Stellar. Stellar's interactions with the money transfer industry have been minimal, focusing mainly on partnering with new fintechs that might be more inclined to use Stellar's advantages as a cross-border platform and Lumens, its cryptocurrency. The partnership between Stellar and MGI might be a step forward in the use of crypto by MTOs.

Stellar's CEO, Denelle Dixon, announced in August 2023 a minor investment in MGI[324]. Dixon now has a seat on MGI's Board of Directors. MGI

---

318 Connor Sephton: What is XRP? Your simple guide to Ripple's cryptocurrency, Legal battle with the SEC, currency.com, jul 18, 2022 - https://bit.ly/3Pwybw7
319 Ripple and MoneyGram Partner to Modernize Payments; PR Newswire, January 11, 2018 - https://prn.to/3tjIuOJ
320 Jeran Wittenstein: MoneyGram Doubles After Blockchain Startup Ripple Buys Stake; Bloomberg, June 17, 2019 - https://bloom.bg/3PFmRje
321 Blockchain firm Ripple to end partnership with MoneyGram; Reuters, March 8, 2021 - https://reut.rs/3LLzPux
322 MoneyGram: whack-a-mole of money transfers?: MoneyGram Discovers Blockchain; updated sep 13, 2021 - https://bit.ly/3KDoY4p
323 Daniel Webber: MoneyGram's global crypto opportunity: CEO Alex Holmes on enabling crypto-fiat interoperability; FXC Intelligence, jan 2, 2022 - https://bit.ly/3coeVU1
324 Mat Di Salvo: Stellar Invests in MoneyGram in Bid to Be a 'Digital-Forward' FinTech Leader; Decrypt, August 15, 2023 - https://bit.ly/45iLlVp

allows customers to convert physical currency into digital cash using USDC in 34 cash-in and 180 cash-out-enabled countries. Using Stellar blockchain with Circle's USDC stablecoin is the idea behind the MGI product. USDC is a widely accepted and highly liquid digital dollar. Additionally, the company has a deal with Coinme that allows the purchase and sale of cryptocurrencies across the US through its large agent network.

Cryptocurrencies are criticized for their volatility, namely the rapid rise and fall of their prices, posing a risk that is difficult to predict, which is crucial for cost and price management in a company. The transaction can, however, occur instantaneously if both ends have liquidity.

Mexican fintech Bitso has been very active in the US-Mexico corridor, impacting the country's remittance market. The company reported[325] that, as of June 2022, it had processed US$1 billion and expected to double it by the end of the year, aiming to capture 10% of the remittance market by 2023. Bitso operates in Mexico, Brazil, Argentina, and Colombia.

> **Linking their value to a fiat currency and backed by real-world assets, stablecoins, such as USDC, are likely to improve the acceptance of crypto in the industry.**

Entrepreneur Brandon Zemp, in a Forbes article[326] makes the case for the advantages of stablecoins and why he believes they will become the standard for remittance, payments, and cross-border transactions. Suppose stablecoins, besides their advantages in terms of liquidity, speed, transaction cost, etc., can help MTOs bypass banking rails. In that case, it might realize Zemp's vision of stablecoins' role in the international money movement.

New fintechs, such as Roxe, are using blockchain without cryptocurrencies to develop an advanced cross-border payment system and hiring other fintechs to create an international network of instant payments. The company

---

325 Andres Engler: Bitso Processed $1B in Crypto Remittances Between Mexico and the US so far in 2022; CoinDesk, jun 16, 2022 - https://bit.ly/3TdUFVO
326 Brandon Zemp: The Power Of Stablecoins - Enabling Fast And Efficient Cross-Border Transactions; Forbes, Apr 5, 2023 - https://bit.ly/3ZHqnOA

announced in June 2022 that it would merge with Goldenstone Acquisition Ltd to go public with a capital of US $3.6 billion and list on Nasdaq[327].

CENTRAL BANK DIGITAL CURRENCIES - CBDCS

CBDCs are virtual, digital currencies or cryptocurrencies issued by national central banks, cryptographic versions of their fiat currency in a digital version intended for centralization and control. A CBDC would be legal tender. Most CBDCs are using blockchain technology slightly different from the original developments. Some central banks are using permissioned blockchains, which are centralized variations with additional layers of access control.

The CBDC Currency Tracker of the Atlantic Council reports 11 CBDCs launched, 21 active pilots, and 33 in development[328]. Caribbean island nations such as Bahamas, Jamaica, and Anguilla, as well as Nigeria, are among the 11 countries where CBDCs have launched.

The key findings of the Currency Tracker on its 2023 report are:

- CBDC development is in fast-track mode. If in May 2020 there were only 35 countries considering a CBDC, in October 2023, 130 countries are exploring a CBDC, representing 98 percent of global GDP.

- Nineteen of the G20 countries have made significant progress and invested resources in CBDC projects in 2023; nine countries are already in the pilot phase.

- China's pilot, which currently reaches 260 million people, is being tested in over 200 scenarios, some of which include public transit, stimulus payments, and e-commerce.

- The European Central Bank is on track to begin its pilot for the digital euro. Over 20 other countries will take steps towards piloting their CBDCs in 2023. Australia, Thailand, and Russia intend to continue pilot testing. India and Brazil plan to launch in 2024.

- In the US, progress on retail CBDC has stalled. However, it is moving forward on a wholesale (bank-to-bank) CBDC.

---

327 Press Release: Roxe Holding Inc., a Blockchain Payment Company, Announces Plans to List on Nasdaq Through Business Combination With Goldenstone Acquisition Limited; jun 21, 2022 - https://bit.ly/3Ax0MMh
328 Central Bank Digital Currency Tracker; Atlantic Council, updated October 5, 2023 - https://bit.ly/46hcSry

Since Russia invaded Ukraine and with the G7 sanctions response, wholesale CBDC developments have doubled. There are currently 12 cross-border wholesale CBDC projects. For the World Bank, the cross-border use of CBDCs is a collective, cooperative undertaking and its potential to facilitate cross-border payments is part of a report[329] published in 2021. The highlights of the report are:

- A peer-to-peer payment into a country using a CBDC should go from the remitter at the origin account or wallet to the central bank of the receiving country and then directly to the payee or directly to the payees' account or wallet without having to go through a network of commercial banks.

- If both countries were to issue interoperable CBDCs, payments would only need an exchange market to function across borders. However, any cross-border arrangement necessarily involves two (or more) partners and requires them all to agree on the rules and procedures needed to make the underlying exchange process possible.

- CBDCs could not be used for cross-border payments without the central banks being intimately involved in setting up and operating the interlinking or common infrastructure and making its various (legal, technical, operational, financial, risk management) components mutually consistent or commonly shared.

Instant Cross-Border Payments (ICBPs) need the existence of Domestic Instant Payment Systems. Domestic Instant Payment Systems (DIPS) are known as fast, instant, real-time, immediate, or rapid payments since they make funds immediately available to beneficiaries around the clock, on a 24/7 basis. We call them DIPs to differentiate them from ICBPs. DIPs are supported by central infrastructures, which enable banks and non-banks to connect and to build additional overlay services for end users.

The Payment Systems Development Group (PSDG) of the World Bank has played a leading role in global research and technical assistance to countries DIPS, and Project FASTT —Frictionless, Affordable, Safe, Timely Transactions— tracks all these developments. The FASTT site has information on each DIPs development with downloadable data and per-country details.

---

[329] WorldBank Group: Central Bank Digital Currencies For Cross-Border Payments: A Review of Current Experiments and Ideas, November 2021 - https://bit.ly/3AejlEO

Every DIPS is gaining traction. In its August 2023 guide to real-time payments, Mastercard reported that India, which launched its rapidly growing Unified Payments Interface in 2016, is the largest market by volume, with 89.5 billion transactions, followed by Brazil, China, Thailand, and South Korea[330]. Graph 7 visualizes the countries per region with a DIPs system in place using data from FASTT[331].

GRAPH 7: Percentage of Countries with DIPS by Region (2023)

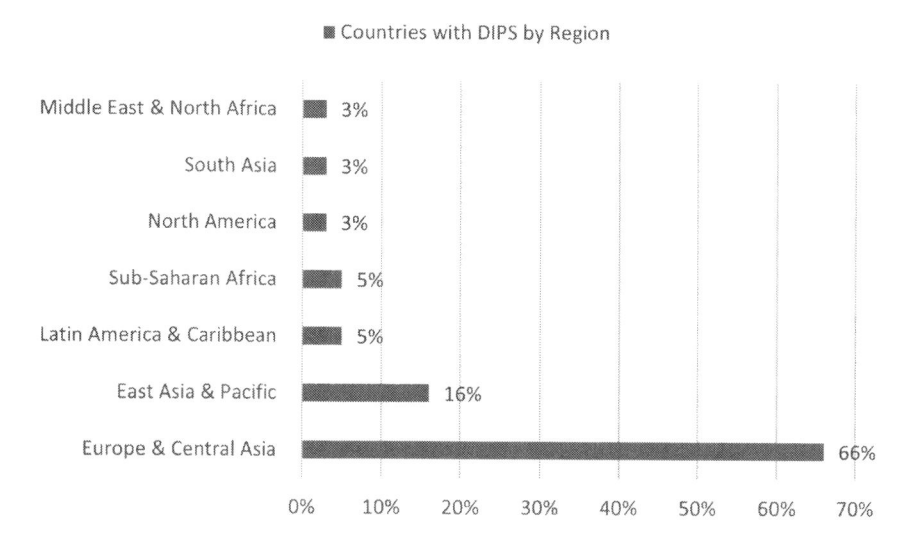

Region	Countries with DIPS by Region
Middle East & North Africa	3%
South Asia	3%
North America	3%
Sub-Saharan Africa	5%
Latin America & Caribbean	5%
East Asia & Pacific	16%
Europe & Central Asia	66%

Some ICBP projects have been tested, linking DIPS and pilots are in the works. These projects mainly test cross-border settlements using Wholesale Central Bank Digital Currencies (wCBDCs).

In 2021 Project Jura investigated using two wCBDCs —Euros and Swiss francs— for cross-border settlement of trades between Swiss and French financial institutions on a DLT platform. A six-minute video[332] developed by the consortium is highly informative and summarizes the pilot's success.

In 2022, Project Nexus connected three DIPS[333]:

---

330 Vicki Hyman: Your real-time guide to real-time payments; Mastercard, August 25, 2023 - https://mstr.cd/3rHm0Xl
331 Project FASTT; World Bank Payment Systems Development Group (PSDG), Data Visualization - https://bit.ly/3RKe566
332 Project Jura: Cross-border settlement using wholesale CBDC (Video) - https://bit.ly/46BwKFr
333 Project Nexus: enabling instant cross-border payments; BIS - https://bit.ly/46C8i72

- The Eurozone's TARGET Instant Payment Settlement (TIPS) system[334]
- Malaysia's Real-time Retail Payments Platform (RPP)[335]
- Singapore's Fast and Secure Transfers (FAST) payment system[336]

Comparatively, there are few projects testing cross-border settlements linking Retail Central Bank Digital Currencies (rCBDCs). There are trials between France and Tunisia, and between China and Hong Kong; Project Icebreaker between the central banks of Israel, Norway, and Sweden is also in the works[337].

Tobias Adrian, Financial Counsellor, discusses the private sector's role in using CBDCs and what he calls *Synthetic CDBC* or *eMoney*. In his remarks[338] at the IMF-Swiss National Bank Conference in Zurich in May 2019, he explained: *Central Banks can be responsible for settlement between trust accounts and for regulation and close supervision, including eMoney issuance, while it outsources several steps to the private sector: technology choices, customer management, customer screening, and monitoring, including for Know Your Customer and AML/CFT purposes, regulatory compliance, and data management — all sources of substantial costs and risks.*

The OMFIF, an independent think tank for central banking, economic policy, and public investment, published an article[339] by CBDC experts Roman Hartinger and Daniel Nagy about the importance of monetary unions and rCBDCs. These monetary unions in Africa can impact cross-border payments by sharing a common CBDC. Two sets of nations in west and central Africa use two versions of the CFA franc, and four countries in the

---

334 TIPS is operated by the Bank of Italy on behalf of the Eurosystem and overseen by the European Central Bank.
335 RPP is operated by Payments Network Malaysia (PayNet) and overseen by the Central Bank of Malaysia.
336 FAST is operated by Banking Computer Services (BCS) and overseen by the Monetary Authority of Singapore.
337 Roman Hartinger, Daniel Nagy: Financial inclusion across borders with retail Central Bank Digital Currencies; Whitepaper by Giesecke+Devrient, 2023 - https://bit.ly/48CJWvI
338 Tobias Adrian: Stablecoins, Central Bank Digital Currencies, and Cross-Border Payments: A New Look at the International Monetary System; IMF-Swiss National Bank Conference, Zurich, IMF, May 14, 2019 - https://bit.ly/3PNruI2
339 Roman Hartinger, Daniel Nagy: Cross-border retail CBDCs can help financial inclusion for migrants, OMFIF (Official Monetary and Financial Institutions Forum), nov 28, 2022 - https://bit.ly/3AUW7ER

south use, or link their currencies to, the South African rand. The African Union is discussing plans to develop a euro-like common currency, administered by the African Central Bank, called the Afro or Afriq.

The impact of regional and international trade using CBDCs that lets governments ensure centralized control while fostering the use of new technologies, accelerating the use of cryptocurrencies and blockchain platforms within traditional finance might be one way forward to the financial ecosystem to benefit from the creativity and innovations of the fintechs in our industry.

I am confident that the use of CBDCs will impact cross-border business payments favorably if the rails are not restricted to banking entities. Maybe it is too early to estimate the impact of CBDCs on remittances and other services the money transfer industry offers migrants. But as we move forward, more pilots and integrations will make it feasible for this potential to be realized sooner rather than later.

CHAPTER 5

CROSS-BORDER PAYMENTS 2030

Sitting on a bench outside the CorpArtes Cultural Center in Santiago, Chile, during a break from LABITCONF 2018, a Latin American Blockchain and Cryptocurrency event, I opened my lunch box: a sandwich, chips, and juice. I was waiting for the Descentralizados team to prepare the cameras for an interview on a comfortable and attractive outdoor terrace. My presentation that morning had discussed the remittance industry, and I knew they would ask me the usual questions that come to young innovators' minds. There is an understandable difficulty in comprehending a sector that appears to be an old, rusty, disjointed, and pedal-driven system for a generation so fascinated by new technologies. The frustration they experience with regulations and structural barriers can't be explained until they are confronted with them.

Meeting Rodolfo Andragnes, Diego Gutierrez Zaldivar, Efrain Barraza, and all who have developed this event over the years has been inspiring. The challenging ideas Andreas Antonopoulos presented in that event took me back to the early struggles we endured in the 1990s that I detailed in Part 1 of this book. After my presentation that morning, I attended talks that were well worth listening to while I marveled at the technological creativity of fintech innovators. It is easier to comprehend that change will come, even in the walled-in financial services sector. Companies like Amazon, Apple,

Lime, Airbnb, Uber, Bolt, etc., have changed the world. Riding a scooter rented using my mobile, from my Airbnb to the CorpArtes Cultural Center in Santa Fe, is a technological gift where logistics and payments interact.

The guys from Descentralizados are ready for the interview[340]; Luis Bustamante inquires: *Hugo, let's dig deeper into this topic. Can you tell me about your background? What does it mean to work with NFBIs for thirty years?* I speak, I express my opinion, and I answer their questions. I want to help them change the industry for the better, but I also want to channel their frustrations. After the cameras are off, I chat with them informally and ask them questions; then, I go back to the crowd, the conference rooms, and the commercial area, where I will visit each booth and do my best to understand what they offer. I do not hide my ignorance, and I question everything. Everyone is eager to explain and help me understand their ideas and proposals.

Predicting industry trends in the third decade of the millennium is challenging. The *global industry*, as a whole, differs from *the regional* and even more from the evolution of payments within specific countries. No country has figured out *the best solution*, and the diversity of systems, ideas, trials, pilots, and sandboxes is undeniable; the payment revolution *is alive and kicking*.

All opinions regarding trends and what the future holds are valid in such a dynamic environment. My thoughts and those of the colleagues I advise, consult, and have interviewed for this work are based on our biases, determined by our experiences, preferences, and location. Country trends are shaped by local history, sector regulation, market freedom, barriers to entry and freedom of competition, maneuvering room of commercial banks and NBFIs (the possibility of partnerships between banks and fintechs), and a variety of socio-economic and political factors that influence cross-border financial services.

Part 1 (1987-2000) and Part 2 (2001-2023) of this book summarize 35 years of industry history; it is hard to predict how things will turn out by 2030. I will focus on the global trends of this decade, which can be more significant to global fintechs than regional or local ones.

In this chapter, I will almost exclusively use the term *fintech*, leaving the acronym NBFI behind. The distinction between banks and non-banks is

---

[340] Descentralizados (Chile); Luis Bustamante interviews Hugo Cuevas-Mohr (n Spanish), December 5, 2018 - https://bit.ly/3AovgQl

rapidly evolving, too. The definition of non-banks is evolving too. No fintech wants to be called an *MSB* or *Money Transmitter*, and larger MSBs are changing their name in the US, adopting fintech names. Payment Institution (PI), EMI, bank, payment bank, exchange bank, or payment processor might only describe the license type or the regulatory framework of the products and services financial services institutions offer the public. Additionally, as international transactions become easier, the distinction between domestic and cross-border payments will gradually fade.

> **I now use the term crosstech to designate fintechs specializing in cross-border payments.**

The future of cross-border products and services depends on the customers and their expectations. Customer demands will continue to rise; innovative technologies, creative solutions, and operational excellence, combined with a commitment to providing solutions that are flexible enough to evolve based on criticisms and complaints, will distinguish winners from losers.

Therefore, we should begin by asking ourselves: What will our customers want in the next seven years? How can the service or the product be improved? In the view of most executives, digital customers are increasingly demanding and want better experiences with less friction and more transparency. As institutions have realized, huge marketing investments do not always translate into active customers who generate income: stickiness is a measure of success, so to achieve it, fintechs must build a closer relationship with the customer, nurture a sense of belonging, and try to make them become fond of the brand and the service.

In my experience, I have met many executives who firmly believe in these concepts but do not create a sense of belonging among their team that manifests itself in more humane and supportive actions, both internally and externally. Retaining qualified and committed team members is becoming, in fintechs, just as important as bringing in new customers[341].

For the forecasts to be realized and the industry to thrive we need innovators to continue bringing their ideas forward and find supporters, investors,

---

341 Vasyl Soloshchuk: Talent Shortage and High-Rate Turnover Force Fintech Market Squeeze; June 17, 2021 - Fintech CTO Club, Insart - https://bit.ly/3tjIDBD

tech hubs, incubators, accelerators, and all types of programs, some in existence and thriving, some in the works. As part of making South Florida my home, Miami's initiative to build a collaborative ecosystem, where partnerships between startups, corporations, academia and government entities are built and encouraged, makes me pleased, and being part of some of these developments makes me proud. I believe in fostering innovation through knowledge, and expertise sharing with effective mentorship, not only for companies or ideas, but also in the growth of individuals as the business and community leaders of tomorrow.

MARKET GROWTH

Using data from FXC Intelligence's report published on April 27th, 2023, the overall cross-border payments market is $190.1tn in 2023 and is expected to grow 53% to $ 290.2tn in 2030.

Close to 77% of this market is wholesale —transactions for currency trading, institutional investors, hedge funds, government, and central banks— and it is valued at $146tn in 2023.

Consumer and business payments or the retail market accounts for 23%, and it is valued at $44.1tn in 2023, estimated to grow 47% to $65tn in 2030. Protectionist policies in developed markets, including Brexit and trade tensions —US, China, Russia— are going head-to-head with the growth in emerging markets in Africa, Latin America, and Asia.

While the forecast for the consumer retail markets predicts growth above 80% for the three categories —83% for P2P (C2C), 81% for P2B (C2B), and 88% for B2P (B2C)— the growth for the B2B sector is more modest, 43%. However, B2B Ecommerce is estimated to reach $21,9tn in 2030, an increase of 119% in 7 years. I prepared Graph 8 based on the data provided by FXC Intelligence.

GRAPH 8: Size and Growth of the Cross-Border Retail Market (2023-2030)

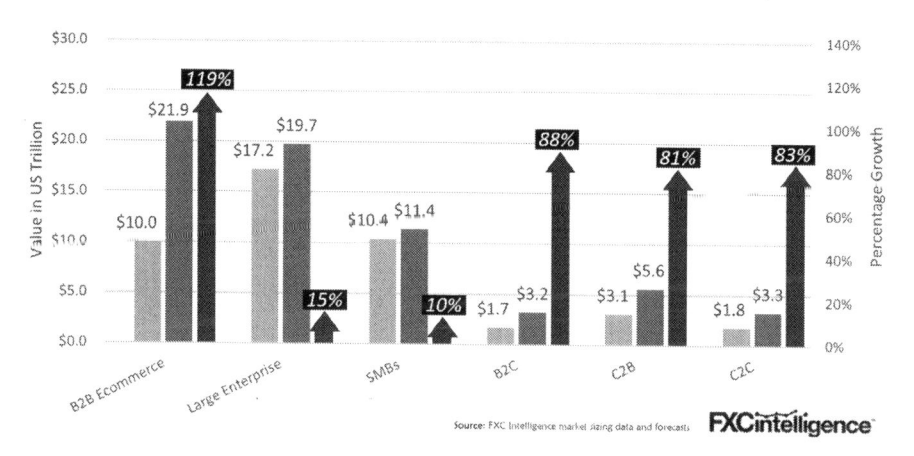

Size and Growth of the Cross-Border Retail Market (2023-2030)

Category	Value 2023 (US Trillion)	Value 2030 (US Trillion)	Growth
B2B Ecommerce	$10.0	$21.9	119%
Large Enterprise	$17.2	$19.7	15%
SMBs	$10.4	$11.4	10%
B2C	$1.7	$3.2	88%
C2B	$3.1	$5.6	81%
C2C	$1.8	$3.3	83%

Source: FXC Intelligence market sizing data and forecasts — **FXCintelligence**

The estimated market growth will undoubtedly be supported by innovation and fierce competition from fintechs and banks willing to capture a larger share of consumers and business clients. New or improved use of existing technologies, new products, and creative solutions will be key to the companies that want to grow and expand. Regulators are running behind on a tightrope between innovation and stability, liberalization and control, and their decisions, as well as the political events and policies —migration policies, for example— also play a role in what the future will hold.

I believe M&As will accelerate in the next seven years.

Some regional and local service providers have been acquired in Latin America, Europe, Asia, Africa, and Oceania to consolidate the market and join synergies to make these conglomerates more competitive. The next step is trans-regional acquisitions and mergers.

The EFCD merger between Australian firm Assembly Payments and Irish fintech CurrencyFair is one example. Assembly Payments was founded in Melbourne, Australia, in 2013 under the name PromisePay by Darren McMurtrie, Simon Jones, and Simon Lee aimed at systematizing payments through technology to make scheduled transactions securely within predefined parameters. The addition of new services and its expansion into the US, New Zealand, and Singapore led to the company's name change in 2017: Assembly Payments. Meanwhile, CurrencyFair was founded in 2009 by Brett Meyers and several Irish-based Australians. A client, Irish entrepreneur Paul Byrne, discovered the foreign exchange fintech in 2016 and decided to invest. He later became the company's CEO. The company had already exceeded US $10 billion in transaction volume. Assembly Payments and CurrencyFair merged in 2021, creating Zai, the new conglomerate's brand that now offers services in Australia and Europe and plans to expand globally.

This is only one example. A strong dollar might also contribute to acquisitions from US companies in Europe, Africa and Asia.

REMITTANCES (P2P) WILL CONTINUE THEIR UPWARD TREND

At the beginning of this chapter, we mentioned that the forecast for the consumer cross-border retail markets predicts growth above 80%. P2P (C2C) money transfers, which include remittances and other personal transfers, are estimated to grow 83% from $1.8tn to $3.3tn in 2030.

Although the growth is expected to be global, there will be regional differences. As young people join the working-age population in Africa and South Asia and aging populations in advanced economies increase, this demographic imbalance will contribute to the growth of cross-border payments to these two regions. Climate change is also a migration driver that will contribute to impact migration and, hence, increase remittances to North Africa. As payments become cheaper and simpler, that will also drive growth[342].

Since more than two-thirds of cross-border migration in Africa occurs within the continent, the flow of these regional remittances will continue to expand. If the interoperability of mobile networks increases, lowering the cost and easing the transaction flow, it will certainly contribute to this growth.

Political developments in Europe and Latin America will continue to drive the movement of migrants, professionals, and millennials, who will use cross-border payments: P2P, P2B and B2P.

---

342 Dilip Ratha: Resilient Remittances, IMF F&D Magazine, September 2023 - https://bit.ly/3RQigO3

People inside and outside the industry share this view. As migration increases, the industry will continue to grow according to Francisco Sánchez Apellániz:

> First, there is the problem of the birth rate in developed countries; that is, there will continue to be a labor shortage in both the United States and Europe, where the birth rate is low, as opposed to underdeveloped countries where birth rates are high. If Europeans or Americans want a high quality of life, they should open their borders: so business will continue to grow. The online remittance business is already there, it has been developed, and customers are using it. The classic business is still there for a different type of client, and a large part of the business is also growing: service for companies, which is even more important. Those who want to send money with a system like ours, faster and cheaper, will do it instead of using the traditional banking system. In my opinion, development never ends: someone is always left behind when you move, and you have to send them money[343].

Some MTOs will continue to specialize in migrant remittances, either through agents in sending countries where cash still circulates. Digital MTOs will keep improving their apps to attract more remitters, and global players will see competition from focused players with regional, ethnic, or age specialties. Consolidation will continue in the market, but new innovators will carry on challenging the barriers to entry, bringing more competition with improved products and services.

Expansion of distribution networks, entry into new markets, and M&As will be the key to the growth of the P2P sector.

We cannot rule out that a digital fintech may successfully develop a system that rewards agencies for enticing their clients to join a digital platform, earning revenue, maybe not directly from transactions but from referrals, as price and rate comparison sites already do. Agencies are finding ways to use digital domestic payment systems to serve clients remotely, a trend that will transform competition between money transfer agents.

---

343 Virtual interview, recorded and transcribed, with Francisco Sánchez Apellániz on April, 12, 2022, by Lucía Salazar.

Fintechs also specialize in sectors, whether students or temporary or permanent workers, who may require tailored solutions. Traditionally, port agents served personnel on cruise ships and freighters, who spent many weeks at sea. Digital solutions are now available, such as Brightwell, a company based in Atlanta, Georgia, whose app allows these employees to receive salaries digitally in partnership with OceanPay, to send remittances to their families, and to use a debit card at the ports (or the ship), etc.[344]. Remitly[345] and Martrust[346] have also created solutions for these workers.

Fintech companies are developing better online foreign exchange services to serve customers who need a high-value money transfer to invest abroad and similar services. Typically, they offer a single attractive rate without necessarily charging for the transaction, provided it exceeds certain limits. To ensure KYC compliance, the company or person must create an account to conduct due diligence and monitor their risk level. Fintechs seek to attract these bank clients by offering convenience, efficiency, and greater exchange transparency. Banks will not sit idle and will improve their exchange rate transparency and pricing. For fintechs to compete fairly, solid financial positions and banking partners with reliable payment rails are essential. In the end, competition will benefit the clients of high-value cross-border transactions.

Several fintechs compete in this sector. In the UK, Currencies Direct, established in 1996, is a new-generation foreign exchange house. Since being acquired by Palamon Capital Partners and Corsair in 2015, the company has achieved earnings growth of over 20% CAGR, with EBITDA increasing from £13 million to £43 million. It received a strategic investment from Blackstone in March 2022 of £140 million[347]. The company's website invites its 325,000 customers to make transactions online, similar to HiFX, which was acquired by Euronet in March 2014 for £145 million.

Established in 1962, MoneyCorp is a foreign exchange finance company that has evolved to compete with digital solutions while still providing traditional foreign exchange services.

---

344 Brightwell: OceanPay Card: Salaries at sea solved - Splash 24/7 - https://bit.ly/3QFtG2E
345 Michelle Winny: A custom money transfer service, aimed at crew, has been designed by digital remittance company Remitly; Seatrade Cruise News, April 5, 2019 - https://bit.ly/3eJ4ATm
346 Martrust: https://bit.ly/3U1pTzT
347 Currencies Direct scores £140m investment from Blackstone; Finextra, March 8, 2022 - https://bit.ly/3CJ2Umh

The differentiation between the provision of money transfer services to migrants (small, repetitive amounts) and currency exchange (movement of large sums for investments and other purposes) will not change drastically in the next few years, even if digitization provides the ease and flexibility to target both consumer groups at the same time.

BUSINESSES & INDIVIDUALS, B2P & P2B

Cross-border payments between individuals and companies is a fast-growing sector. With a very similar dollar value to remittances, cross-border payments from businesses to individuals, B2P (B2C), is expected to increase by 88%, from $1.7tn to $3.2tn. A larger market is cross-border bill payments, P2B (C2B), estimated to grow 81% from $3.1tn to $5.6tn.

Different fintechs have different targets, but the mechanisms will be very similar because the rails are merging and integrating rapidly. Trolley, for example, a Canadian fintech founded by Andreas Farina Vaz and Tim Nixon in 2015 as Payment Rails, shows on its website[348] the transparency of all payment integrations it performs through an API connection it offers in several markets.

Bill payment (P2B) is an integration of an additional service to remittance sending. To make these payments from abroad, a domestic digital invoice payment system must be functional and efficient: public services, banking (mortgages, loans), education, and health centers need to be easily integrated into the cross-border payment. An agile and secure technological bridge through full digitization is the key. Treasury management and excellent forex trading are the revenue drivers.

The cross-border payments market share of Mastercard, Visa, and UnionPay is significant and will continue to grow. Not only because the cards, with their brands and rails, are the heart of thousands of mobile and virtual wallets, but all digital MTOs use them to process debits for their users. Traditional MTO agents are also increasingly accepting payments with debit cards instead of cash. At the same time, these companies are offering cross-border solutions, which they are developing in a determined attempt to provide cross-border payments for businesses and individuals such as Visa Direct and Mastercard Send.

---

348 Trolley: https://trolley.com/

> The increased presence of Mastercard, Visa, and UnionPay in the cross-border payments market will continue, and their alliances with industry players will create new opportunities, driving growth.

BUSINESS PAYMENTS (B2B)

As I discussed at the beginning of this chapter, B2B accounts for the majority of cross-border payment flows. Banks are expected to continue to dominate this arena for high-value B2B transactions (above US $50,000) due to comparatively low costs and efficient and reliable correspondent banking networks. The large competition of banks and fintechs will come in the area of payment services for SMBs, a $10.4tn market.

> New payment management options developed by innovative fintechs will drive the transition and growth in this sector.

In 2022, we launched CROSSTECH PAYMENTS, a conference designed to bring together cross-border business payment fintechs and further develop the ecosystem that is needed for the non-bank sector to successfully partner and compete. *Coopetition* with banks, and between fintechs is essential; I will develop this further in this chapter. In the B2B Payments Workshop that I moderated with innovation expert Erick Schneider at this event, we analyzed how every sub-sector of the cross-border B2B is experiencing a dynamic and unprecedented change[349].

Although I have no empirical data to challenge the excellent work of the FXC Intelligence Team that I condensed in Graph 8, the growth of the SMB sector might be larger than the 10% predicted, possibly reaching at least a 20-25% increase in the next seven years. The shift from SMBs utilizing fintech payments instead of bank payments, while being faster and offering better fees and exchange rates, is providing systems to speed invoicing, accounting,

---

[349] Hugo Cuevas-Mohr: Cross-Border Payment Highlights; LinkedIn Post, June 14, 2023 - https://bit.ly/3M5ECqO

tracking, and overall management. A better cross-border payment experience can present incentives to SMBs to engage in international trade.

At the same time, the growth and development of migrant SMBs has been well documented[350]. Migrants contribute disproportionately to entrepreneurship. In the US, where they represent 27.5% of all entrepreneurs — and only 13% of the population— we see a contribution that outpaces the entrepreneurship of native-born citizens twofold. Migrants are not only creating more businesses; they are building more successful ones.

> Many of these ethnic SMBs are trading internationally, which can be an attractive segment to tap for innovative crosstechs.

Chinese migrant entrepreneurship worldwide is a phenomenon that is important to note[351]. Will Chinese SMBs use formal cross-border payment services to trade and develop? As Chinese fintechs are developed in Europe, Africa, and the Americas to serve the China corridors —and other Asian corridors as well— they could bring a significant formalization to this market.

It will be a decade of new ventures in different markets and stronger competition with banks. I look forward to watching fintechs succeed in this segment.

GOVERNMENT PAYMENTS

All government institutions, local or national, make or receive payments from individuals and companies. These can be categorized as P2G (Person to Government) and B2G (Business to Government) - taxes, fines, permits, certificates -, G2P (Government to Person) - pensions, social benefits, welfare - and to a lesser extent G2B (Government to Business). Due to their socioeconomic implications, G2P payments have generated the most interest among these categories. The P2G bill payment system, which we discussed earlier, has incorporated some of these features when governments enable digital payments, and integration with existing platforms is possible.

---

350 Nataly Kelly: Research Shows Immigrants Help Businesses Grow. Here's Why; Harvard Business Review, October 26, 2018 - https://bit.ly/46zJZGA
351 Migrant Entrepreneurship: Journal of World Business, Science Direct, 2021 - https://bit.ly/46JEFRj

The CGAP published a paper[352] in September 2019 entitled *The Future of G2P Payments: Expanding Customer Choice*, which states:

> In line with the expansion of digital payments, governments have increasingly begun to channel the payment of social assistance benefits directly to beneficiaries' financial accounts. However, if these advances in the digitization of payments are to aid beneficiaries, their scope must be expanded. The next step is to develop delivery systems that provide beneficiaries with more control and representation by allowing them to choose where and when they receive payments and withdraw money. This provides policymakers with an opportunity to better address beneficiaries' needs. Modernizing payments of social assistance benefits to the poor and disadvantaged also encourages better customer service by promoting competition among multiple financial service providers.

This document was followed by a World Bank initiative called G2Px[353] in early 2020. The Covid pandemic and the need for rapid distribution of social benefits and economic incentives to meet the crisis sparked an enormous interest in using digital distribution tools. As Samir Kiuhan[354] of the Robert Schuman Centre for Advanced Studies points out: *The number of government assistance programmes went from 103 in March 2020 to 1,841 in May 2021, reaching more than 1.5 billion people.* Not all programs used digital channels, but most did: *Of the 202 cash transfer programmes studied [by Kiuhan], 58% were disbursed through digital payments and 22% through manual and digital payments. Interestingly, low-income countries display the highest share of digital payment deployment with 63%.*

The G2P Network[355] was created in 2021, an organization involving several public and private institutions such as the Center for Global Development (CGD), MicroSave Consulting (MSC), the Better Than Cash Alliance, and the Bill & Melinda Gates Foundation, plus the World Food Programme, CGAP, and the World Bank. As part of its mission, the organization seeks

---

352 The Future of G2P Payments: Expanding Customer Choice; september 2019, CGAP; english: https://bit.ly/3SNvokz - spanish: https://bit.ly/3ecKy3W
353 World Bank: G2Px: Digitizing Government-to-Person Payments - https://bit.ly/3T4PvKI
354 Samir Kiuhan: The pandemic, Government-to-person (G2P) programs, and digital wallets; Robert Schuman Centre for Advanced Studies, The Florence School of Banking and Finance, June 21, 2022 - https://bit.ly/3Cj44U7
355 G2P Network: https://g2p-network.org/

to support the development of a new generation of government-to-person (G2P) payment systems in Africa, Asia, and the Pacific.

This development is an excellent incentive for fintechs entering or planning to enter this segment, competing against banks that have more influence on government policies. This type of program is more competitive locally than internationally. It is important, however, to use the expertise of crosstechs when making cross-border payments, for instance, as part of multilateral agency assistance programs.

G2Ps are being targeted by critical analysts[356], since they involve privatizing public services and generate concerns from observers, which must be heard to ensure that the intended benefits are well managed at the societal level. Fintechs may find themselves under severe scrutiny. as happened with South African fintech Net1 and its subsidiary Cash Paymaster Services (CPS).

Net1 was commissioned to distribute benefits to 17 million people by the South African Social Security Agency (SASSA) in 2009[357]. There have been many complaints, press publications, accusations, civil lawsuits, and audits claiming that Net1 used information about these individuals to provide them with loans, deducting interest from profits and performing unauthorized debit deductions. Net1 received a capital injection from the World Bank in 2016, US $107.7 million from the International Finance Corporation (IFC) for 19% of Net1shares[358]. The controversy also hit Mastercard and the new World Bank president, Ajay Banga, who was Mastercard's CEO at the time, visiting Soweto to champion the partnership with Net1[359]. Black Sash, the well-known South African NGO, has described[360] its long-standing position to protect the beneficiaries of government grants and pensions.

I cannot judge whether the SASSA program, with all its flaws, encouraged *predatory behavior by financial service companies,* but it is certainly a good

---

356 Nick Bernards: Fintech and Poverty in and Beyond the Pandemic; Bot Populi, March 28, 2022 - https://bit.ly/3EBGa94
357 Press Release: Net1 Announces 12 Month Contract with SASSA,, Johannesburg, March 27, 2009 - https://bit.ly/3yovDKE
358 Erin Torkelson: The World Bank's role in SA's social grants payment system; Bank invested R1.6 billion in Net1 last year; GroudUp, March 23, 2017 - https://bit.ly/3RO2xvb
359 Patrick Bond: Grant distribution failures foil financial inclusion; The African, September 27, 2023 - https://bit.ly/3S3ko5c
360 Lynette Maart, Angie Richardson and Rachel Bukasa: Hands Off Our Grants — Black Sash's Long Battle for Justice against SASSA and Cash Paymaster Services; Black Sash Blog, May 31, 2022 - https://bit.ly/3tyVPmi *Published on 19 May 2022 by Daily Maverick* - https://bit.ly/3RYPzyt

lesson for fintech companies to analyze if they are competing in this market. Financial inclusion is an important undertaking for financial service companies partnering with governments, and there is a fine line between making a profit and taking advantage of the most vulnerable members of society. Fintechs must remember that they will be more scrutinized than banks when participating in such government programs.

Gerardo Una, Senior Economist at the IMF's Fiscal Affairs Department, and co-authors have addressed the risks and benefits for fintechs and state: *The use of fintech in public finance could bring various benefits—including strengthening fiscal transparency, improving budget planning and execution, and upgrading cash management— if public sector institutional and technological capacities are strengthened, and risks are adequately mitigated*[361].

The importance of agents has been revealed by implementing these programs in developing and crisis-stricken countries, not only for distributing cards or encouraging people to use digital media but also for access to cash, which is important to creating digital ecosystems alongside ATMs.

The growth of this sector in this decade will be incremental, even with the obstacles to adoption that many experts perceive[362]. For our industry, there can be no development of government-related cross-border services without a functioning G2P and P2G domestic payment ecosystem. There are many instances where multilateral grants, relief efforts, and charity programs can benefit from fintechs developing cross-border services that tap into government payment systems.

HUMANITARIAN AND RELIEF PROGRAMS

The experience and creativity of fintechs has reached one of the most critical aspects of the need for support of vulnerable communities worldwide. In a blog at the end of 2021, Save the Children, the 1919 post-World War I founded NGO, wrote: *The emergence of fintech for the humanitarian sector comes at a time of unprecedented need and is being driven by the convergence of several major technological advancements including widespread internet connectivity,*

---

[361] Gerardo Uña, Alok Verma, Majid Bazarbash and Naomi N Griffin: Fintech Payments in Public Financial Management: Benefits and Risks; IMF eLibrary, February 3, 2023, eISBN: 9798400232213 - https://bit.ly/3PZOMun

[362] Ian Hall: Government use of fintech solutions: what's next?; Global Government Fintech, November 25, 2022 - https://bit.ly/406k2g4

cheap smartphones and other devices, cloud computing, mobile money platforms and biometric identification.

Many programs have been developed recently, and others are in the works, where the cross-border experience of our industry is converging with the need for a new wave of humanitarian and relief programs that places funds in the hands of the most needed individuals and grassroots organizations. Some experts in this field believe that the future of humanitarian action stands in the hands of *the fintech revolution powering aid*[363].

The total international humanitarian assistance from governments and EU institutions and estimated contributions from private donors has stalled after the Covid pandemic, at around US$31 billion. It is expected to grow as the domestic needs of government and donors shift to the international need for assistance. Hopefully the growth realized pre-covid, averaging 12% per year, will soon materialize. Appeal requirements have grown faster than ever and the appeal gap stands around 52%[364].

Some of these humanitarian aid funds are counted in the cross-border transfer statistics. What is new is the increasing number of these funds that are managed by fintechs, some of them in *coopetition* with banks.

Two banks, Barclays and Standard Chartered, teamed up with Save the Children to create the social fintech enterprise Fintech for International Development (F4ID) to help deliver humanitarian assistance to hard-to-reach communities, with a digital platform for cash and voucher programmes[365]. The program lets families select the goods and services they need from local merchants and providers, ensuring those vendors are paid on time. The F4ID announcement mentions that cash and voucher programming worldwide, totalling US$6.3 billion globally in 2020, has more than doubled in the past five years.

---

363 The future of humanitarian action: The fintech revolution powering aid; Devex, October 7, 2020 - https://bit.ly/45JMCoM
364 Fran Girling and Angus Urquhart: Global Humanitarian Assistance Report 2021; Development initiatives, June 22, 2021 - https://bit.ly/45x0Ust
365 New Fintech company creates tools to help communities thrive; Save the Children Press Release, November 22, 2021 - https://bit.ly/3tDXR4E

The US$17.9 million UNICEF's Venture Fund[366], launched in 2016, has provided technical and strategic support to fintech startups that can benefit humanitarian efforts. The Portfolio currently includes 72 investments, including 33 to startup companies in countries where UNICEF is active. One of these fintechs, Leaf Global Fintech, participated in our 2020 RemTech Awards[367], successfully graduated from the Fund and was acquired by a leading company in the industry, IDT. Leaf developed a *virtual bank* for refugees and vulnerable populations in Africa *to enable storage and transfer of assets across borders even without the need for a smartphone*[368].

Other fintechs in the UNICEF program are Bloinx, a decentralized app by BX Smart Labs, Kotani Pay a crypto to fiat off-ramp platform with no need for internet connectivity, Rahat, by Rumsan, a digital cash and voucher assistance (CVA) management system, Treejer an open protocol that empowers local communities who protect forests and Xcapit, a smart crypto wallet with investment and simple loan applications.

The International Federation of Red Cross and Red Crescent Societies (IFRC) published in December 2022 a report titled *Global Payment Solutions for Humanitarian Cash Assistance*[369] where 17 payment solution providers were shortlisted, mostly for comparison purposes and guidance: Celo, Vital Wave, BPC Technologies, RedRose, World Line, Leaf Global, Eversend, Nagad, Papara, Zwipe, Squid and Grassroots Economics were evaluated. It's a good report that should be consulted by fintechs in this space.

As always, it is easier said than done, especially with humanitarian aid for refugees, and consultant Joris Lochy gives a summary of the need and the risks facing fintechs that want to enter this field of work. He notes how traditional financial institutions have failed to serve the needs of refugees; every industry colleague certainly understands the financial barriers, account setup documentation requirements, risk and regulatory concerns and the management of fees, foreign exchange and the costs involved.

---

366 UNICEF Venture Fund: Flexible funding and networks for innovators on the ground - https://uni.cf/3Qq9Agg
367 2020 Remtech Awards Entries organized by IMTC (now CrossTech) - https://bit.ly/492ccIb
368 Meghan Warner: UNICEF Venture Fund: Five Blockchain Startups Graduate from UNICEF's Venture Fund, September 5, 2022 - https://uni.cf/46Zs10F
369 Global Payment Solutions for Humanitarian Cash Assistance; IFRC, December 2022 - https://bit.ly/3rNXMeh

Revolut experienced such risks and rewards with Ukrainian refugees. Many fintechs, besides Revolut, have done their best to help Ukranians such as Monese, Bunq, TransferGo, Zopa, Vantage, Bunq, Picnic and MessageBird, as reported[370] by Alex Guts, Chief Business Officer at Banxe, a UK based, EMI backed platform that provides banking and crypto services.

The UN High Commissioner for Refugees (UNHCR) and the Stellar Development Foundation (SDF), Stellar blockchain network's NGO, is piloting a blockchain cash distribution system for internally displaced persons (IDPs) and other war-affected people in Ukraine. The digital wallet provided by Vibrant uses Circle USDC and the more than 4,500 MGI agents in Ukraine will be providing cashout services.

Since most of these fintech pilots and solutions are fairly new and their future in this area looks promising, the road to 2030 will see an increase of solution providers and the volume of funds being managed and transacted will surely grow.

INTRA-REGIONAL REMITTANCES

As South-South migration increases, intraregional remittances will rise as well. Intraregional migration in Africa is the largest in the world, with internal displacements that will continue as some countries achieve greater stability and their neighbors experience crises, socio-political, ethnic, climatic, etc. According to the World Bank, internal migration in Africa represents 70% of international migration.

In many corridors, transactions are conducted through IVTs with intermediaries at borders, using MMOs to transfer money from one country's mobile wallet to another. Technology simplifies Hawala systems. For families moving overseas in search of a better life, these wallets offering cross-border services are extremely important, and there are many programs underway in Africa that we have mentioned throughout this book.

Most European migration is within the EU; the Ukraine war is an example of this internal displacement, and the formal and informal movement of funds to and from Ukraine is still being documented. Migration was allegedly one of the reasons for Brexit, but the UK will still face the same challenges

---

370 John Reynolds: Fintechs Fast Out of Blocks in Helping Ease Refugee Crisis but Experts Call for More Action; The Fintech News, November 19, 2022 - https://bit.ly/3M6GtMf

as before, turning the English Channel into a barrier for migration, much like the wall President Trump tried to construct along the US southern border. As internal EU P2P money transfers continue to grow, fintechs continue to develop solutions using the available banking rails, SEPA, and TARGET for these EU transfers.

As Manuel Orozco and Matthew Martin report, intraregional migration in Latin America[371] has expanded to countries such as Chile, Colombia, Costa Rica, Panama, the Dominican Republic, and Mexico. Domestic remittances from the continent increased exponentially in 2021 due to these movements. Most significantly, remittances from Chile to Haiti have grown by over 50%. Colombia to Venezuela and Costa Rica to Nicaragua money transfers will increase as long as the socio-political situation remains the same. While P2P transfers help the family members remaining in the country, a counterflow of funds takes place as individuals seek to sell their homes, farms, and businesses before or even after they are gone. What will happen to Argentina will surely cause a movement of funds in and out of the country.

Uruguayan consultant Daniel Trias highlights some of the main reasons why South Americans migrate to neighboring countries: *Intraregional migration in Latin America accounts for more than 45% of general migration and has several factors that favor it: the first one is language, even with Portuguese in Brazil, because you can understand it; and the second one is the easy return: even if things go wrong, you can take a bus, walk, or whatever, but you still get back to your country. The third is family reunification, which also becomes simpler after one member is successful*[372].

In Asia, COVID had a bigger impact on intraregional migration[373] than in other continents. Many countries in the region maintain strict controls over visas and illegal migration, so they have been able to manage their quotas and admit migrants who meet their criteria. Thailand and Indonesia, for example, attract migrants with special qualifications, and almost all visas are issued to residents of neighboring countries.

---

371 Manuel Orozco, Matthew Martin: Family Remittances in 2021, Is Double-Digit Growth the New Normal? The Dialogue, March 2022 - https://bit.ly/3Apn2rf
372 Virtual interview with Daniel Trías, May 12 and 17, 2022, recorded and transcribed by Lucía Salazar.
373 Asian Development Bank Institute (ADBI) International Labour Organization (ILO), Organisation for Economic Co-operation and Development (OECD): Labor Migration in Asia: Covid-19 Impacts, Challenges, and Policy Responses; 2022 - https://bit.ly/3AoIYTz

A steady number of individuals from Bangladesh and, to some extent, Nepal, migrate to GCC countries (Gulf Cooperation Council) like Saudi Arabia and the Emirates, and the policies to attract citizens from these countries are expected to continue in the current decade. Japan and Korea remain popular destinations for intraregional migration, and the Philippines is their largest supplier of foreign workers. The volume of cross-border payments through fintechs has more than doubled the percentage increase in migration flows, a sign of their ability to gain market share. Competition among Chinese fintechs for acquiring local payers reflects this region's optimistic view of the sector.

The growing *transient migration*[374] of individuals moving from one country to another in the hope of reaching a previously defined destination is worth noting: migrants crossing the US border from Central America to reach the United States or waiting in Turkey to reach Europe, etc. In some cases, transitory migrants may become permanent if conditions are particularly right. This is the case with Dominicans, Cubans, Haitians, Sudanese, Nigerians, and Venezuelans, for whom academics and researchers[375] predict a substantial increase over the next few years. The number of temporary workers traveling internationally for harvests, construction of facilities, or specific projects is expected to increase as well. The discussion that brought up the book[376] by Myron Weiner and Tadashi Hanami, published in 1998 and reprinted in 2017, is back: *Temporary Workers or Future Citizens?* which reflects on the dilemma of permanent versus temporary migration to benefit host countries, specifically Japan and the US.

Sometimes, these *transient migrants* do not have the ability to send or receive funds due to local restrictions in terms of IDs needed or legal status, and they resort to informal channels.

---

374 Transient migrants include students, knowledge workers, migrant workers, itinerant workers, backpackers, tourists, refugees and asylum seekers.
375 Gioconda Herrera & Carmen Gómez (eds) Migration in South America. IMISCOE Research Series. Springer Cham, ago 17, 2022 - https://bit.ly/3ARCb6b - IOM: Grandes Movimientos de Migrantes Altamente Vulnerables en las Américas Provenientes del Caribe, Latinoamérica y Otras Regiones; November 16, 2021 - https://bit.ly/3KtL1Kv
376 Myron Weiner, Tadashi Hanam: Temporary Workers or Future Citizens?; Japanese and US Migration Policies, Palgrave MacMillan, 1998/2017, ISBN: 978-1349144198 - https://bit.ly/3RPxDlT

COOPETITION: BANKS AND FINTECHS

In the chapter on technological innovation, I referred to a text[377] written by Professor Purnanandam from the University of Michigan. I take it up to continue with his analysis, which begins with the question: *Will banks survive fintech's challenge?*

> A deeper look at the cost of the traditional finance sector makes it evident that it has been ripe for disruption for quite some time. Research has shown that the cost of financial services is surprisingly high at about 2% of the asset value on average. Moreover, this cost has remained remarkably similar for a century despite all the technological improvements during this period. So why didn't banks pass on some of these benefits to their customers by lowering transaction costs and fees?
>
> Imperfect competition in the banking market explains a big part of this behavior. Indeed, regulatory restrictions make it really hard for a new player to enter the financial services industry, providing the incumbent banks with a lot of market power. With higher market power came higher rents that the banks have enjoyed for decades. But imperfect competition doesn't tell the complete story. Banks also enjoyed rents from having access to information that others could not have. Additionally, they benefited from the explicit or implicit government guarantee, making them a trusted counterparty for financial transactions.
>
> The loss of *global market power* experienced by banks following the 2008-2009 financial crisis is real. As a result, politicians and regulators have begun to view financial services in a new light, which has helped fintechs enter the market. The concept of *Too Big To Fail*, which pushed governments to bail out banks financially with public funds to avoid a financial collapse, is a specter still haunting.
>
> I believe relationships between banks and NFBIs will continue evolving in all countries, although friction will likely persist in most markets, causing distortion and difficulties. Banks' acquisitions or creation of fintechs, their specialization in providing services to fintechs (safeguard accounts for e-wallets and other products), and digital banks are trends we'll continue to see as we carve out the future.

---

377 Amiyatosh Purnanandam: Will Banks Survive FinTech's Challenge?; Forbes, July 21, 2021 - https://bit.ly/3SJcI5Q

Professor Purnanandam believes that in order for banks to survive the challenge from fintechs, there are three strategies that they are following:

- Acquire fintech firms to enhance the efficiency and speed of banking.
- Make investments in fintech startups through VC investments.
- Enter into strategic partnerships.

In the cross-border payments sector, strategic partnerships seem to be the trend that we will see moving forward in this decade. Acquiring fintech firms to diversify and complement the services provided by banks seems to be another path being followed, and we need to be attentive to M&A announcements to understand market tendencies. Seeing the increasing percentage of banks attending events such as CrossTech World, CrossTech Payments, and other payment events, I can't help observing a pattern developing.

According to Suman Bhattacharyya's article at PaymentsDive[378], the analyst defined the relationship between banks and fintechs as more of a *coopetition* based on collaboration rather than competition. In this context, he mentioned Payoneer, a fintech company that has designed a payment system that facilitates cross-border transactions through banks. Rapyd is another fintech that uses banks but creates online solutions for easier B2B payments.

If regulators don't understand and encourage the *coopetition* between banks and fintechs, we will continue to see market distortions and suffer the consequences.

Additionally, regulations are changing, and new types of banks are being created in a number of countries, removing the distinction between banks and non-banks through service integration. European regulation allows NBFIs to offer services previously reserved for banks, such as opening accounts and handling bank transfers. In Europe, the benefit of SEPA[379] and TARGET continues to grow, making the transfer of domestic and cross-border funds easier and less costly. This makes international and domestic payments equally easy, largely due to the use of a common currency.

---

378 Suman Bhattacharyya: Fintechs attack cross-border business payments as banks and legacy players rush to innovate; PaymentsDive, May 25, 2021 - https://bit.ly/3KxCciU
379 Qué es SEPA - https://bit.ly/3JSOvWx

In 2011, SWIFT sponsored the IMTC in Miami, launching SWIFTRemit and inviting MTOs to connect to the system. During this event, Director Olivier Denis told Nabil Kabbani in an interview[380] about SWIFT's efforts to attract fintechs and help them connect directly with the system to make payments. The system failed to achieve the relevance they expected. Whether SWIFT manages to reinvent itself with SWIFT Go and build on the system's inclusiveness or remain only as a banking rail will be interesting to see. SWIFT launched its SWIFT Go system in 2021[381], built on SWIFT gpi's high-speed rails, designed for high-value payments. It would be a scaled-down version of SWIFT gpi, tailored for small businesses.

As I mentioned in the last chapter, Africa is gradually moving toward one goal: monetary unification. With MMOs leading the way and collaborating with banks to have a digital interoperable system, the path forward seems easier than in Latin America and Asia. The Economic Community of West African States (ECOWAS, or CEDEO in French) comprises 15 East African nations united to create a single currency. Despite several postponements in the past, this plan is getting renewed momentum and is set for 2027.

Digital banks, Neobanks, or Challenger Banks will probably have more room for action, and, like Brazil's NuBank, they can open branches in several countries and move money among them more easily. Neobanks will surely face great challenges as they grow.

NEOBANKS

BBVA, one of the most technologically involved traditional commercial banks, offers an insightful explanation of Neobanks that I would like to use as a starting point. Their website explains[382]:

> Neobanks are banking entities that use the *fintech* (financial technology) philosophy to offer a better customer experience, with closer contact through mobile phones and other remote channels, focusing on transparency and lower commissions. BBVA Research published a report titled *Neobanks: creating a digital bank from scratch* pointing out that compared

---

380 IMTC (CrossTech) Interview by Nabil Kabbani at IMTC Miami 2011 to Olivier Denis, Sr Product Manager at SWIFTRemit, October 27, 2011 - https://bit.ly/3PTk3gG
381 SWIFT Launches SWIFT Go, a Fast, Cost-Effective Service for Low-Value Cross-Border Payments; Business Wire, July 7, 2021 - https://bwnews.pr/3TkFtGa
382 BBVA: Neobancos: ¿Qué son y cómo operan? - https://bbva.info/3QN6CzA

to the traditional banks, *these new banks have the advantage of not having a complex legacy technology burden, with data that is hard to exploit through being organized into silos, and the cost-saving that comes from not having a physical distribution network.*

Atom, a UK-based firm, is an example of this policy; BBVA owns 39% of the company (as of March 2018), up from 29.5% in 2015 when it entered the organization as a stakeholder.

To clarify, Neobanks are financial entities with banking licenses, which hold client money on deposit and provide services exclusively through digital means, primarily through mobile devices. Nonetheless, some analysts do not consider neobanks founded by commercial banks as such. Although closely related and sometimes confusing, *Open Banking* should be treated separately. Open Banking refers to the right to access our financial information in full transparency regardless of our bank of choice. Therefore, we can authorize apps to access our data via APIs and use it to the extent we want. As Claran O'Malley explained[383], Open Banking poses a significant challenge:

> Banking is structurally anti-competitive. There is always a drive towards stability, which crushes competition. You don't want thousands of small banks that could go bankrupt at any point – that's why regulators typically prefer larger, more stable banks. Stability is, of course, a good thing, but it stifles competition. Open Banking is the antidote to this. It allows us to have financial stability, but also new and innovative products.

Regulation is opening up the anti-competitive practices and structural conservatism in the banking sector.

Fintechs' access to banking rails is on the line and will determine the future of coopetition as fintechs seek to serve more customers, providing the innovation needed and relegating banks to the role of *financial back-offices*. It is a new era of BOPs (Back-Office Providers), B2B fintechs and banks, performing functions for direct customer-oriented fintechs.

---

383 Claran O'Malley: The Next Chapter in Open Banking; Trustly, August 1, 2022 - https://bit.ly/3ZTjz0J

Neobanks are competing for bank customers. This decade will be interesting to watch, as statistics predict that the proportion of young, millennials with traditional bank accounts[384], will continue to drop, leading to an unprecedented expenditure of bank resources on appearing like fintechs. Millennials want banking products and services that offer perks and rewards, such as a higher interest rate on deposit accounts, cash-back on purchases, and foreign ATM fee refunds. There are many surveys on millennials and banking: 40% of millennials abandoned mobile banking activities when they took too long, and 94% said that no-fee banking was a priority[385]. Will traditional banks be able to compete with Neobanks? For how long?

Electronic Money Institutions (EMIs) in Europe are NBFIs authorized to issue, distribute, and refund electronic money, and they also act as payment intermediaries by providing virtual wallet services. Although listed as Neobank, Wise (formerly Transferwise) is an EMI, along with Revolut and Monese. EMIs may become banks in the future if they wish to offer other banking products or find themselves in conflict with business partners. EMIs provide debit cards, i.e. plastic cards that may be branded by Visa or Mastercard and used with Visa Direct, Mastercard Send, Swift Receive, and ATM networks for debit and credit transactions. As contactless payments become more common, plastic cards will increasingly be kept in wallets or at home.

Revolut was founded in 2015 by Russian entrepreneurs Nikolay Storonsky and Vlad Yatsenko in London. Through its *financial supper app*, the company offers a variety of services provided within the same application. After obtaining a license from the Bank of Lithuania in 2018, it started operations in Australia and Singapore and in 2020, expanded to Japan, Lithuania, Poland, and the US[386]. To operate in the US, the company needed to establish a commercial partnership with a banking institution, which it did with Metropolitan Commercial Bank and Cross River Bank. In March 2021, the company announced the application for a state charter bank license in the

---

384 Emmanuel Dooseman: How Traditional Banks Can Compete with Fintech Disruptors; Finextra, October 11, 2022 - https://bit.ly/3eDO8E8
385 Rebecca Lake: Surprising Millennial Banking Trends; Millennial banking habits set them apart from other banking customers, The Balance, April 19, 2021 - https://bit.ly/3tlyjJj
386 The world's biggest financial super-app: Revolut; Nuclei, April 21, 2022 - https://bit.ly/3eQocoH

state of California[387]. In the UK, it seems that Revolut is finally getting its banking license. The Bank of England had demanded Revolut to simplify its ownership structure —collapsing its six classes of shares into one— which led to more than 2 years of negotiations with its shareholders[388].

The Revolut case illustrates the difficulties a growing fintech faces looking to provide financial services in different markets: you can be an NBFI in one market and a bank in another, a practice that will likely become more common as financial services evolve and regulations change. WU has faced the same challenges and operates a bank in Austria and Germany and another bank in Brazil.

How can Neobanks benefit the industry? Most of them attempt to grow in their domestic markets to attract large numbers of users that make their shares valuable, making investors happy.

This is how fintech banks define their success. In the end, their ability to deepen their relationship with these customers, either by offering more profitable products or providing services to SMEs, will determine their success. Users are increasing daily, and the 2022 list[389] below is just a sample of the millions of people who used its service at one point in time. Although the data are obsolete due to the sector's dynamism, it offers a comparative perspective:

TABLE 15: Main Neobank Comparaison; users and countries covered, 2022

Name	Users (millions)	Presence
NU Bank	34	Brazil, Argentina, Colombia, Mexico
Chime	13.1	USA
N26	7	Germany

---

387 Romain Dillet: Revolut applies for bank charter in the US; Techcrunch, March 22, 2021 - https://tcrn.ch/3BiCtSy
388 Revolut strikes share deal with SoftBank to remove barrier to UK licence - FT Reuters. October 3, 2023 - https://reut.rs/3rBjaDo
389 I have compiled this list using various sources, referenced in this chapter as well as: Insider Intelligence: What neobanks are, how they work and the top neobanks in the US & world in 2022 - https://bit.ly/3A6t0gy, Africa currently has 21 digital banks which in total serve more than 18 million customers, Ecofin, mar 24, 2022 - https://bit.ly/3A5aS6S

Name	Users (millions)	Presence
Bettr	6	South Africa
Monzo	5.8	UK
TymeBank	4	South Africa
Current	4	USA
Aspiration	3	USA
Varo	2.7	USA
Current	2	USA
Kuda	2	Nigeria
Tangerine	2	Canada
Ualá	2	Argentina
Starling	1.9	UK
Orange Bank	1.8	France, Spain and some African countries

The case of NU Bank in Brazil raises the question of whether digital banks in Latin America will be able to break the monopoly of traditional banks. *Unless new players come in to challenge the way things are, I don't see the financial industry having much incentive to change*, says Christine Chang, a director at Finnovista in Mexico City[390].

The Philippine Central Bank approved six digital banks[391], including OfBank, Overseas Filipino Bank, owned by Land Bank of the Philippines, which provides banking services to Filipino migrants abroad. With remittances accounting for 9.2% of GDP, they will likely develop cross-border products and services, as these two companies are sure to do: UNOBank and MayaBank.

The Brazilian Neon, with more than 9 million users, and the US Square should be considered Payment Institutions, even though Square has obtained a state bank license in Utah through its subsidiary Square Financial Services. The seven African digital banks described in Pay Space Magazine's

---

390 Wesley Tomaselli: How digital banks are breaking up Latin America's finance monopolies, The Daily Dose, OZY, July 11, 2019 - https://bit.ly/3woxePK
391 Regina Liezl Gambe, Ranina Sanglap: Philippine virtual banks to ride on remittance flows, digital payments; S&P Global, November 10, 2021 - https://bit.ly/3CgtBz0

article[392], should be examined individually to determine whether they are licensed banks or payment entities. This includes Eversend and Chipper cash from Uganda, Lidya, Cowrywise and PiggyVest from Nigeria, LSOL wallet from South Africa, and 7aweshly from Egypt. We should apply the same criteria to analyze Middle Eastern Neobanks such as Bankino of Iran, Halade Saudi Arabia, Ila of Bahrain, Xpence, Mashreq Neo and Liv of the Emirates.

Non-banks and banks will continue to blur the lines between them. LendIt's founder, Peter Renton, explained in an interview[393]:

Fintech and banking are converging. There will be a time in the near future when there will be little distinction between banks and fintech companies. Even those companies that are happy without a banking license use partner banks to offer various services to their customers. The future of fintech is in banking And the future of banking is in fintech.

Many countries will have to modify their regulations to facilitate their implementation, but they are already doing so. As stated in a report[394] on digital banking in Latin America:

In many Latin American countries, oligopolistic tendencies of banking markets have inhibited innovation and competition. As an example, 83% of Brazilian commercial banking assets are held by its top five banks. Recent market developments, however, have reduced exclusive access to information and financial services, following a global trend evident in the growth of digital banking [...] In Latin America, regulators' positive interventions have contributed to the expansion of neobanks. In Brazil, for example, one of the world's most ambitious open banking frameworks is under development.

Using the experience of a crosstech, a Neobank could establish an agreement with commercial partners to provide services such as international funds transfers or currency exchange. The industry is experiencing all these shifts, which will increase even outside of Europe and the UK, where regulations are most advanced.

392 Leading neobanks in Africa: top 7 digital-only banks; PaySpace Magazine, January 22, 2021 - https://bit.ly/3Pwf319
393 Everyone wants to be a bank: The Big Story, Why fintechs want to become banks; Protocol, March 5, 2021 - https://bit.ly/3w9TE6Y
394 Jeroen de Bel, Benjamin Kral, Santiago Egas, Nadia Benaissa: Banca Digital en América Latina; BPC Banking Technologies y Fintech Consultancy Group (Fincog),201 - https://bit.ly/3QOUgH5

Furthermore, Neobanks are offering bank account services in different currencies and converting them, thus entering the foreign exchange business. They all will eventually end up trading with cryptocurrencies and becoming crypto-exchange business competitors.

In terms of foreign exchange services, some Neobanks are providing bank account services in different currencies and allowing currency conversion between them. Some are offering the purchase or sale of cryptocurrencies, such as stablecoins, which would also make them competitors in the cryptocurrency exchange business.

The Covid pandemic allowed Neobanks to evolve rapidly and strengthen their relationship with users, making this global crisis an opportunity to grow. In this regard, Eric Barbier, member of the board of directors of the STC of Saudi Arabia, one of the largest digital banks in the country, stated:

> STC was doing well but Covid made us grow much more: branches were closed and clients were forced to use technology. In my experience with remittances, it is a bit complicated if you want to innovate because we are not targeting the most literate people. Users had to learn to send money through their mobile phone because there was no other solution for a while. People who send money generally do not change their habits, they know a company and they know that their money is delivered to the beneficiary without any problem, they cannot afford to change companies and wait for the money to arrive because the money may not reach their destination. The beneficiary might have to change habits too, so they are afraid to take risks. Payment expectations are very high for remittance senders and as a user, you don't want to innovate, that's why I think the pandemic was very good for innovation[395].

THE FUTURE OF DERISKING AND DEBANKING[396]

The contentious relationship between banks and NBFIs when we are dealing with the provision of bank accounts is a completely different matter from the partnerships mentioned before. I extensively reviewed the history of derisking, and now we must ask: *Will Derisking and Debanking significantly change in this decade?*

---

395 Virtual interview with Eric Barbier, April 11, 2022, recorded and transcribed by Isabel Cortés.
396 Hugo Cuevas-Mohr: Derisking o Debanking; Llegaremos a una solución?- Crosstech Blog, junio 16, 2021 - https://bit.ly/3bS9psy

> Derisking and debanking will continue to be an issue affecting the provision of financial services to cross-border payment companies.

According to analysts, regulators must address derisking, as has been demanded for almost two decades. *Is it going to happen?* Certainly not in many countries since it is not considered a major problem. However, many industry consultants, like me, spend a large portion of their time seeking and consulting for banks willing to provide banking services to crosstechs and helping crosstechs obtain bank accounts, both in their domestic markets and in the US and Europe.

A simple solution, as it has been discussed in Australia (see Chapter 2) would be for banks and NBFIs to report account closures to the regulator so they can intervene or investigate and determine what happened, the reasons, and the arguments. *Is it possible for the regulator to force the financial institution to open an account?* Almost certainly not, but it could provide an important view of this inconvenient truth.

THE FEDWIRE, RTP AND FEDNOW BATTLEFRONT

Access to banking rails by fintechs is a confrontational issue in the US. Still, with the necessary precautions and clear requirements, as European regulations seek to do, moving forward with Open Banking and Fast Payments seems to be the only path to follow to lower costs, speed payments, and break down the barriers to entry for innovative players.

In Unfiltered, Paiak Vaid commented: *Open banking payments are already a fact of life in Europe. In the US, not so much. It's a classic tortoise-and-hare tale. The EU is the hare that bolted from the starting line and maintained a rapid pace ever since. That's left the US playing the tortoise, consistently lagging behind. Europe is still streets ahead in terms of adoption. Spurred on by regulatory mandates and robust ecosystems, Europe hit 12.2m open banking users in 2020. That's nearly half of all global users*[397].

---

397 Paiak Vaid: Europe's open banking is leaving the US in the dust; Unfiltered, May 3, 2022 - https://bit.ly/45nzeq2

The Federal Reserve Banks in the US approve the connection to the national interbank rail systems as well as the newer systems being implemented and tested, from FedWire, Real Time Payments (RTPs) to FedNow.

After submitting its intentions and receiving dozens of comments, the Federal Reserve Board published new guidelines[398] on August 15, 2022. The intentions were to establish a transparent, risk-based, and consistent set of factors for Reserve Banks to use in reviewing requests to access Federal Reserve accounts and payment services. At the same time, new legislation requires the Fed to create a database of institutions that hold or have applied for access to Federal Reserve accounts and payment services.

The new database showed 28 pending applications; one of the oldest was filed in October 2020 by Kraken Financial, which has a Wyoming SPDI charter and is affiliated with Kraken, the world's third-largest cryptocurrency exchange. Two rejected applicants are Custodia Bank (former Avanti) and PayServices, a fintech facilitating international money transfers for the export and import of commodities by small and medium-sized businesses. The delays and rejection have led to regulatory and political jousting and litigation[399].

In a July 12, 2021, letter[400] to Ann E. Misback of the Fed Board of Governors, Kraken (Payward Inc.) complained about the guidelines and the grounds for denials, stating: *Given their vagueness, these denials could be based on any number of grounds that are just as likely to be politically-driven as prudential. Even then, there are no assurances that Reserve Banks will apply the factors consistently. They [the guidelines] will serve as hollow justifications for denial.*

There is no clear sight if or when the US Fed will approve access for fintechs and other alternative banking companies. The barriers to entry continue in place. Fintechs can access the Fed accounts and payment services facilities through already approved banks. The question is: *What is preventing fintechs and traditional NBFIs from establishing these partnerships with banks?*

---

398 Press Release: Federal Reserve Board announces final guidelines that establish a transparent, risk-based, and consistent set of factors for Reserve Banks to use in reviewing requests to access Federal Reserve accounts and payment services; August 15, 2022 - https://bit.ly/3cCBXGU
399 Emily Mason: Fintech And Crypto Firms Stew And Sue As Fed Moves Into The 21st Century without them; Forbes, August 10, 2023 - https://bit.ly/3Q9r9RB
400 Kraken (Payward Inc.): Letter to Ann E. Misback, Secretary, Board of Governors of the Federal Reserve System RE: Proposed Guidelines for Evaluating Account and Services Requests (Docket No. OP-1747), July 12, 2021 - https://bit.ly/3RSTHQm

The question is also: *What deter banks from establishing these partnerships with fintechs and traditional NBFIs?* The answers might be the same: *regulatory uncertainty and the lack of transparency by regulators and examiners.* In a panel that I moderated one panelist raised a question: *Are banks behind the unwillingness of the regulators to find a solution?*

The creation by the Fed of a Novel Activities Supervision Program (NASP)[401] in October 2023 *will focus on understanding novel activities related to crypto-assets, distributed ledger technology (DLT), and complex, technology-driven partnerships with nonbanks to deliver financial services to customers.* NASP might primarily look at domestic payments; I hope they also look at cross-border payment services.

International Financial Entities (IFEs) —also called International Banking Entities (IBEs)— international banks licensed in Puerto Rico, have long attempted to connect with the Fed but have not been granted master accounts; they have been forced to look for correspondent banks with just a handful of them obtaining them. Most of them are inactive or folded. FinCEN's first enforcement action against a Puerto Rican IFE was announced on September 15, 2023. FinCEN assessed a $15 million civil money penalty against Bancrédito for willful violations of the Bank Secrecy Act (BSA) and its implementing regulations[402]. Libertarian magnate Peter Schiff's Euro Pacific Bank's closure in September 2022, following a joint action of five countries[403], does not improve the situation of IFEs, nor the financial stability of the island, which is facing an all-round crisis[404].

RTPs in domestic markets are important for further developing digital cross-border payments as they are critical as the first and last mile. To quote Erick Schneider, a digitization expert: *crosstech companies depend on banks to access the traditional financial system and on fast payments to lower costs and speed payments.*

---

401 SR 23-7: Creation of Novel Activities Supervision Program, Board of Governors of The Federal Reserve System, August 8, 2023 - https://bit.ly/45psJ5U
402 FinCEN Announces $15 Million Civil Money Penalty against Bancrédito International Bank and Trust Corporation for Violations of the Bank Secrecy Act, September 15, 2023 - https://bit.ly/3RL6MeB
403 Frances Robles: Peter Schiff Has a Deal With Puerto Rico to Liquidate His Euro Pacific Bank, He Says; NY Times, aug. 9, 2022 - https://nyti.ms/3SILbkp
404 Amelia Cheatham, Diana Roy: Puerto Rico: A US Territory in Crisis; Council on Foreign Relations, September 29, 2022 - https://on.cfr.org/3ylDfha

Banking institutions in the US that understand the benefits of partnering with fintechs and develop very tight relations that enhance the existing compliance requirements —and the lack of transparency and guidance of federal agencies— will likely create win-win partnerships that can impact the industry. Hopefully, we can witness this change on the road to 2030.

INTEGRATING SERVICES AND PARTNERING

One of the major trends in the industry over the current decade is the incorporation of products and services into the money transfer portfolios of crosstechs and the incorporation of cross-border payment services by other service providers. Companies will use different approaches depending on the markets they serve or want to serve, whether they are in origination or destination countries or decide to operate on both ends of the corridor. The use of intermediaries in integrating these services is also an important component in the ease and cost of these service integrations.

I will categorize these *integrations* to help understand the most important trends. Some companies combine one or more categories horizontally and vertically. The ease or difficulty of entry barriers, such as regulations or finding available business partners, play a role in the supply of the different services and products. As these barriers are lifted, product and service integration will speed up change:

1. Domestic Payments and Cross-Border Payments
2. Embedded Finance
3. Integration of Complementary Services
4. Integration of Communication and Payment Services
5. eCommerce and Payments

DOMESTIC PAYMENTS AND CROSS-BORDER PAYMENTS

I already mentioned the importance of domestic fast payment solutions for further developing digital cross-border payments as they are critical as the first and last mile.

Some payment fintechs have been able to grow in local markets, gaining customers who use their domestic services regularly, whether it is a mobile payment, a prepaid card, or an associated mobile application (a virtual wallet or a connection to a bank account). The same fintech may be inclined to offer cross-border payment services as well.

A few MMOs in Africa have incorporated cross-border payments into their domestic services offering, sometimes only on the recipient side (remittance deposits) and, increasingly, both sending and receiving services. Fintechs located in remittance destination countries can funnel payments into cards, mobile wallets, bank accounts or agents, establishing commercial alliances with local institutions.

For fintechs in remittance source countries, the institution can integrate international payments into its local offering, partnering with a crosstech, as Walmart (WM) did with Walmart2Walmart (US domestic) and Walmart2World (international). The key to WM's success was to offer financial services in their customer service counters that manage claims and returns, reducing and transforming this cost center by adding a revenue stream. Many retail chains have tried to incorporate money transfers as part of their offerings with inconsistent success.

Elektra's success in Mexico with remittances is widely recognized. Elektra combined the sale of appliances with international payment services, which worked for both the company and the beneficiaries, who were able to use remittances to make purchases or down payments. In Central America, Costa Rican Importadora Monge, owner of well-known retail chains like El Gallo más Gallo, set up a remittance business using its large regional store footprint. During a meeting I moderated between their CEO and World Bank Payments Area representatives, he commented that the bank that provided credit lines to the group feared that family remittances would pose a risk, and they were forced to shut down the service. Even if it was not a money-maker, the company was happy to help remittance families with safe and convenient ways to receive their remittances in the stores. Another case of bank derisking that will never be part of any statistic.

White Label Service (WLS) offerings are important to expand the integration of cross-border payment solutions into apps. There is a large variety of WLS offerings in the market, and new ones are coming online. Some of them are basically technological integrations, while others provide a full range of services, including licensing, KYC, risk management, AML compliance, fraud prevention and liability, customer service, etc. Several terms are used by providers of WLSs, including RaaS (Remittance-as-a-Service) in the P2P segment and PaaS Payment-as-a-Service) for business payments.

Some cross-border payment institutions with a large client base in their home country (remittance families) will be the ones that will mostly benefit from WLS as they can enter markets in countries and regions where their diasporas are located. Cebuana, a leading remittance payment company in the Philippines, has ventured into the US market using a WLS provider[405]. Bantrab, a Central American bank, has partnered with Uniteller to enter the US[406].

European WLSs are also coming online. Looking for the best WLS partner is still a complex undertaking that needs a detailed analysis to evaluate the pros and cons. In the next few years as early adopters reap the newcomer benefits, and successful initiatives and partnerships are developed, WLS will become more common in the industry.

EMBEDDED FINANCE

Embedded Finance (EFin) is the integration of financial services like payment processing, lending, or insurance products into non-financial offerings. Some embedded financial services have been around for a while, like company-branded credit cards and payment plans for high-priced items, such as *Buy Now, Pay Later* (BNPL) services in shopping sites. EFin is also the integration of financial services that require special licensing into payment offerings. Crosstechs are integrating savings, investing, debit card use, etc. into their apps.

If EFin services have been around, why are they trending? It is because technology is making it easier for any company to improve their customer experiences by adding financial service offerings —an added revenue stream — and this huge market opportunity for businesses is expected to produce $384.8B in revenue by 2029—a nearly 17x increase over the $22.5B in revenue generated in 2020.

EFin is enabled by third-party *banking-as-a-service* companies that use API integrations to embed financial services into the user experience

---

405 Pangea Partners with Cebuana Lhuillier to Simplify Remittances in the Philippines; Business Insider, July 2, 2019 - https://bit.ly/3rLw6CZ
406 Remesas Bantrab - Uniteller - https://bit.ly/3MowK2B

of other financial as well as non-financial companies. The are two examples worth noting that Tom Sullivan, a fintech industry writer, presents in a Plaid Blog[407]:

- The ride-sharing app Lyft offers a checking account and associated debit card exclusively to its drivers. Using this account, drivers can get paid immediately after every ride rather than have to wait weeks to get a lump sum payment. They can then spend those funds from their Lyft debit card and get cash back and rewards.
- Shopify Balance allows Shopify store owners to *skip the bank* by getting paid faster and eliminating the need to open a separate business bank account. It also offers a debit card with exclusive rewards for purchases made towards growing their Shopify business.

Cross-border payment companies are also actively pursuing EFin deals. WU has partnered with Google Pay, initially in the US, India and Singapore, to offer seamless peer-to-peer in-app money transfer experience[408]. WU has also partnered with STC Pay[409], a subsidiary of Saudi Telecom Company (STC), a company where WU invested $200 M for a 15% stake. WU is also using EFin entering in an agreement with BNPL fintech Beforepay to enable its clients, access to short-term lending[410].

These in-app experiences are very common in China. *Super apps* – a term sometimes loosely used – are based on mini-programs, lightweight applications that run inside another and allow one app to do the work of many. The mere existence of many different types of products and services in a mobile application does not necessarily make it a Super App[411].

Within a decade, Chinese WeChat super app has become one of the strongest global brands with 1.32 billion monthly active users or 80% of

---

407 Tom Sullivan: What is embedded finance? 4 ways it will change fintech; Plaid Blog, October 3, 2022 - https://bit.ly/3LRlooS
408 Western Union Launches Cross-Border Payments on Google Pay; Press Release, May 11, 2021 - https://bit.ly/3F8pbuh
409 Western Union and STC Pay Collaborate; WU Press Release, October 3, 2018 - https://bit.ly/3ZK6s1J
410 Western Union, Beforepay team on 'send now, pay later' offering; FinTech Global, February 27, 2023 - https://bit.ly/3rI6udP
411 Ron Shevlin: Super Apps Aren't Going To Make It In America; Forbes, August 1, 2022 - https://bit.ly/3BdGRSQ

China's total population[412]. For its clients, the super app is a survival tool: it is the home screen for social media, money exchange, shopping, ride-hailing, food delivery, dating, and much more, such as payments and cross-border payments. WeChat achieved an 88% daily usage rate and a penetration rate of 89% in its mini-programs in 2022. It might not be able to hold its place in the market with competition stepping-up their game and the Chinese government cracking down on big tech monopolies.

Other successful super apps are motorcycle ridesharing app Gojek, mobile payment platform Alipay, mobile food and package delivery app Grab, and mobile payments and financial app Paytm[413].

dLocal, the first Uruguayan unicorn, is a crosstech founded by Andrés Bzurovski and Sergio Fogel in 2016 with initial operations in Brazil, Colombia, Argentina, Chile and Mexico to later expand in Uruguay, Paraguay, Peru, Ecuador, Bolivia and rest of the world. The service allows fintechs, marketplaces, and other companies to charge customers in multiple markets using local options adapted to the end user. In June 2021, it made its IPO and was valued at US $6 billion, starting at US $21 per share, a price that reached US $70 in a few months to drop in 2022 back to the initial quote.

INTEGRATING COMPLIMENTARY SERVICES

MTOs have been integrating complimentary services into their service offerings for quite some time now, especially digital-first ones. At one point, remittances (P2P) was the only service provided. However, new options were introduced: cross-border phone recharges or Top-Ups (crediting minutes to a cell phone account in a different country) and later making bill payments at the destination (P2B).

Discussing market growth, I presented an estimated increase in P2B (C2B) payments of 81% for 2030, from $3.1tn in 2030 to $5.6tn at the end of the decade.

XOOM, a P2P provider, acquired BlueKite (a P2B provider) in 2014 for US $15 million[414], a fintech that developed a novel way to pay bills abroad.

---

412 Lai Lin Thomala: Leading startup in China: WeChat - statistics & facts; Statista, August 31, 2023 - https://bit.ly/3F6v4rI
413 Ben Lutkevich: super apps; WhatIs.com, October 2023 - https://bit.ly/3rLM97p
414 Press Release: XOOM Corporation Acquires BlueKite; BlueKite Team Brings Expertise in Cross-Border Bill Pay, Mobile Phone Top-Up Payments; February 4, 2014 - https://bit.ly/3e8lYRk

Bobby Aitkenhead, BlueKite's CEO, subsequently led XOOM Bill Pay and XOOM Top Up (recharges). Other crosstech companies have chosen WLS such as Reloadly or DT One, which offer top-up services to many fintechs.

Cross-border business-to-person payments (B2P) are also growing rapidly, expected to increase by 88%, from $1.7tn to $3.2tn. As firms that contract services overseas, hire remote workers, pay commissions, etc., have emerged in the market, the demand for B2P payment providers has flourished. Thousands of individuals, with the most varied skills, offer their specialties from anywhere on the globe on marketplaces such as Upwork and Fiverr.

Upwork was founded in 2015 through the merger of oDesk (founded in 2003) and Elance (1998). In 2022, Upwork was the world's largest service marketplace platform with revenues of US $374 million, 150,000 customers, and US $2.5 billion[415]. Fiverr, more oriented to creative jobs, has 3.4 million companies as clients and generated US $700 million in sales in 2020 with annual earnings of US $190 million[416]. A Fiverr designer created this book's cover, and an Upwork designer did the layout.

Fintech companies are increasingly offering payment services to individuals in more and more markets. Rapyd, Tipalti, PMI Americas, TransferMate, PMI Americas, are competitors in a segment with a growing specialization and potential for expansion.

An example of an integration of P2B and B2B payments is the advanced system conceived by Flywire. The fintech developed in 2009 by Spanish entrepreneur Iker Marcaide, previously known as peerTransfer, was initially designed to solve the problem of international students in the US[417]. It was a typical situation: a Chinese student had to pay his annual tuition at Boston University. With a wire transfer, he couldn't determine how much the institution would credit his college account and ensure it was posted before the deadline. By solving the problems of students and universities one by one, peerTransfer became the preferred option and captured a large part of the

---

415 Luisa Zhou: Upwork Revenue, User, and Growth Statistics (2022); January 6, 2022 - https://bit.ly/3AAl2wv
416 Brian Dean: Fiverr Usage and Growth Statistics: How Many People Use Fiverr in 2022?; apr. 20, 2021- https://bit.ly/3CK6zRf
417 Jeff Kauflin: Startup Raises $100 Million To Allow College, Hospital And Business Bills To Be Paid In Foreign Currency; Forbes, July 26, 2018 - https://bit.ly/3Asq2Da

college market share in the US The company was rebranded as Flywire[418] in 2015 and received new investments and the necessary funding to expand into new markets like hospitals and businesses in need of cross-border payments. It will certainly continue to grow.

Many financial service institutions are now dealing with the decision to provide services directly to consumers, individuals or businesses, or to offer them to other companies, as WLS, either outside or within their sector. Direct-to-consumer businesses rely heavily on their brand as a primary asset. Creating it and keeping it at the *top of mind* involves high advertising costs in highly saturated and competitive markets.

I believe, however, that the most significant development we will see in this decade will be fintechs solving *pain points* for customer-facing companies. The recent development of aggregators is an example of these B2B fintechs that provide back-office solutions to customer-facing companies. Euronet's RIA is now offering the cross-border network it has developed since the founding of the company in 1987, for banks and businesses, with a new service and a new brand: Dandelion.

Although there will continue to be large NBFIs developing the entire payment chain and striving to provide in-house solutions, new *back-office fintechs* are partnering with *customer-facing firms* to enhance their capabilities, including operational and functional, financial and treasury, distribution and market expansion, regulatory compliance, technology, and cybersecurity.

INTEGRATING PAYMENT AND COMMUNICATION SERVICES

In the industry, the integration of communication and cross-border payments have always existed, going back to the origins of the industry with agents having calling booths, offering calling cards and top-ups etc. Migrants needed both services, and they still do. As a result, remittance companies incorporated communication services in the origination countries. Sometime later, communication companies in the destination countries incorporated payment services.

When Digital-First MTOs appeared most of them were eager to offer communication products and the availability of Top-up or Mobile Reload

---

418 Press Release: peerTransfer Expands in US and Europe; Rebrands as Flywire; September 16, 2015 - https://bwnews.pr/3AVSizI

providers made these partnerships successful for WorldRemit, WU, and others. Xoom, besides sending money, offers mobile reloads through DT One.

DT One began as Transfer-To, founded in 2005 to offer mobile top-ups to MTOs and other companies. It began offering money transfer services in 2015 and announced in 2019 that it would split its communications and payment services into two separate entities: DT One, driving the company's growth with recharges and rewards, and Thunes, a new P2P cross-border payment service[419]. Thunes is one of the industry's largest aggregators.

Eric Barbier, a TransferTo founder recalls the journey in an interview for this book:

> I started my career in 1999, working at a company that manufactured SIM cards. I worked on the software that goes inside the SIM card, we were building the first services that added value to mobile phones. With my partners, we had the idea of Mobile 365, a global SMS (Short Message Service) network that connected different mobile providers in the world with Content Providers. Our first client was Yahoo! After the Mobile 365 sale, I found a business opportunity in the Philippines by helping people send their family and friends a recharge of US $1, $2 or $5 from another country and we created the first TransferTo product. It was an additional service that didn't compete with traditional remittances, allowing the sending of a few dollars at a low cost. Then we decided to get into the remittance business; It was a logical step. The idea was to create a remittance hub which we did[420].

There has been a lot of speculation about the entrance of the most widely used communication App in the world (outside China), WhatsApp, into the payments sector. The smartphone messaging app was created by Brian Acton and Jan Koum in 2009 and in just two years it was handling one billion messages every day. Facebook, now Meta, acquired it for US $19 billion in February 2014, its largest purchase ever and one of the highest-value technology acquisitions in history. The app is undoubtedly the most popular among migrants worldwide[421].

---

419 Press Release: TransferTo announces rebrand with the creation of two market defining companies: DT One and Thunes; February 18, 2019 - https://bit.ly/3wJeNW6
420 Virtual interview, recorded and transcribed, with Eric Barbier, April 11, 2022, by Isabel Cortés.
421 Tamlin Magee: 'It's a WhatsApp life': how the messaging app became a critical financial service; Raconteur, November 25, 2021 - https://bit.ly/3AAydxt

Is it possible for WhatsApp to conquer the payments market? WhatsApp has been unable to launch its payments button[422]. The company has attempted to enter Brazil's and India's markets, but both have been filled with regulatory obstacles, often politically motivated. I believe this showed a severe lack of strategic management and handling the concerns about the potential monopoly that might exist. Novi, WhatsApp wallet pilot program, launched in the US December 2021[423] but months after, both the Novi app and Novi on WhatsApp were closed in September 2022. I guess the vision of using crypto was also a reason for its shutdown. I consulted briefly with Novi, and my main question never got an answer: *Why not partner with various local strategic partners for payments in specific countries and run pilots to test the system and make improvements over time?*

Google Pay, Samsung Pay, Apple Pay, Amazon Pay, and Alipay, are developing their domestic payment systems. Whether and how they will enter the cross-border payments industry is unknown. It is unlikely that they will have a greater impact unless they develop business partnerships with industry participants and integrate services.

Can China's largest mobile app, with over 1.6 billion monthly active users worldwide as of 2023, succeed beyond its borders? WeChat was launched in 2011 as Weixin, Mandarin for *micro-messaging* as a simple messaging app comparable to WhatsApp. WeChat was developed by Chinese technology giant Tencent, one of the world's most valuable companies. Tencent has become one of the country's largest investors, second only to Sequoia China, with hundreds of stakes in other companies such as Snapchat, Fortnite and Tesla Motors.

The only app in China to exceed one billion users is WeChat, and it is among the five apps globally to achieve that feat[424]. Unlike WhatsApp, WeChat successfully developed a payment system, WeChat Pay, which reached 900 million active users by 2021. WeChat Pay has displaced Alibaba Group's AliPay as China's most popular mobile payment system. Using WeChat Pay and Alipay has become a part of daily life for Chinese people.

---

[422] George Iddenden: Meta suffers new setback with WhatsApp payment plans; Charged Retail, April 20, 2022 - https://bit.ly/3RFwyxJ
[423] Meta extends Novi payments trial to WhatsApp; Finextra, December 9, 2021 - https://bit.ly/3Cjz6LB
[424] Mansoor Iqbal: WeChat Revenue and Usage Statistics (2022), Business of Apps, updated August 15, 2022 - https://bit.ly/3AAMTfZ

An interesting strategy of WeChat is to host thousands of mini-applications, such as Pinduoduo, JD.com, DiDi, and mini-apps, such as Pinduoduo, JD.com, DiDi, and Meituan, all very popular in China. By providing the payment platform, WeChat earns revenue from each of these mini-programs.

WeChat and AliPay are currently expanding to nearby countries and in other continents. At first, WeChat's strategy was to provide Chinese tourists with a payment method for their vacation trips. Therefore, through local agreements, they can use WeChat Pay at duty-free stores and malls in their favorite cities. The company has partnered with a local fintech, Tramonex, to enter the UK market. Consequently, an international transaction is generated by each payment of Chinese tourists.

As for remittances, WeChat launched WeRemit in Hong Kong to enable migrants from Indonesia and the Philippines to send money to their relatives partnering with EMQ[425], an aggregator that integrates correspondents throughout the region to process remittances. AliPay has also developed its platform and the two are competing in Hong Kong[426]. In Singapore, WeChat has teamed up with local fintech AletaPay to offer payments in China[427] for more than 400,000 Chinese residents. In Korea, the company has partnered with WireBarley; thus, the fintech will be able to process remittances to China from these countries: US, Australia, New Zealand, Canada, the UK, France, Germany, Italy, Netherlands, and Ireland[428].

WeChat use is growing in many countries; it has over 2 million users in the US, most of them Chinese migrants. A WeChat deal with US fintech Paysend will also expand this crosstech's payment services to China[429].

---

425 Press Release: EMQ Partners with WeChat Pay HK to Expand Remittance Services in Southeast Asia, November 17, 2017 - https://bwnews.pr/3B04Fe9
426 Fanny Potkin, Venus Wu: Tencent & Alibaba chase remittances in battle for Southeast Asia, Reuters, September 27, 2018 - https://reut.rs/3e4qArv
427 Tyler Pathe: Singapore Residents Can Now Send Money to Weixin Users in Mainland China, The Fintech Times, December 13, 2021 - https://bit.ly/3Rpoukw
428 PYMNTS: Korean FinTech WireBarley Collaborates With TenCent on Payments to China; February 15, 2022 - https://bit.ly/3TuM4Ol
429 PYMNTS: Paysend, Tencent Collaborate on Cross-Border Payments; December 29, 2021 - https://bit.ly/3RmmB8a

> **I hope every crosstech dealing with the China market is making sure that their systems know how *to dot all the i's and cross all the t's*. Big Brother is certainly watching.**

The complexity of handling payments to China has caused many headaches for companies in the West, as evidenced by Operation Emperor, which involved allegations of money laundering at MTO agencies. This operation dismantled a huge network in Spain and other countries, affecting hundreds of businesses and industries and involving Chinese businessman Gao Ping[430].

WU was sanctioned by the federal government for its transactions with China - including human trafficking - in 2017 (US $586 million[431]) 643) and the state of New York in 2018 (US $60 million[432]). In March 2022, MGI was fined US $8.25 million for failing to monitor agents in New York sending remittances to China[433]. I concur with many risk analysts that the Chinese market poses a great deal of risk to all financial companies, including MTOs and FECs.

Over the next ten years, the continued competition between WeChat Pay and AliPay and their expansion into other markets will be very dynamic, and the potential for growth of the fintechs partnering with them is huge. However, geopolitical tensions between the Asian giant and the rest of the world might curtail this progress.

MOBILE MONEY AND WALLETS

Integrating Payment and Communication Services has been the essence of MMOs. MMOs' presence in Africa and Asia as remittance-payers and remittance-senders will continue to grow. MMOs such as M-Pesa, MFS Africa, Airtel, Terrapay, and Orange will continue to develop cross-border

---

430 Heriberto Araújo, Juan Pablo Cardenal: Chinese mafia's "state within a state"; El País (Madrid), October 24, 2012 - https://bit.ly/3S4pdat
431 Department of Justice: Western Union Admits Anti-Money Laundering and Consumer Fraud Violations, Forfeits $586 Million in Settlement with Justice Department and Federal Trade Commission, January 19, 2017 - https://bit.ly/3Org8qA
432 Western Union Financial Services, Inc. Resolves Previously Disclosed Investigation by New York Department of Financial Services, WU Press Release, January 04, 2018 - https://bit.ly/48Z71cc
433 MoneyGram Fined $8 Million in NY Over China Transfers Oversight; Bloomberg Law, March 16, 2022 - https://bit.ly/3Tbnu4B

payment options and build partnerships with fintechs at the origin and destination, an ongoing evolution throughout this decade.

Mobile wallets processed over $16 billion in remittances in 2021, despite only making up 3% of the total global volume[434] according to the GSMA. By the end of this decade, I am confident they will exceed 12 to 15%, accounting for their growth and the fact that remittances to Mobile Operators are the cheapest, 4.5%, while MTOs are at 5.4%, Post Offices at 6.3% and Banks at 11.8%[435].

Interregional remittances in Africa and Asia will be the major reason for this expansion. In Asia, MMOs will increase their market share in Indonesia, Thailand, and Vietnam and in sending countries such as Malaysia and Singapore; the expansion of digital ecosystems will lead to easier cross-border payments and, as a result, a significant increase in their market share.

For users of smartphones, the difference between mobile wallets and digital or e-wallets is minimal. Mobile Operators implement Mobile Wallets using their platforms; digital wallets are apps that connect to the cloud, but users may not necessarily use them on mobile devices, and they are offered normally by fintechs.

According to GSMA, Latin American mobile operators entered the market in 2020, such as Telefónica Brazil with its Vivo Pay virtual wallet, in partnership with banks or financial technology companies. A few examples are provided: Claro Brazil and Banco Inbursa, owned by the same company, launched Claro Pay; AT&T Mexico, in collaboration with Broxel, launched AT&T ReMo and Movistar Mexico and Banco Sabadell joined forces to develop Movistar Money[436].

The barriers to entry in Central and South America have been significant. Tigo Money has been seeking to compete in markets such as Honduras, El Salvador, Guatemala, Bolivia, Paraguay, and Panama for many years and has had to deal with many bumps along the way. Most governments prefer to protect their banking institutions rather than develop financial inclusion

---

434 GSMA: State of the Industry Report on Mobile Money 2022 - https://bit.ly/3KkSR9c
435 KNOMAD: Remittances Remain Resilient but Are Slowing; Migration and Development Brief 38, June 2023 pp.8 - https://bit.ly/3PPB7Gb
436 GSMA: La Economía Móvil en América Latina 2021 - https://bit.ly/3qowrLl

through MMOs. In a letter[437] from Mauricio Ramos, CEO of Millicom TIGO highlighting the importance of the Covid pandemic to spur change, it expressed the need for dialogue to bring down barriers: *The time has come for Telecommunications providers to continue to work closely with governments and legislative bodies to develop also long-term solutions to bridge the digital gap.*

Piero P. Coen, president of AirPak, explains his experience with digital wallets and the growth they have found after the appearance of Covid:

> We are operating with our digital wallet in Nicaragua and Costa Rica, and we are adapting it to Guatemala, El Salvador, and Honduras. Mexico will be next. The growth has been more aggressive than we had imagined; the Covid pandemic changed clients' behavior out of necessity or convenience. We have also made the service more friendly: the fewer steps, the better. We have earned trust since we have been paying WU remittances for many years. We have also grown our clientele with the functionalities we add to the digital wallet. We are even seeing that they are using us as savings: I mean that they leave their money in the wallet. They know that we do not pay them interest, but instead of having the money under the mattress, their money is kept safe in the wallet[438].

In North America, Europe, and other regions (i.e., Australia, New Zealand), digital wallet success is unpredictable due to the popularity of different payment apps. Despite the tremendous growth of digital payments, whether domestic or cross-border, a wallet may not necessarily be preferred over all the other options available now or in the future.

What advantages can wallets develop to encourage digital payment users to adopt them? What advantages can they offer over leading remittances and payments apps? Can migrants' use of wallets make a difference in the market?

Remittance apps such as Remitly offer cross-border payments to an increasing number of wallets around the world, mostly Asia and Africa: M-Pesa, MTN Mobile Money, Airtel, GCash, bKash, PayMaya, Gopay, Paga, OVO, Vodafone, eSewa, Link Aja, EZ Cash, EU Mobile, Coins.ph, Dana, helloCash, Vimo, Orange Money, Tigo and DaviPlata.

---

437 Mauricio Ramos: COVID-19 could widen the digital gap. Here is what is needed now, Millicom TIGO - https://bit.ly/46M1a85

438 Virtual Interview with Piero P. Coen on July 5, 2022, conducted, recorded and transcribed by Lucía Salazar.

Will MTOs decide to launch their wallets in partnerships with other fintechs, or will wallets just integrate a *money transfer send button* to their offerings? Whichever way is done, the use of wallets for cross-border payments will increase in the next few years.

Welcome Tech has developed a virtual wallet specifically for Hispanic migrants in the US After launching SABEResPODER, co-founders Amir Hemmat and Raul Lomeli raised investments totaling US$73 million for further development and market expansion[439].

Wallets are more than payment channels, and their use as marketing tools will also increase their usage. A report from Forrester Research predicts the payment options of mobile wallets transformation into a viable marketing channel will be a driver for change in developed markets[440]. This can also be true in developing markets and wallets designed for migrants.

ECOMMERCE AND PAYMENTS

Even before the pandemic, eCommerce, the process of buying goods and services online or via mobile devices and picking them up or dropping them off at home or office, was booming. As a result of the pandemic, people with some eCommerce experience were very inclined to expand its use, but more remarkably, it brought thousands of new users who ventured out to try and learn.

Also, as a result of the crisis, countless businesses started to offer their products online, both locally and internationally, dramatically expanding their product range. Therefore, the payments industry, responsible for moving money between buyers and sellers, and their intermediaries in the chain, saw a huge increase in funds transferred and consequently in commissions and fees. Providing easy payment methods, channel options, and other payment or shipping alternatives has become a guarantee of success for eCommerce companies.

The predicted growth of B2B Ecommerce from $10tn in 2023 to 21.9tn in 2030, a 119% increase, will drive up investment in this sector. Companies that entered the world of eCommerce had the chance to choose from marketplaces (online shopping malls) or operate independently. Whatever the

---

439 Press Releases: News from Welcome Technologies; PR Newswire - https://prn.to/3ExWzLK
440 Alex Samuely: Mobile wallets are more marketing channel than payments, Mobile Commerce Daily, 2017 - https://bit.ly/3GyQwrr

way of accessing the market, local, regional, and international fintechs have developed interconnections to make payments and accept debit, credit and prepaid cards, access to bank payments, cash or installments, mobile wallets, and even cash payments through agents. Consequently, this has encouraged innovation and curiosity about customer preferences. Competition implies lowering costs, and there are plenty of opportunities for the segment to mature. The race to increase volume and ensure survival will give us some losers and, certainly, many winners.

Marketing research firm Juniper Research predicts[441] by mid-decade eCommerce market size in 2023 will be $5.3tn, increasing to $8.0tn in 2027, a market growth of 51.4%. This estimate is lower than the FXC's predictions, placing the current market size of 2023 at $10tn.

The massive Juniper Research report is based on a regional-level analysis of 17 countries in 8 key regions; a key forecast of 60 countries covering the state of Ecommerce, preferred payment methods, legislation, and regulations. Also, it analyzes payment vendors' capabilities and a capacity assessment for key players from ACI Worldwide, Adyen, and Amazon to Trustly, Verifone, and WePay. A complimentary whitepaper titled *How Alternative Payments are Disrupting eCommerce*[442], examines the benefits of providing the frictionless payment options that fintechs are developing for this sector.

Additionally, there are other types of payments in the service supply chain for eCommerce companies that do not directly involve the buyer but rather the means of delivery to the end user. A growing eCommerce industry has resulted in intense competition among shipping companies, from large companies to an increasing number of regional players; since these intermediary services must be paid, fintechs are also emerging to improve the efficiency of the reconciliation process, reduce costs, and be the best option for supply chains, couriers and brokers.

The tax and customs front, from fees to charge and payment collection, is complex and fintech creativity and innovation will certainly be at the heart of these developments. In this context, fintechs will play a crucial role in B2B

---

[441] Juniper Research: Ecommerce Payments Market: Trends, Analysis and Market Forecasts 2023-2027; May 2023 - https://bit.ly/3FbJhUz
[442] Juniper Research: How Alternative Payments are Disrupting Ecommerce, May 2023 - https://bit.ly/3trk3Pk

and B2G payments. This sector still faces many difficulties -and costs- and each solution will increase eCommerce's market size, speed, and profitability.

As for the last mile, the Covid pandemic expanded the number of companies providing home and office delivery services, contributing to global eCommerce's growth.

The vision of a not-so-distant future can be seen in developments such as IoTs (Internet-of-Things). Technology is allowing connected devices to communicate with the cloud and among themselves, enabling the efficient connection to payment systems.

Marketplaces, in turn, allow users to make local payments to their international suppliers via crosstechs that handle the cross-border segment of transactions. At one point, Amazon decided to pay its suppliers in China using specialized fintechs. Since then, it has let suppliers choose payment options from a wide range of Payment Service Providers (PSP) programs. In June 2022, Currenxie, a crosstech founded by Riccardo Capelvenere in 2014 in Hong Kong, announced[443] an agreement with Amazon as a global payments provider, enabling sellers on its platform to send and receive payments to and from more than 40 countries through a multi-currency virtual account without incurring any correspondent bank fees.

It is worth mentioning that Amazon has built a continuous strategy as an NFBI, providing financial services of all kinds, both in the US and in other countries[444]. As a reminder, Amazon launched its first payment product, *Pay with Amazon*, in 2007, the same year it acquired TextPayMe, a mobile P2P service that was relaunched as Amazon WebPay in 2012. Webpay was shut down in 2014, unlike Venmo (now part of PayPal), which managed to grow; Bill Me Later (I4 Commerce) was also acquired by PayPal in 2008, despite Amazon's investment the year before. It is not my intention to list all the acquisitions and exits this company has made but given the number of cross-border payments it generates (just like Chinese competitor Alibaba), I cannot ignore its relevance.

One of the company's primary business partners is WorldPay. It was founded in 1997 in the UK and acquired by FIS in March 2019 after several

---

[443] Currenxie joins Amazon's Payment Service Provider (PSP) Program; Bloomberg UK, June 28, 2022 - https://bloom.bg/3T5FOf6
[444] Everything you need to know about what Amazon is doing in 2022 financial services; CB Insights Report 2022 - https://bit.ly/3eeZEpC

iterations for US $43 billion (cash and stock). PayPal, which I have barely mentioned despite being the world's largest NBFI, still generates billions in cross-border payments. It accounted for 64% of all online payments in the US, followed by Visa Checkout with 22% and Amazon Pay in third place with 14%.

eCommerce competition increases the availability of cross-border payments. It is common now to see NBFIs, some of Chinese origin, being licensed in the US or Europe to bridge the gap between the vendor in one market and the manufacturer or distributor in another. The Asian giant is estimated to generate 37% of the world's eCommerce volume, demonstrating its potential for developing solutions worldwide. Geopolitical tensions could affect eCommerce at any moment; however, crises also create opportunities.

Migrants also play an important role in eCommerce, although they contribute a relatively small amount. The nostalgic products they remember from their homelands and wish to continue consuming, formerly found only in neighborhood stores where diasporas gathered, are now available online. The market is expanding, regardless of whether the product is imported or transported from origin to destination. Likewise, increasing racial and ethnic diversity in developed countries has led restaurant chains, food stores, and other businesses to offer exotic flavors and smells to appeal to a wider audience. A 2012 study[445] estimated that a 10% increase in a country's immigration would increase trade by 1.5% on average, resulting in a rise in cross-border payments.

Purchasing goods for delivery to their home countries is another way migrants provide for their families. This method, called *Cash to Goods* (CTG), allows migrants to order products to be delivered to their families through an agency or online. This product can be food - grains, grains, oil, etc. - construction materials or agricultural products. In an article for La Vanguardia, Josep Arroyo, a Catalan entrepreneur, called CTG, *The eCommerce of the Poor*[446]. Baluwo, his fintech in Spain, has developed a marketplace that offers African migrants secure, prompt, and efficient product delivery, as well as options for prepaid electricity services and call minutes.

---

[445] Migration and trade (last updated on 5 October 2021): Migration Data Portal - https://bit.ly/3CL1Hey
[446] Josep Arroyo: Cash-To-Goods, el eCommerce de los pobres; La Vanguardia, May 1, 2019 - https://bit.ly/3RcS64k

An article in the French newspaper Le Monde[447], commented in 2019 on the low traction of CTG services in Africa, where the sender would buy vouchers at the origin to be redeemed for products at a chain store, including discounts for the beneficiary. It appears that fintechs such as Afrimarket, Yenni, Moods or Mergims, which were expected to increase the US $48 million made by this sector before Covid, have failed to deliver. In other regions, such as in Latin America, vouchers have also failed to gain traction[448].

We must distinguish CTGs from IKRs (In-Kind Remittances), products taken by migrants to their native countries. Temporary migrants are entitled to take a limited amount of goods back to the country without customs duties. In many countries, these permits are also extended to parcel delivery services, which have given rise to the well-known *Balikbayan boxes* (Balikbayan in Tagalog means *the one who returns*) in the Philippines. These are government-approved boxes of a predetermined size, which can contain goods of any kind (with certain restrictions) sent by companies specializing in this type of shipping. In 2018, Filipinos shipped more than 400,000 Balikbayan boxes per month[449] according to the association representing these companies, DDCAP (Door To Door Consolidation Association of the Philippines), in constant negotiations with the Philippine government about regulating a service vital to thousands of migrants.

Latin American customs authorities are expected to analyze the importance of allowing migrants, particularly women, to send gifts to their relatives through these free-of-charge packages. Regulating the market would prevent the use of *baggage bribers* and travelers with suitcases who bribe airport employees to let dozens of suitcases through. In 2019, I actively participated in supporting Hispanic parcel entrepreneurs in the US to establish their association, ICSA, International Courier Services Association[450], based in Miami, enabling ICSA to be represented before regulatory authorities, and measures can be agreed upon among members for increased professionalization.

---

447 Marie des Verges: En Afrique, les espoirs déçus du "cash-to-goods"; Le Monde, dic 15, 2019 - https://bit.ly/3dYiQHw
448 Cash-to-goods services have evolved to meet the recurring and urgent financial needs of receivers but have yet to prove themselves (p. 53): in Demand analysis on remittances in West African Francophone countries: Côte d'Ivoire, Mali, and Senegal, Microsave Final report, October 2020 - https://bit.ly/3wESAID
449 Frank Shyong: These boxes are a billion-dollar industry of homesickness for Filipinos overseas; The Los Angeles Times, April 28, 2018 - https://lat.ms/3AU04Kz
450 International Courier Services Association - https://icsassociation.org/

Seeing a daughter's or a mother's picture wearing a new dress sent from abroad is not the same as sending money to buy it. However, the growing eCommerce sector will continue its steadfast march with the support of cross-border payment firms.

TRAVEL & TOURISM

The T&T industry reached $11.1tn in 2022 and is predicted to grow to $16.9tn by 2030. *The market's expansion is primarily attributable to the world's expanding air transportation networks, increased consumer spending power on travel-related expenses due to rising personal disposable income, and a steady rise in international tourist arrivals*[451]. The world tourism market has changed significantly; emerging economies hold a larger market share than developed ones, and this market share will continue to rise.

The relationship between the T&T industry and cross-border payments has been analyzed extensively. A country's Foreign Exchange Earnings (FEEs) are directly related to Foreign Tourist Arrivals (FTAs). They act similarly to exports and remittances, increasing the country's foreign reserves. FEEs come from payments made by tourists on goods and services such as tours, hotels, restaurants, etc. Every expenditure made by an international tourist carries a cross-border payment, from buying or exchanging currency to using a credit, debit, or pre-paid card[452]. The contribution of T&T to international trade and eCommerce is also well documented[453].

Two-thirds of revenue in global T&T came from online sales in 2022, a volume of $475 billion, forecasted to reach over $1tn by 2030. eCommerce has impacted the T&T industry, and the overlap has created an unprecedented expansion in sales. Mobile eCommerce T&T sales accounted for 56.1% in 2022, with desktop users taking 43.9% of the market share. However, 73% of airline reservations and sales came from desktop users due to the gaps in the customer's mobile journey. T&T eCommerce falls short of the general

---

451 Tourism Market to Reach USD 16.9 Trillion By 2030; The Emerging Notion of Adventure Tourism Reflects Strong Growth: The Brainy Insights; February 24, 2023 - https://bit.ly/3FjPKwE
452 Aman Mishra: Growth of tourism and its impact on gdp and Foreign Exchange Earnings; Journal of Emerging Technologies and Innovative Research (JETIR), March 2018, Volume 5, Issue 3 - https://bit.ly/3gpn7Fy
453 Jitin Sharma, Parveen Kumar Garg, Tourism Contribution To Global Trade And Economic Growth Post Covid-19; Guru Kashi University, Talwandi Sabo, Journal of Critical Reviews, Vol 8, Issue 03, 2021 - https://bit.ly/3rOdvtN

eCommerce average in the cart abandonment rate, with an 87.9% abandonment rate compared to 80.68%.

Fintech innovations and creativity will seek to provide solutions for many of the gaps, friction, and pain points, as well as the rails for the B2B cross-border payments needed.

Card companies are very active in the T&T sector. UnionPay partnered with TripLink to introduce a UnionPay Virtual Commercial Card in Singapore, allowing TripLink's customers to pay merchants and partners using the card[454]. Mastercard launched a tourism innovation hub in Spain in 2022[455]. Visa announced in 2022 that its profit beat expectations as payment volumes surged on travel demand[456].

We should not overlook the importance of migrants in the T&T industry, not only as workers in cruise ships, hotels, and tourist venues but as tourists themselves. Some airlines cater to their diasporas, finding ways to attract them and compete with global airlines. Return migrants are very active in many countries and have contributed to the tourism development of many resort areas, cities, and towns, investing locally and, in many cases, managing their businesses remotely. Many of these migrants use P2P channels to manage their cross-border financial needs. Fintechs may soon find ways to attract these customers by providing products and services tailored to their needs.

Ajay Singh of BCD Travel is very optimistic about the prospects of fintech companies innovating and improving business travel management: *Adopting fintech-based solutions can help remove the friction and pain points experienced by travelers, travel managers, and finance teams related to travel and expense payment, invoices, reimbursement, and reconciliation*[457].

---

[454] Unionpay and Triplink Launch Unionpay Virtual Commercial Card in Singapore, UnionPay International, Press Release, Oct 10, 2023 - https://prn.to/3FiDVH8
[455] Press Release: Mastercard Launches Tourism Innovation Hub in Spain; January 20, 2022 - https://mstr.cd/3ELV8Jr
[456] Mehnaz Yasmin: Visa profit beats as payment volumes surge on travel demand; Reuters, October 26, 2022 - https://reut.rs/3EqlKOS
[457] Fintech's role in the future of business travel; BCD Travel Blog - https://bit.ly/46OdTac

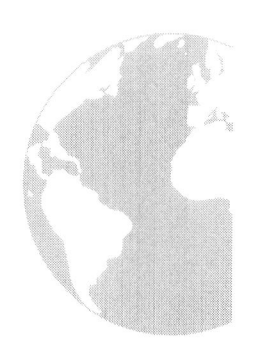

CLOSING REMARKS

Predicting the socioeconomic and political challenges humanity will face by the end of this decade is not an easy task. The sector will, however, continue to grow and consolidate in all aspects, as I have tried to present in the last chapter of this book.

It is unclear which technology innovation will differentiate service providers and what will be the drivers that will make some companies increase their market share as the industry expands and the forecasted growth is realized.

How regulators will help or hinder innovation and how banks and fintechs will develop partnerships are issues that will continue to impact the industry. Fintech companies' creativity that enables faster and easier international payments and money transfers will connect people and businesses in ways never imagined as globalization continues.

People's tendency to explore new frontiers and exchange goods and services is bringing the world closer together, and interactions will surely become more frequent. And the cross-border payments industry will be at the very core of these interactions.

APPENDIX ONE

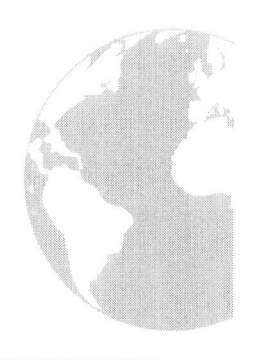

CONFERENCES

IMTC - CROSSTECH

The events we developed for the cross-border industry began in 2010. IMTC (International Money Transfer Conferences) was rebranded as CrossTech in 2021 to reflect the cross-border payments evolution. I have categorized the events that we organized by decade.

The First Decade (2005-2009)

I consider the *First Continental Congress of Money Remittance Companies* held on July 25-26, 2005, in Miami as the seminal business event of the remittance industry, as described earlier. It was organized by industry leaders Ernesto Armenteros, Jorge Guerrero, and Carlos Grossman. Before this event, seminars and meetings geared to the development and social impact of remittances took place. The first IDB event was held a month prior.

These three pioneers wanted to create the *American Confederation of Money Remitters* (ACMR), and the Congress was a way to launch it. It was the first time that many of us, colleagues, regulators, and business executives met. ACMR was not established. In Spain, the Ibero-American Association of Remitters (AIBER) was formed in 2008 with 15 members from Spain, Uruguay, Ecuador, Bolivia and Paraguay. The first meeting was in Madrid on November 5-7, 2008. In 2011, AIBER hosted its third and last convention. I was involved with these earlier efforts that didn't materialize.

After ACMR could not get off the ground, the NMTA, the association founded in New York in 1999, decided to hold an event in South Florida in 2006, a seminar organized by David Landsman. The first events were focused on compliance and regulation. I became involved in 2009 crafting business-oriented sessions, and in 2010, David and I developed our first event together, IMTC MIAMI, which became IMTC WORLD some years later.

The Second Decade (2010-2020)

By 2010, IMTC had taken off, and the event in Miami was already an industry benchmark. The flagship conference in South Florida gained global significance as all institutions, banks, and nonbanks realized the importance of attending an event where they could meet and conduct business with partners from the many countries where delegates came from. Companies and individuals providing services to the sector, such as technology, fintech, regtech, foreign exchange, currency settlement, distribution networks, and legal and regulatory support, started to realize the importance of the event for meeting clients and networking.

That year, we also organized the IMTC Mexico 2010, together with *RemesAmericas, Remittances for the Future*, held by the IDB in May in Mexico City, attended by its president Luis Alberto Moreno, Banco Mexico's governor Agustin Carstens, and numerous attendees. The main topic was the effect of the 2008-9 financial crisis and U.S. immigration policies, which were impacting remittances[458].

Besides the WORLD event, we began to develop more focused regional events in other US cities, such as Los Angeles (2011, 2012 and 2013), San Diego (2014), Las Vegas (2015 and 2016) and San Francisco (2017 and 2018). West Coast conferences were designed to attract the emerging fintech sector.

Two IMTC LATAM events were held in Mexico, one in Mexico City in 2011 and one in Cancun in 2019. In 2017, we organized the LATAM event in Antigua, Guatemala. As a Guatemalan native, speaking at the conference in my home country was an honor. A large press conference held weeks earlier was widely reported in the local press[459]. The *Trump-Effect* on remittances and migration was at everyone's top of mind. In 2016, we held our IMTC

---

458 José Manuel Arteaga: Control Migratorio afectará Remesas; El Universal, México, May 7, 2010 - https://bit.ly/3pcOX8N
459 "It is the migrant, often forgotten, who is financing the entire economy"; Diario La Hora, Guatemala; January 20, 2017 - https://bit.ly/3SHUUYG

CUBA event, the first of its kind in this country. The Obama presidency had made it feasible to formalize the handling of remittances to this island nation despite the US embargo.

ABRACAM, a Brazilian association we will discuss later in this Appendix, hosted the IMTC BRASIL in São Paulo in 2012, 2014, 2016, and 2018. Although country-specific IMTCs were significant in many countries, nothing compared to their impact on the Brazil cross-border payment market. As a result of the IMTC's efforts to transition remittances from the informal to formal sectors in 2012, the market has experienced dramatic changes. A cautious regulatory approach and strong support for NBFIs have been crucial to Brazil's digital transformation of domestic and cross-border payments.

In Europe, we held our first event in Istanbul in 2015, followed by Barcelona (2016), Madrid (2017), Brussels (2018), and London in 2019, before Covid emerged and had a major impact on all meetings and presential gatherings.

IMTC AFRICA 2017 was held in Kenya with the support of M-Pesa (Vodafone-Safaricom). Many participants remembered the *field day*[460] in which participants walked through Nairobi in groups, experiencing how mobile wallets work in all kinds of businesses, including street vendors; we also sent and collected remittances, and a video captured the best moments of this experience.

Lagos, Nigeria, hosted IMTC AFRICA 2019 at a time when new regulations implemented by the Central Bank caused high tension in the market. My colleague and friend Leon Isaacs' support in Nairobi and Lagos was crucial; his extensive knowledge of the African continent and cross-border payments was invaluable.

The first event in Asia, IMTC ASIA, was held in New Delhi in 2016, and the second one in Manila in 2018. Both countries were eager to support the events to gather the industry and discuss the evolution of their cross-border payment corridors.

The Third Decade (2020)

In 2020, the COVID pandemic marked a worldwide dramatic beginning of the third decade. Although we successfully managed to run the IMTC

---

460 Mobile Financial Services Field Day - M-PESA @IMTC AFRICA 2017 - https://bit.ly/498dMbO

LATAM 2020 virtually, broadcasting from Mexico City and then IMTC WORLD 2020 broadcasting from Miami, networking, our core event component, did not work as effectively online as our participants expected.

In 2021, we successfully held the IMTC WORLD in Miami and introduced our new brand, CrossTech, backed by the vision that crosstechs —fintechs specializing in cross-border payments-— are the industry's future. We will continue organizing our CROSSTECH WORLD, as we have done in 2022 and 2023, as I transition my role in the organization. These events are a tribute to the industry we have built and the companies that will lead it into the future.

In May 2023, we organized the first CROSSTECH PAYMENTS event in Miami, gathering the new fintechs that are shaping the future of cross-border business payments, the industry's fastest-growing sector if we account for B2B Ecommerce, estimated to reach $21.9tn in 2030, an increase of 119% in 7 years. The growing B2B market serving SMBs is $10.4tn a year, forecasted to grow in 2030 to $11.4tn. B2B payments are developed from the experience and the networks built for remittances and P2P money transfers.

REMTECH AWARDS

The Remittance Innovations Awards (Remtech Awards) were created in 2017 and were first held in cooperation with IFAD for the Sixth Global Forum on Remittances, Investment, and Development (GFRID) hosted at the United Nations headquarters in New York. The awards are intended to highlight the most innovative ideas, models, and projects designed to improve remittance services worldwide. This first edition had 36 participants, 11 prizes awarded, and ten mentions from the judges.

Azimo, a UK crosstech, won the *Judges Overall Favorite Award*, while Safaricom M-Pesa, received the *Mobile Creativity Award*, and another crosstech, Xoom, won the *Digital Pioneer Award*. Regtech Trulioo, EcoCashDiaspora, ComplyAdvantage, Moneytis, Airpocket, and Everex received honorable mentions. Crypto company Bitso received the award for its *Pioneering Spirit* in the quest to offer cryptocurrency solutions to the industry[461].

---

461 The 2017 Remtech Awards: https://bit.ly/3Rc6Rog

A second edition of the RemTech Awards[462] was held at the GFRID in Kuala Lumpur, Malaysia, again in support of IFAD. On May 8, with coordinator Olivia Chow[463], we presented the awards to the winners from 38 participants. RemitONE, Trulioo, Paykii, ValYou, Koibanx, Mahindra Comviva, TransferTo (Thunes), Rewire, and Afbit won awards and received public acclaim. Remtechs were presented virtually at IMTC WORLD in Miami in 2019 and presentially at CROSSTECH WORLD in November 2022.

At the ninth GFRID held in Nairobi[464] from May 14 to 16, 2023, the RemTech Awards 2023[465] were held. The Remittance Evolution Award was presented to European fintech MoneyTrans, the Innovation Remittance Solution to RemitOne, the Best in Class Compliance Solution to Regtec ThetaRay, and the Partner of the Year Award to MFS Africa. A special mention was presented to Yida Financial Services for his work with African Refugees[466].

FINTECH CONFERENCES AND EVENTS

The Las Vegas Money20/20, held for the first time in 2012 at the Aria Resort & Casino, is the largest global fintech event, and its events in Europe and Asia have been growing since they were first launched. The number and the variety of fintech events worldwide are impressive, and it is difficult to differentiate one from the other. Very few offer sessions on cross-border payments, especially on P2P and remittances. However, the magnitude of the wholesale and retail of business cross-border payments market has gained the attention of fintechs event organizers.

Lists of fintech events are gathered by FintechLabs[467] and Fintech Weekly[468], and Lawrence Wintermeyer, the Chair of GBBC Digital Finance (GDF), a global NGO promoting fair and transparent markets for crypto and

---

462 GFRID2018 Report; International Fund for Agricultural Development (IFAD); Global Forum on Remittances, Investment and Development 2018, May 8 to 10, 2018 p.36 - https://bit.ly/3Qbgxyr
463 Olivia Chow: LinkedIn - https://bit.ly/3zIPGVk
464 GFRID Summit: Global Forum on Remittances, Investment and Development, May 14-16, Nairobi, Kenya; Recognition of the RemTech Awards - https://bit.ly/3Qs4EHy
465 GFRID Summit 2023 & RemTECH Awards - https://bit.ly/45Jt9o7
466 RemTECH Awards Winners 2023 - https://bit.ly/471QAK6
467 FintechLabs: Fintech Conferences & Events - https://bit.ly/3tMMebJ
468 Fintech Weekly: Worldwide events with fintech and finance focus - https://bit.ly/3Qw7vPy

digital assets, published in Forbes[469] his top 10 fintech events in September 2023. Lawrence included the Benzinga Fintech Awards and Fintech Week in New York, FinTech Connect and IFGS Global Summit in London, Fintech World 24 in Berlin, FinTech Festival Tanzania, Singapore FinTech Week, Dubai FinTech Summit and even the World Economic Forum in Davos!

REMITTANCES AND DEVELOPMENT

As we noted in Part I of this work, migration and remittances go hand in hand. As widely recognized, migration brings both benefits and drawbacks. These may be reflected differently in the country of origin and destination. Sending money is part of these benefits, both for families and communities. Many academics and researchers have discussed and analyzed the relationship between remittances and development, strengthening the existing knowledge.

I did not discuss the importance of cross-border payments to development in Part I or II of this work since many authors have already explored it in sufficient detail[470]. I believe it is necessary here to recognize the efforts of many organizations in this field. They provided great help to the industry in its formative years.

I would like to mention Donald Terry and Natasha Bajuk at the Inter-American Dialogue in Washington for their work at the bank, as well as the work of Manuel Orozco at the Interamerican Dialogue. The first publications of remittance statistics had a considerable impact on the industry, both in understanding the sector and in driving remittance support policies within sending and receiving countries.

CEMLA[471] made a decisive contribution under the leadership of Jesus Cervantes González, Coordinator of the Forum on Remittances in Latin America and the Caribbean, and the General Principles for Latin American and Caribbean Remittance Markets. In appreciation for their extensive and

---

469 Lawrence Wintermeyer: The Top 10 Global Fintech Conferences: From AI To Zombie Unicorn; Forbes, September 24, 2023 - https://bit.ly/473PIFa
470 There are so many academics whose insightful works on the subject I have read, such as Matt Bakker at Marymount University (https://bit.ly/3ziKPc4). Their insights are important to remittance families and the industry that serves them, as well as the policymakers and development initiatives. Bakker's book *Migrating into Financial Markets: How Remittances Became a Development Tool* traces part of this history.
471 CEMLA: Directorio 2022 - https://bit.ly/3Cdkjng

significant work, Mr. Jesus Cervantes González and Salvador Bonilla, now retired, deserve much gratitude.

Dilip Ratha and his team at the World Bank, and Pedro de Vasconcelos and his team at IFAD, had been crucial for remittance senders and recipients and the industry's development.

GLOBAL FORUM ON REMITTANCES, INVESTMENT AND DEVELOPMENT

In Washington, D.C., from June 28-30, 2005, the Inter-American Development Bank's Multilateral Investment Fund (MIF) held the first international forum on remittances[472] and their nexus to technology, financial services, and housing for immigrants and their families in their native countries. The second forum was held in 2007[473], also in Washington, D.C., at the IDB headquarters.

At the third forum in 2009[474], IFAD took the initiative and started the Global Forums, with Tunisia hosting the first one. The event took place during the 2008-2009 economic crisis when fears of a downturn affected the sector. Remittances' relative resilience during this time of economic instability was nonetheless proving to be a stabilizing force for many nations.

These Forums have been supported by the World Bank, UNDESA (UN Department of Economic and Social Affairs), as well as collaboration agencies from several countries, such as Switzerland (Swiss Agency for Development and Cooperation - SDC), Germany (German Cooperation) and different governments: Luxemburg, Spain, Sweden, etc.

I should note that Pedro de Vasconcelos[475] joined IFAD in 2007 as Program Manager of the FFR and led it to acquire a global perspective aimed at creating synergies between governments, civil society, and the private sector, which were considered critical from that moment on to maximize the

---

[472] Interamerican Development Bank (IDB) Multilateral Investment Fund (MIF); IDB fund to hold an international forum on remittances, June 28-30, 2005 - https://bit.ly/3Bq90I9
[473] International Fund for Agricultural Development (IFAD), Multilateral Investment Fund (MIF); International Forum on Remittances 2007, Washington; October 18 - 19, 2007 - https://bit.ly/3cIlL6q
[474] International Fund for Agricultural Development (IFAD); Global Forum on Remittances 2009, Tunis, October 22 - 23, 2009 - https://bit.ly/3Q6JbAR
[475] International Fund for Agricultural Development (IFAD); Pedro de Vasconcelos - https://bit.ly/3zKRxcf

impact of migration and remittances on development, particularly in rural areas. This new dimension is important not only because it acknowledges the industry in front of governments, regulators, and banks but also because it acknowledges the members of the sector who felt isolated and marginalized.

The explicit call of the Group of Eight (G8), followed by the G20, on the importance of remittances and the reduction of their cost by 50% provided a framework for collaboration with goals, data gathering, statistics, discussion of the reasons for high rates, competition, regulation, derisking, and technology. Originally from Portugal, Pedro de Vasconcelos, who studied in France, had previously worked at UNCTAD (United Nations Conference on Trade and Development) in Geneva, and during his time at IDB-IFM, he gained knowledge of remittances.

Four years later Thailand hosted the fourth forum[476]. Participating at the 2013 GFRID, I was able to get to see the country and participate actively in the event, understanding and appreciating its importance for the industry. I would like to mention Alessandra Casano[477], who joined IFAD in 2010 and helped organize the 2013 GFRID in Bangkok and subsequent forums; she made everyone welcome.

The fifth edition was held in 2015 in Milan, Italy[478], parallel to MILAN EXPO 2015, with the theme Food and Energy (Feeding the Planet, Energy for Life). Several private sector organizations took part in this event for the first time as partners, including IMTC, the International Association of Money Transfer Networks (IAMTN), the association of mobile telecommunication companies, GSMA (Groupe Spécial Mobile), CGAP (Consultative Group to Assist the Poor) and the World Savings and Retail Banking Institution (WSBI).

The sixth forum was held in 2017 in New York[479] at the United Nations headquarters in Manhattan, where we hosted the first Remittances Innovation Awards (Remtech) in collaboration with IFAD. With Bank

---

476 International Fund for Agricultural Development (IFAD); Global Forum on Remittances 2013 Bangkok 20 - 23 may 2013 - https://bit.ly/3JhO7k6
477 Alessandra Casano LinkedIn - https://bit.ly/3oKW7Rr
478 International Fund for Agricultural Development (IFAD); Global Forum on Remittances, Investment and Development 2015; June 16 - 19, 2016 - https://bit.ly/3oO7iZn
479 International Fund for Agricultural Development (IFAD); Global Forum on Remittances, Investment and Development 2017, June 15-16, 2017 - https://bit.ly/3bfWznJ - PDF Report: https://bit.ly/3QXbvX7

Negara Malaysia promoting the event, the seventh edition[480] was held in Kuala Lumpur from May 8-10, attracting over 400 professionals from public and private organizations. During this GFRID, the Remtech Awards were presented at the Sasana Kijang, a gorgeous convention center.

In 2021, the eighth forum was held virtually due to the Covid pandemic, and in 2023, the ninth edition was held in Nairobi, Kenya, and the Remtech Awards were held on the third day of the event[481].

Forum reports[482] from 2007 onwards illustrate the topics and evolution of remittances and development. They also discuss government and international agency policies and programs that have contributed significantly to the support of migrants to ensure that remittances not only provide immediate support to families but also have a long-term impact on their communities.

The work of IFAD is grounded on the Sustainable Development Goals (SDGs)[483], which are a series of targets that the United Nations has set for 2030. These guidelines are divided into 17 targets; among them, number 10 relates to reducing global inequalities. Target 10.c contemplates remittances since it aims to reduce transaction costs: *By 2030, reduce to less than 3 percent the transaction costs of migrant remittances and eliminate remittance corridors with costs higher than 5 percent.* The goal is not easy to achieve, and a lot needs to be done by international organizations, regional developments, local governments, regulators, industry, and companies to bring technological innovations that break through the structural inefficiencies, barriers, and friction that exist. As I mentioned, *coopetition* is crucial to achieve these goals.

In response to Covid, IFAD created the Remittance Task Force (RTF)[484] on March 24, 2020, addressing the UN Secretary General's request for global solidarity, stating that *remittances are a lifeline in the developing world*. Forty-one organizations participated in the RCTF, including international and intergovernmental agencies, industry associations, member networks of diasporas, and international remittances experts, who have continuously worked together.

---

480 International Fund for Agricultural Development (IFAD); Global Forum on Remittances, Investment and Development 2018, May 8-10, 2018 - https://bit.ly/3vtmNKe
481 GFRID Summit: Global Forum on Remittances, Investment and Development, May 14-16, Nairobi, Kenya; Recognition of the RemTech Awards - https://bit.ly/3Qs4EHy
482 International Fund for Agricultural Development (IFAD); Global Forum on Remittances, Investment and Development Reports - https://bit.ly/3bgBv0m
483 SDG #10: https://bit.ly/3dWlOfJ
484 IFAD: The Remittance Community Task Force (RTF): https://bit.ly/3L2oaGq

International Day of Family Remittances (IDFR)[485] —an IFAD-generated initiative— is celebrated on June 16 every year. The 176 member states of IFAD unanimously proclaimed the date in February 2015, and the first celebration was in Milan, Italy, in June 2015. Since then, government agencies, regulators, financial institutions, and development agencies have acknowledged it yearly.

This celebration recognizes and seeks to raise global awareness of the contributions that migrants worldwide make to their families and local economies. It commemorates the dedication, sacrifice, and generosity of international workers who provide sustenance for their loved ones and contribute to the sustainable development of their home countries. The IDFR also honors those of us who have worked in both the public and private sectors to help migrants send and receive family remittances.

---

485 IDFR: International Day of Family Remittances - https://familyremittances.org/

APPENDIX TWO

THE ASSOCIATIONS

Associations are crucial to any industry. Even if the cross-border payment industry is merging the traditional NBFIs with the new NBFIs (fintechs) that have joined the industry, the existing associations still have a way to go in terms of working together for the common goals that the industry, in their partnerships, has already been developing.

That is why I have to divide associations into two main categories: the associations of new NBFIs (fintechs) and traditional NBFIs. While there are some associations with members from both groups, there isn't much interaction or joint work between them. It is imperative that we work in unifying goals and developing a common path forward.

NFBIS ASSOCIATIONS

This is a list of the major money transfer and exchange associations. The only international associations are IAMTN and the new cTech Network. I have categorized the associations by continent and country, with a brief overview highlighting their work over time.

IAMTN

Founded in 2005 in London, the International Association of Money Transfer Networks (IAMTN)[486] gathers bank and non-bank companies involved in the cross-border payment industry. IAMTN works with its

---

486 IAMTN: https://www.iamtn-network.org/

members and partners to create safer, cheaper, more accessible, and transparent payment systems and mechanisms.

Until 2008, the association was led by English journalist and politician Lady Olga Maitland, with Conservative politician Lord Norman Lamont as honorary president[487]. At the time of the foundation, Lady Maitland stated: *We see our role as highlighting a major financial services sector which has been largely overlooked. Money transfers, and in particular the remittance market, play a crucial role in the economies of emerging markets.* After becoming CEO of the organization, she would serve on industry boards and associations, including Earthport. Lord Larmont was a major contributor to Brexit as he was one of the politicians who first promoted the idea.

Veronica Studsgaard assumed leadership of the IAMTN after working with the Russian money transfer company Unistream, a major sponsor of the organization in its early years. Born in Argentine Patagonia and living in Denmark, Veronica developed an organization of the top multinational MTOs worldwide. In the past, Leon Isaacs and Mohit Davar provided valuable support and collaboration as conference and event organizers in London, Cape Town, Dubai, etc. Veronica works in close collaboration with Nikila Punnoose, Head of Partnerships.

cTech Network

Founded in 2023 in Miami, cTech's[488] mission is to serve the networking needs of all its members, companies, and industry executives, promoting communication, collaboration, cooperation, and collective support to build a thriving and engaged community of cross-border payment professionals.

One of the association's aims is to be the bridge that interconnects the payments industry with other NGOs, multilateral agencies, civil society organizations, consumer groups, and government agencies, developing a supporting entrepreneurial ecosystem that works for the common good.

---

487 Finextra: International Association of Money Transfer Networks established; January 14, 2006 - https://bit.ly/3qdDjuD
488 cTech: https://ctechnetwork.org/

THE US

NMTA (1999-2018)

The National Money Transmitter Association (NMTA) was founded in 1999 in New York City by a group of industry insiders led by attorney Jorge Guerrero to boost the reputation of money transmitters in the US, seek legal reform, and promote compliance standards.

Five years later, in 2004, the Board of Directors appointed David Landsman as Chief Executive Officer. He led the association to publish a well-recognized newsletter, organize compliance seminars, participate in conferences, and testify before congressional committees while seeking to promote constructive dialogue with banks and regulators. From 2007 to 2010, David represented the NMTA on the FinCEN Advisory Group (BSA Advisory Group - BSAAG). Alan Friedman, who had worked for WU, MGI, and The National, was NMTA's chairman for many years. In 2018, the NMTA became part of the MSBA.

MSBA

The Money Service Business Association (MSBA)[489] was founded in 2015 after several meetings where Connie Fenchel, former director of FINCEN and now in private practice, attorneys Andrew Ittleman and Judie Rinearson, and myself, as a consultant, decided to create an organization to bring together MSBs (Money Services Businesses) in the US, not only MTOs. After several consultations with potential members and the engagement of top company CEOs, we began looking for a candidate to organize the association. Judie Rinearson recommended Kathy Tomasofsky, who had been the manager of NBPCA (Network Branded Prepaid Card Association) for seven years and was the most qualified candidate.

In October 2015, the MSBA was launched. Under Kathy's leadership, the organization has grown and established itself as a respected interlocutor among the authorities, both state and federal, engaged in constant discussion to monitor laws, regulations, and measures that may be affecting the industry.

---

489 MSBA: https://www.msbassociation.org/

THE MONEY SERVICES ROUNDTABLE

The top companies in the industry, WU, MGI, RIA, and American Express, created a group in 1988, The Money Services Round Table (TMSRT), represented for many years by Ezra Levine from Morrison & Foerster. The group was responsible for representing these companies to regulators and expressing their opinions on proposed legislation and other measures that require their input.

They occasionally issue joint communiqués, such as the one announced in May 2022 involving four associations: The Electronic Transactions Association (ETA), INFiN, the Financial Services Alliance[490]; the MSBA and TMSRT, containing an important document: *Best Practices for U.S. Money Services Businesses: Anti-Money Laundering and Counter-Financing of Terrorism Compliance Program*[491].

MTRA

The Money Transmitters Regulators Association (MTRA)[492] is a U.S. non-profit organization, unique in its kind, as it comprises the regulators that monitor money transmitters (as well as other non-bank services) in each state. MTRA's objective is to achieve a uniform and efficient regulation that is similar and congruent across all states to the extent possible. The MTRA, founded in 1989, is governed by a Board of Directors elected every two years. It holds an annual conference for companies in the industry, although some sessions and courses are only open to regulators. Their efforts to standardize procedures led them to sign an agreement in 2021 to conduct Joint Examinations, eliminating the need for each state regulator to audit companies licensed in more than one state.

The MTRA works closely with the Conference of State Bank Supervisors (CSBS)[493], initially founded in 1902 as the National Association of State Bank Supervisors and renamed in 1971 to expand beyond financial services

---

[490] INFiN represents more than 350 companies, including check cashing, pre-paid cards, money transfers, electronic bill payments, and small-dollar consumer loans, among others: https://infinalliance.org/
[491] Leading MSB Industry Associations Unveil Anti-Money Laundering Best Practices; Press Release, May 11, 2022 - https://prn.to/495a9TH
[492] MTRA: https://www.mtraweb.org/
[493] CSBS: Who is CSBS? - https://bit.ly/3U1SGEo

banking. The CSBS has also worked to harmonize state regulations and achieve better coordination among the 50 states. States prefer to maintain their relative independence despite attempts by the federal government to intervene by creating federal regulations.

The MTRA has been crucial to the development of the NMLS System. The NMLS was established in January 2008 as part of the CSBS program for monitoring and licensing mortgage companies and providing better consumer protection. After starting as a voluntary system among seven states, it eventually gained acceptance among all of them, and by Puerto Rico, the Virgin Islands, and Guam. Following the licensing of mortgage companies, the same system has been used to manage the state licensing of money transmitters and other NBFIs[494].

IOREM

The International Organization for Remittances and Migration (IOREM) is a network of academics with expertise in remittances and migration, aiming to conduct research, exchange knowledge with public and private entities, publish publications, organize events, and offer graduate training programs. We founded it in 2019 with Sabith Khan, a professor at California Lutheran University, with the support of its initial board of directors: Sue Smock, an independent researcher with extensive experience in NGOs, Daisha Merritt from Embry-Riddle Aeronautical University in Jacksonville, Florida, and Sulayman Njie, a researcher and professor of Political Science at Bluefield State University in West Virginia.

In the coming years, we hope to continue advancing this project, still in the planning stages, by integrating dozens of researchers involved in this field, bringing their work closer to industry, and promoting students' interest in the subject.

EUROPE

After the approval of the PSD 2011, the European Payment Institutions Federation (EPIF) based in Brussels was created to bring together the associations of payment institutions in each European country. EPIF's associate Members include associations from Spain, France, Portugal, Belgium, and

---

[494] NMLS: About the NMLS - https://bit.ly/3qyG0ag

Poland. Full Members and Corporate members include large multinational companies. The Electronic Money Association (EMA) is the trade body representing the interests of over 90 e-money issuers across the EEA since 2001, with local branches in the UK where it was founded, Belgium, Ireland, Lithuania, Luxembourg, Malta, and the Netherlands.

From ANAED to AENPA

In 1997, the Spanish Association of Payment Institutions (AENPA)[495] was first established as the Spanish Association of Money Transfer Agencies (ANAED) by payment institutions from Spain and other European Union countries. This association, which has more than 20 members (2022), has been a constant and permanent voice for the industry under the leadership of lawyer José Hervás, who has managed ANAED alongside his law firm from the beginning.

Former associations and groups

REMESAS.ORG

The network remesas.org was formed in November 2004 when a group of Spanish economists decided to analyze the potential use of remittances as a development booster in recipient countries[496]. The first measurement of remittance prices from Spain was carried out on March 15, 2005, and the first seminar at Casa de América was held on September 16, 2005[497]. Casa de América was founded in the 1990s to bring Spain and Portugal closer to the Americas. In subsequent years, seven meetings were held in Spain and one in Casablanca, Morocco, which gathered public and private players involved in this migratory phenomenon and provided information and analysis helpful to the industry and its context. remesas.org ceased to exist in 2017-2018.

AUKPI (UKMTA)

AUKPI (Association of UK Payment Institutions), known before as the UKMTA (UK Money Transfer Association) until 2014, ceased to exist in 2021. Its director was found guilty of failing to detect fraudulent transactions

---

495 Asociación Española De Entidades De Pago (AENPA) - https://bit.ly/3dtx6I9
496 Remesas.org: ¿Qué somos? - https://bit.ly/3AYGzPQ
497 Remesas.org: Primer Encuentro Iberoamericano sobre remesas; Las remesas de los emigrantes en Iberoamérica; Casa de América, Madrid, Viernes 23 de Septiembre de 2005 - https://bit.ly/3x2ezcS

involving money movements to Hong Kong and China in a company he controlled[498]. We hope the PIs in the UK will soon work together to create a new association. AUKPI was very active in defending the industry against derisking.

SOUTH AMERICA

While I have met and collaborated directly with the associations I mention here, they are not the only ones in the remittance and exchange sector.

ABRACAM - BRAZIL

The Brazilian Exchange Association (ABRACAM)[499] was founded in 2001 to represent the interests of the foreign exchange segment in Brazil. A Code of Ethics was developed with 12 associates the following year, along with meetings with various ministries to discuss ideas and solutions. In 2012, ABRACAM reached 58 members and held its first international conference with IMTC in Sao Paulo, IMTC BRAZIL 2012. With great success, the association organized its first Compliance Day in 2015. In 2018, Kelly Cristina Gallego Massaro was appointed as the first Executive President.

As per the agreement with the Association, IMTC BRAZIL continued to be organized every two years, holding events in Sao Paulo in 2014, 2016, and 2018. In 2022, following the pandemic, CROSSTECH BRAZIL2022 held its first event with the new branding of IMTC, hosting more than 200 participants from around the globe.

CIASEFIM - SOUTH AMERICAN CONE

In November 2016, at IMTC WORLD, entities representing the Southern Cone foreign exchange market institutions identified the need to conduct studies to curb the practice of derisking and advocate on behalf of the sector before regulators and multilateral agencies. In December of the same year in São Paulo, the associations of four countries, ABRACAM (Brazil), CADECAC (Argentina), CESFUR (Uruguay) and ACCP (Paraguay) met and created the International Commission of Associations of Money

---

498 Lyddon Consulting: My involvement with the Association of UK Payment Institutions (AUKPI) - https://bit.ly/3RyixSs - CPS (The Crown Prosecution Service): Anti-money laundering expert sentenced for allowing criminal money to be sent abroad, July 31, 2021 - https://bit.ly/3BjuKoo
499 ABRACAM: Historia - https://bit.ly/3S43WhN

Transfers Companies, Non-Bank Financial Services Companies, Foreign Exchange Firms and their Agents of Mercosur - CIASEFIM[500].

ADEREDI and ADOCAMBIO - THE DOMINICAN REPUBLIC

The story of foreign exchange and remittances in the Dominican Republic sounds like a science fiction novel. No one can tell the story better than Freddy Ortiz, writer, publicist, and former director of ADEREDI, the Dominican Association of Foreign Exchange Remitter Companies (which, as Ortiz states, should have been called "Dominican Association of Remittance Companies"). The association, founded at the end of the 1980s, is probably the oldest grouping of remittance companies. Because of his friendship with Victor Mendez Capellan of Vimenca, WU's paying agent in the DR since 1987, Freddy was appointed president in 1995.

Freddy is the author of the book *Errores Gubernamentales En Las Crisis Cambiarias - El Caso De Las Empresas Remesadoras*[501]. The work extensively narrates the experiences of the foreign exchange and remittance sector during a coordinated siege backed by the government and regulators under pressure from commercial banks that sought to control the foreign exchange market and, therefore, remittances. Another publication worth mentioning for anyone interested in this country's difficult history is *El Seductor* by Francisco Canahuate, attorney and former executive director of the Association of Exchange Agents. The book was published by Editora Corripio in 1993.

The history of the Dominican Republic and its exchange association will make an excellent documentary someday due to its tragic overtones, such as the kidnapping and murder on January 4, 1985, of influential money changer Héctor Méndez and his driver Napoleón Reyes[502]; allegedly, the murder was ordered by President Salvador Jorge Blanco's government officials.

The Dominican Association of Foreign Exchange Intermediaries (ADOCAMBIO)[503] was formally incorporated on August 15, 1995, as a representative guild of the sector. In 2021, it consisted of 17 member entities. In April 2022, ADOCAMBIO and the Association of Commercial Banks

---

500 CISEFIM: https://ciasefim.com/
501 Freddy Ortiz: Errores Gubernamentales En Las Crisis Cambiarias - El Caso De Las Empresas Remesadoras, ASIN: B005TKZIZ8, oct 2011, Amazon Kindle: https://amzn.to/3fF7oBn
502 Sin castigo 34 años después asesinato de Héctor Méndez; El Nacional, January 4, 2019 - https://bit.ly/3Canaf5
503 ADOCAMBIO: https://bit.ly/3RFEfUM

of the Dominican Republic (ABA) signed an inter-institutional cooperation agreement, bringing these sectors closer together for the benefit of the country's financial sector.

ANCEC-TD - MEXICO

The National Association of Exchange Centers was founded in May 1996 in an effort to provide stronger representation before authorities and other organizations. Exchange Centers are small establishments that sell and buy foreign currency in cash. In September 2005, the National Association of Money Exchange Centers and Money Transmitters, ANCEC-TD, updated its bylaws, corporate name, and logo to include Money Transmitters and strengthen the membership. However, this organization has not yet succeeded in gathering Money Transmitters, who are not represented in Mexico, despite attempts by industry insiders to develop ASOTRANS.

MAMSB - MALASIA[504]

The Malaysian Association of Money Services Businesses or MAMSB (Persatuan Perniagaan Perkhidmatan Wang Malaysia) was formed in 2013 to bring together all institutions licensed under the 2011 Money Services Businesses Act. In 2022, there were almost 200 licensed companies in this country, sending $2.2 billion, with 40% coming from digital remittance providers. This law requires foreign exchange, remittance, and payment companies to be licensed and comply with specific requirements. One of the few instances I know of where the regulator successfully worked to gather the industry and serve as its intermediary when enacting the law.

FINTECH ASSOCIATIONS

Fintech organizations worldwide strive to build a community of like-minded individuals trying to bring down regulatory barriers and having a unified front to bring change. Networking and developing a supportive ecosystem is also a crucial point.

In my attempts to bring traditional NBFIs and fintech together, I have tried unsuccessfully to create a dialogue between associations. In a Latin American country, the local fintech association did not accept a traditional NBFI as it did not yet have a digital channel available to the public. Since the channel was under development, the association's director was not convinced

---

504 MAMSB - https://mamsb.org.my/

that the company was indeed *a fintech*. There is a perception by some fintechs that building ties with traditional NBFIs is a burden.

Using an article[505] by Mark Walker, the Editorial Director of The Fintech Times, which summarized the importance of fintech associations and organizations worldwide, they can be categorized as follows:

1. International Associations and Association Federations:
2. National Associations
3. Thematic Associations
   a. Business Practices and Education
   b. Interoperability and platform development
   c. Technology

The International Associations and Association Federations are:

- World FinTech Association
- European Fintech Alliance
- European Digital Finance Association
- FintechLAC (IDB-supported public-private group)
- Africa Fintech Network (AFN)
- The MENA Fintech Association
- Financial Data and Global Technology Association (Europe)
- Iberoamerican Network of Women (Latin America)

Findexable has created one of the best lists summarizing the existing fintech associations[506], as well as the Global Fintech Index City Rankings and other rankings that give a detailed view of the development of hubs, incubation programs, supporting ecosystems, etc.

---

505 Mark Walker: We're All in This Together – The Value of Associations in Fintech; The Fintech Times, July 4, 2019 - https://bit.ly/3RZTMPc
506 FIDEXABLE: List of fintech associations - https://bit.ly/3dg4iTt

TABLE 16: Fintech Associations around the world

Acronym	Name	Country
AFG	Fintech Association of Guatemala	Guatemala
AFIK	Associations of Fintechs in Kenya	Kenya
AFIP	Associations of Fintechs in Portugal	Portugal
AFP	Fintech Association of Peru	Peru
ASSOFINTECH	Italian Association of Fintech & Insurtech	Italy
AWFP	African Women in Fintech & Payments	Africa
BFA	The Bulgarian Fintech Association	Bulgaria
BFB	Bahrain FinTech Bay	Bahrain
DLAI	Digital Lenders´Association of India	India
EFA	Egyptian Fintech Association	Egypt
FA	Fintech Australia	Australia
FAFW	Financial Alliance For Women	USA
FALS	Fintech Association of Sri Lanka	Sri Lanka
FAS	FinStepAsia	Hong Kong
FC	Fintech Cadence	Canada
FD	Fintech District	Italy
FIA	Fintech Association in Georgia	Georgia
FINDEC	Findec - Fintech/Decentralized	Sweden
FinHam	Fintech Hamburg	Hamburg
FinTech-Aviv	The Israeli FinTech Association - FinTech-Aviv	Israel
FinTechNGR	FinTech Association of Nigeria	Nigeria
FinTechNZ	The New Zealand Fin Innovation and Tech Association	New Zealand
GGH	Global Growth Hub	UK
HFF	Helsinki Fintech Farm	Finland
IAMAI	The Internet & Mobile Association of India	India

Acronym	Name	Country
IBA	The India Blockchain Alliance	India
MAFH	The Mauritius Africa FinTech Hub	Mauritius
MFH	Mumbai FinTech Hub	Mumbai
NCE Finance Innovation	Norwegian Centre of Expertise	Norway
NCFA Canada	The National Crowdfunding & Fintech Association	Canada
PF	Portugal Fintech	Portugal
QCF	Queen City Fintech	Innovation & Connection (*Charlotte, NC*)	USA
SFTA	Swiss Finance + Technology Association	Switzerland
TF	Tokyo FinTech	Tokyo
TFA	The Thai Fintech Association	Thailand
TGCT	The Ghana Chamber of Technology	Ghana
TIPSPA	The Financial Technology Service Providers Association	Uganda
TN	Tech Nation	UK
TQ	TechQuartier - At the Heart of Innovation	Frankfurt
UAFIC	The Ukrainian Association of Fintech and Innovation	Ukraine
	BlockchainNZ	New Zealand
	Colombia Fintech	Colombia
	FinteChile	Chile
	The Fintech Cluster	Iceland
	Fintech Istanbul	Istanbul
	Fintech Saudi	Saudi Arabia
	Fintech Scotland	Scotland

LIST OF GRAPHS

GRAPH 1	Incidence, fatality and injury from terrorist attacks, World, 1970 to 2020	19
GRAPH 2	Western Union's Global Market Share (2006-2022)	70
GRAPH 3	Comparative Revenue between WU Digital and its fintech rivals (2017-2023)	71
GRAPH 4	Use of the word derisking (1997-2019)	79
GRAPH 5	Use of the spanish term bancarización vs inclusion financiera (1990-2019)	93
GRAPH 6	Percentages of Licenses awarded in the last five years in 4 US States (2017-2022)	111
GRAPH 7	Percentage of Countries with DIPS by Region (2023)	159
GRAPH 8	Size and Growth of the Cross-Border Retail Market (2023-2030)	167

LIST OF TABLES

TABLE 1	The Financing of the 9/11 Terrorist Attacks in the US - 2000-2001	14
TABLE 2	Global flow of funds from illicit activities in billions (US $bn), 2000/2001	25
TABLE 3	Number of licenses (PIs & EMIs) issued per country (2019-2020-2021)	112
TABLE 4	Comparing the main crosstechs in the market as of September 2022	113
TABLE 5	WorldRemit Investment Rounds (2014-2021)	119
TABLE 6	Wise investment Rounds (2013-2021)	120
TABLE 7	Remitly Investment Rounds (2014-2021)	122
TABLE 8	TRANSFERGO Investment Rounds (2016-2022)	123
TABLE 9	AZIMO Investment Rounds (2013-2020)	124
TABLE 10	Papaya Global Investment Rounds (2016-2021)	125
TABLE 11	PAYSEND Investment Rounds (2016-2021)	127
TABLE 12	Flywire Investment Rounds (2010-2021)	128
TABLE 13	BITSO Investment Rounds (2014-2021)	130
TABLE 14	Selected Public Company Financial Information (companies involved in cross-border payments) - as of August 2023	135
TABLE 15	Main Neobank Comparaison; users and countries covered, 2022	187
TABLE 16	Fintech Associations around the world	237

LIST OF INTERVIEWS

I appreciate the participation of the following industry colleagues who contributed their stories and insights for this work:

Name	Date of Interview	Page	LinkedIn	
Alberto Guerra	June 29, 2022	64	https://bit.ly/3gEsVKY	CEO UniTeller Financial Services
Amar Das	July 8, 2022	69, 115	https://bit.ly/3DGN1O0	Ejecutivo de Western Union y diversas empresas del sector
Beatriz Navia	April 28, 2022	43	https://bit.ly/3NcHvpc	Oficial de Cumplimiento de Titán Intercontinental, Organicos Cabrita
Erick Schneider	June 14, 2022	54, 84	https://bit.ly/3FluGan	Experto en Innovación (Ejecutivo en AMEX, WorldRemit, Crypto.com)
Ernesto Armenteros	June 28, 2022	53, 57, 58, 92	https://bit.ly/3TQz1XC	Remesas Quisqueyana, Banco de Crédito Unión, DOLEX
Francisco Sánchez Apellániz	April 12, 2022	53, 169	https://bit.ly/3SHG5Ey	Fundador de MoneyTrans
Leon Isaacs		41	https://bit.ly/3sHChbu	SaverGlobal, DMA, MGI
Piero P. Coen	July 5, 2022	94, 206	https://bit.ly/3DGMADm	Fundador del Grupo Coen/ AirPak

Name	Date of Interview	Page	LinkedIn	
Rob Ayers		65	https://bit.ly/3DEOKDj	*Consultor (Ejecutivo en MGI - fundador de Fintech Advisors)*
Salvador Velázquez		56	https://bit.ly/3SK9Swi	*Consultor y Ejecutivo (Consultoría Internacional, Dolex)*
Sergio Pérez	April 12, 2022	134	https://bit.ly/3zoNtO5	*Cofundador de More Money Transfers y Bamboo Payment Systems, Cambios Sir, Redpagos*

ABBREVIATIONS & ACRONYMS

ABRACAM	Associação Brasileira de Câmbio
ABROI	Association of Bank Remittance Officers Inc. (The Philippines)
ACAMS	Association of Certified Anti-Money Laundering Specialists
ACH	Automated Clearing House
ACLU	American Civil Liberties Union
ADEREDI	Asociación Dominicana de Empresas Remesadoras de Divisas (*inactive*)
ADOCAMBIO	Asociación Dominicana de Intermediarios Cambiarios
AENPA	Asociación Española De Entidades De Pago
AIBER	Asociación Iberoamericana de Remesadoras (*inactive*)
AML	Anti-Money Laundering
AMUCSS	Asociación Mexicana de Uniones de Crédito del Sector Social
ANAED	Asociación Española de Agencias de Envío de Dinero (*rebranded as AENPA*)
ANCEC-TD	Asociación Nacional de Centros Cambiarios y Transmisores de Dinero (*México*)
ATM	Automatic Teller Machine
AusAID	Australian Agency of International Development
AUSTRAC	Australian Transaction Reports and Analysis Centre
BACEN	Brazil Central Bank - *Banco Central do Brasil (BCB)*
B2B	Business to Business
B2P	Business to Person
BaaS	Banking-as-a-Service
BID	Banco Interamericano para el Desarrollo (in english IDB)
BNPL	Buy-Now-Pay-Later
BOP	Back-Office Provider

BSA	Bank Secrecy Act
BSup	Colombia's Banking Superintendency (the name was changed to *Superintendencia Financiera*)
CANAFE	Centre d'Analyse des Opérations et Déclarations Financières du Canada
CaSE	UK's Campaign for Science and Engineering
CBDC	Central Bank Digital Currency
CBP	Customs and Border Protection - US Department of Homeland Security
CBR	Correspondent Banking Relationships
CCP	Casa de Cambio Plena - *Colombian NBFIs authorized to offer Forex and Remittance Services (discontinued)*
CGD	Center for Global Development
CELADE	*Centro Latinoamericano y Caribeño de Demografía,* a division of CEPAL/ECLAC
CEPAL	*Comisión Económica para América Latina y el Caribe (ECLAC in English)*
CFC	*Compañía de Financiamiento Comercial - Colombian financial institution category (discontinued)*
CFIUS	Committee on Foreign Investment in the United States
CFPB	Consumer Financial Protection Bureau of the US
CGAP	Consultative Group to Assist the Poor
CIASEFIM	Comisión Internacional de Asociaciones No Bancarias de Transferencias de Dinero, Empresas de Servicios, Casas, Agencias y Corretoras del Cambio del Mercosur *(International Commission of Non-Bank Associations of Money Transfers, Service Companies and Foreign Exchange Brokers of Mercosur)*
CSBS	The US Conference of State Bank Supervisors
CTF	Counter Terrorism Financing
CTG	Cash to Goods
DDCAP	Door To Door Consolidation Association of the Philippines

Abbreviations & Acronyms

DEA	US Drug Enforcement Agency
DFID	Department for International Development
DFS	New York State Department of Financial Services
DIAN	Dirección de Impuestos y Aduanas Nacionales *(The Colombian National Tax and Customs Authority)*
DIPS	Domestic Instant Payment Systems
ECLAC	Economic Commission for Latin America and the Caribbean
EDTF	El Dorado Task Force
EEFT	Euronet Worldwide *(RIA Money Transfer parent company)*
EFT	Electronic Fund Transfer
EMI	Electronic Money Institution
EPIF	European Payment Institutions Federation
EU	European Union
FATF-GAFI	Financial Action Task Force - Groupe D'action Financière - Grupo de Acción Financiera
FBI	US Federal Bureau of Investigation
FCA	Financial Conduct Authority of the UK
FEC	Foreign Exchange Company - *licensed NBFI providing foreign exchange services*
FFR	Financial Facility for Remittances
Fintech	Financial Technology - *NBFI that offers Financial Services*
FINTRAC	Financial Transactions and Reports Analysis Centre of Canada
FIU	Financial Intelligence Unit
FOMIN	Fondo Multilateral de Inversiones *(In english, the Multilateral Investment Fund, MIF of the Interamerican Development Bank, IDB)*
Forex	Foreign Exchange
FSA	Financial Services Authority *(inactive - On 2013 UK's FCA replaced the previous regulator, the FSA)*

FMSB	Foreign Money Services Business
FNUAP	Fondo de Población de las Naciones Unidas, *in english the United Nations Population Fund (UNFPA)*
G2B	Government to Business
G2P	Government to Person
GAFI	Groupe D'action Financière *(Financial Action Task Force FATF)*
GAO	Government Accountability Office of the US
GFRID	Global Forum on Remittances, Investment and Development
GTO	Geographical Targeting Order
HNW	High Net Worth *(as in High Net Worth Individuals)*
IAMTN	International Association of Money Transfer Networks
ICA	MTRA's Industry Advisory Council
ICBP	Instant Cross-Border Payment
ICSA	International Courier Services Association
IDFR	International Day of Family Remittances
IFT	Informal Funds Transfer System (Informal Value Transfer System - IVT)
IKR	In Kind Remittance
INAFI	International Network of Alternative Financial Institutions
IMTC	International Money Transfer Conferences *(former CrossTech Conferences)*
IOREM	International Organization for Remittances and Migration
IoTs	Internet-of-Things
IPS	Instant Payment Systems
IVT	Informal Value Transfer System
JICA	Japan International Cooperation Agency
LEA	Law Enforcement Agency
LMIC	Low- and Middle-Income Countries
MAMSB	Malaysian Association of Money Service Businesses

Abbreviations & Acronyms

MGI	MoneyGram International
MMO	Mobile Money Operator
MSB	Money Service Business *(Term used in the US, Malaysia and other countries - a licensed NBFI)*
MSBA	US Money Service Business Association
MSC	MicroSave Consulting
NMTA	US National Money Transmitters Association *(inactive - merged with MSBA)*
MPI	Migration Policy Institute
MTO	Money Transmitter Operator
MTRA	US Money Transmitter Regulators Association
NBFI	Non Bank Financial Institution
NMLS	Nationwide Multistate Licensing System
OCC	US Office of the Controller of the Currency
OFAC	US Office of Foreign Assets Control
OFC	Offshore Financial Center
OFW	Overseas Foreign Worker
OSS	Office of Strategic Services
OWWA	Overseas Workers Welfare Administration of the Philippines
P2B	Person to Business
P2G	Person to Government
P2P	Person to Person *(Peer-to-Peer)*
PaaS	Payment-as-a-Service
PI	Payment Institution *(Term used in the EU, the UK and other countries - a licensed NBFI)*
POS	Point of Sale
PSD	Payment Services Directive
PSDG	Payment Systems Development Group - *World Bank*
PSR	Payment Systems Regulator of the UK

rCBDC	Retail Central Bank Digital Currency
ROG	Rapid-o-Giros
RPW	Remittance Prices Worldwide
RSP	Remittance Service Provider *(any financial institution providing remittance services)*
RTF	Remittance Task Force
SDGs	Sustainable Development Goals
SEC	US Securities and Exchange Commission
SECO	Swiss State Secretariat of Economic Affairs
SEDPE	Sociedad Especializada en Pagos Electrónicos *(Electronic Payments Entity, a colombian licensed NBFI-fintech)*
SEWA	Self Employed Women's Association *(India)*
SME	Small and Medium-sized Enterprise
SOp	Sting Operation
SPDI	Special Purpose Depository Institution Bank Charter *(Wisconsin)*
TDLC	Tribunal de Defensa de la Libre Competencia *(Chile)*
TIPS	*Eurozone's* TARGET Instant Payment Settlement System
TMSRT	The Money Services Round Table
TSJUE	Tribunal Superior de Justicia de la Unión Europea
UGC	User Generated Content
UIF	Unidad de Inteligencia Financiera
UKAPI (UKMTA)	UK Association of Payment Institutions *(former UKMTA, UK Money Transfer Association)*
UNCTAD	United Nations Conference on Trade and Development
UNFPA	United Nations Population Fund
UNDESA	United Nations Department of Economic and Social Affairs
wCBDC	Wholesale Central Bank Digital Currency
WSBI	World Savings and Retail Banking Institution

WOLA	Washington Office on Latin America
WOM	Word-of-Mouth Marketing
WU	Western Union
WWB	Women's World Banking

Printed in Great Britain
by Amazon